KDI STUDIES IN ECONOMICS

Revised Edition
All Rights Reserved by
THE KOREA DEVELOPMENT INSTITUTE
*P.O. Box 113, Cheong Ryang, **Seoul**, Korea*

Distributed Outside Korea by
The University Press of Hawaii
ISBN 0-8248-0539-9

FACTOR SUPPLY AND FACTOR INTENSITY OF TRADE IN KOREA

By

Wontack Hong

1976

KOREA DEVELOPMENT INSTITUTE

Seoul, Korea

BOARD OF DIRECTORS

Chairman	**Koh, Seung Je**	
President	**Kim, Mahn Je**	
Directors	**Sung, Chang Whan**	
	Kim, Young Hui	
	Rhee, Ki Jun	
	Chang, Duk Chin	
	Cho, Choong Hoon	
	Chang, Duk Hee	
	Shim, Ui Hwan	
Auditor	**Kim, Young Joon**	

◆

The Korea Development Institute was established on March 11, 1971 by President Park Chung Hee. K.D.I. systematically conducts research on policy matters concerning the overall national economy, helps develop the nation's five-year plans, and assists in policy making.

K.D.I. is a non-profit corporate organization operated on an endowment fund. For this reason, its autonomy and independence are guaranteed to the maximum possible extent in the performance of its policy-oriented research activities.

The results of research conducted by K.D.I. will be published and distributed. The contents of reports, however, will represent the opinion of the person in charge of the respective research, and shall not be construed as an official opinion of the Institute.

FOREWORD

This study is the result of a long-term research undertaken in 1972–75 by the author. It may be regarded as a part of the series of continuing KDI research on the general subject of the relationship between Korea's growth and Korea's trade. Dr. Hong explores the relationship between the factor supply and the factor intensity of trade, a subject of great interest in understanding the growth process of Korean economy. I am confident that this study will make a valuable contribution in assessing prospects for other developing countries. I would like to acknowledge the Council for Asian Manpower Studies which partly financed this research project.

The interpretations and conclusions in this volume are those of the author and do not represent the official views of the Korea Development Institute.

Mahn Je Kim
President
Korea Development Institute

TABLE OF CONTENTS

Foreword   *v*

Introduction   *xiii*

CHAPTER 1.   GROWTH AND TRADE IN KOREA *1*

   1. Growth, Trade and Structural Changes
   2. Changes in the Commodity Trade Pattern

CHAPTER 2.   FACTOR SUPPLY AND FACTOR INTENSITY OF TRADE: A THEORETICAL FRAMEWORK *12*

   1. A Generalization of the Rybczynski Theorem
   2. A Two-Factor Multi-Commodity Trade Pattern
   3. Changes in the Wage/Rental Ratio and Sectoral Capital/Labor Ratios

CHAPTER 3.   DOMESTIC AND FOREIGN SAVINGS AND CAPITAL FORMATION *18*

   1. Savings and Investments
   2. Capital Formation

CHAPTER 4.   SUPPLY OF LABOR AND EMPLOYMENT *23*

   1. Labor Force and Employment
   2. Educational Level of the Labor Force

CHAPTER 5. CAPITAL ACCUMULATION, CAPITAL DEEPENING AND THE RISING WAGE/RENTAL RATIO ········· 35
1. The Rising Wage/Rental Ratio
2. The Share of Labor in Total National Income

CHAPTER 6. ANALYSIS OF GROWTH FACTORS ········ 44
1. Factor Share Approach
2. Aggregate Factor/Value-Added Ratios
3. Contribution of Export Expansion to GNP Growth

CHAPTER 7. FACTOR INTENSITY OF TRADE ········ 57
1. Computational Procedures
2. Sectoral Direct Labor Requirements
3. Sectoral Direct Capital Requirements
4. Factor Intensity of Trade

CHAPTER 8. THE IMPACT OF CAPITAL-LABOR SUBSTITUTION ON THE FACTOR INTENSITY OF TRADE ········· 85

CHAPTER 9. FACTOR INTENSITY OF NON-COMPETITIVE IMPORTS ········ 93

CHAPTER 10. SKILL INTENSITY OF TRADE ········ 103

CHAPTER 11. A STATIC ESTIMATE OF GAINS FROM TRADE ········ 112

CHAPTER 12. SUMMARY AND CONCLUSION ········ 124

Bibliography ········ 127
Statistical Appendix ········ 133

TEXT TABLES

1.1.	Growth and Changes in Industrial Structure: 1953, 1962 & 1973	3
1.2.	Exports, Imports and Foreign Aid & Loans	4
1.3.	Major Commodities Exported and Imported: 1961 & 1973	8
1.4.	Commodity Trade by Countries	10
3.1.	Total Available Resources, Consumption and Investment	19
3.2.	Capital Formation in Korea: 1953–73	21
4.1.	Total Population, Potential Labor Force and Effective Labor Supply: Population Census Data (1960, 1966 & 1970)	24
4.2.	Potential Labor Force and Effective Labor Supply: Quarterly Sample Survey Data (1963–74)	25
4.3.	Employed Persons by Industry (14 Years & Over): 1960–73	27
4.4.	Total Number of Employed Persons Adjusted: 1960, 1966 & 1970 (Age Group 14 & Over)	29
4.5.	Population 14 Years Old & Over by Level of Education: 1960 & 1970	31
4.6.	Employed Persons by Occupation and Level of Education: 1960 & 1970	33
4.7.	Employed Persons by Industry and Level of Education: 1966 & 1970	33

5.1.	Per Capita and Per Worker Fixed Capital Stock: 1953–74	36
5.2.	Capital Stock Per Worker and Average Wage Rates: Agricultural and Manufacturing Sectors	37
5.3.	Weighted-Average Interest Rates of Total Domestic Loans and Interest Rate on Time Deposits	40
5.4.	Distribution of National Income: 1953–73	42
6.1.	Analysis of Growth Factors	46
6.2.	Capital-Stock/GNP and Employment/GNP Ratios: 1953–73	49
6.3.	Capital/Value-Added and Employment/Value-Added Ratios in the Agricultural and Manufacturing Sectors: 1960–73	50
6.4.	Direct Contribution of Export Expansion to GNP Growth	52
6.5.	Contribution of Export Expansion and Import Substitution to GNP Growth	54
7.1.	Aggregated Sectoral Labor/Output Ratios	64
7.2.	Comparison of Estimated and Census Sectoral Employments	65
7.3.	Aggregated Sectoral Capital/Output Ratios	71
7.4.	The Coverage of Manufacturing Census	71
7.5.	Comparison of Estimated and Han-BOK Capital Stock Data	73
7.6.	Exports and Employment: 1960–73	75
7.7.	Contribution of Exports to Sectoral Employment: 1960–73	77

7.8. Capital Requirements for Export Production:
     1960–73 ·· 79
7.9. Exports and Sectoral Capital Use: 1960–73 ···························· 80
7.10. Changing Factor Intensity of Trade: 1960–73 (Per
      $100 Million Commodity Exports or Import
      Replacements) ·· 82

8.1. Changes in Industrial Structure and Total Factor
     Requirements Per $100 Million of Export Production
     (Applying the A^d Matrix) ·· 86
8.2. Changes in Sectoral Factor-Output Ratios, Export
     Pattern and Direct Factor Requirements Per $100
     Million (in 1970 Prices) Exports ·· 87
8.3. Impact of Capital-Labor Substitution on Direct
     Factor Intensity of Trade··· 89
8.4. Impact of Capital-Labor Substitution on Total
     Factor Intensity of Trade··· 89
8.5. Changes in the Factor Intensity of Commodity
     Exports Due to Factor Substitutions and Shifts in
     the Composition of Exports: 1966–72 ···································· 90

9.1. Progress of Import Substitution and the Changing
     Composition of Imports ·· 94
9.2. Estimates of Capital and Labor Requirements to
     Replace Non-Competitive Imports: 1968 Basis···················· 97
9.3. Estimates of Capital and Labor Requirements to
     Replace Non-Competitive Imports: 1970 Basis···················· 98
9.4. Factor Requirements Per $100 Million Exports or
     Import Replacements: U.S. (1947), Japan (1951)
     and Korea (1970) ··· 99

9.5. Factor Requirements and Factor Intensity of
Competitive and Non-Competitive Imports: 1968–70 ...... *101*

10.1. Skill Composition of Labor Directly and Indirectly
Employed for Export Production (Based on 1970
Occupational Skill Group): 1963–72 .... *106*

10.2. Skill Composition of Direct and Indirect Labor
Requirements for Competitive Import Replacements
(Based on 1970 Occupational Skill Group): 1963–72 .... *107*

10.3. Skill Composition of Labor Directly and Indirectly
Employed for Export Production (Based on 1971
Monthly Wage Group): 1963–72 .... *108*

10.4. Skill Composition of Direct and Indirect Labor Requirements
for Competitive Import Replacements (Based on 1971
Monthly Wage Group): 1963–72 .... *109*

11.1. Factor Savings Per $100 Million of Trade (1970
Basis): 1966–73 .... *116*

11.2. Exports of Eight Capital Intensive Commodities:
1966–73 .... *118*

11.3. Factor Savings Per $100 Million of Trade Excluding
Capital Intensive Export Group: 1966–73 .... *120*

INTRODUCTION

This paper attempts to continue and extend the investigation into the relationship between factor supply and factor intensity in international trade.

In the confusion following Leontief's finding that American exports are labor-intensive relative to American import-competing industries, an extremely important question has been neglected.[1] That is, even if a country's exports are labor intensive at an early stage of economic development, how will the factor intensity of its trade alter as its overall capital-labor endowment ratio grows relative to that of other countries? The first purpose of this paper is to investigate the changes in the factor intensity of Korea's trade which followed increases in its overall capital-labor endowment ratio. Our investigation will concentrate on the 1960–73 period due to the limited data available. Nonetheless, this period seems to be especially suitable for our investigation, because Korea experienced both very rapid capital accumulation and the rapid expansion of manufactured exports during this period. The Korean experience may provide some clues as to the way comparative advantage may change (albeit at a slower rate in other, less rapidly growing, countries) with capital deepening for the economy as a whole.

Since we naturally expect changes in the factor-output ratios and inter-industry relationships in the course of economic growth, a second purpose of this paper is to examine the extent to which factor substitution occurred in Korea in association with a changing wage/rental ratio, and its impact on the estimates of the factor intensity of trade.

---

[1] W. Leontief, "Domestic Production and Foreign Trade: The American Capital Position Re-Examined," *Proceedings of the American Philosophical Society*, September 1953, and "Factor Proportions and the Structure of American Trade: Further Theoretical and Empirical Analysis," *Review of Economics and Statistics*, November 1956.

Leontief and his followers excluded all non-competitive imports from their computation of factor intensities of trade. In the early stages of economic development most developing countries import a wide range of goods which are not domestically produced, and if one accepts any stylized version of the Heckscher-Ohlin model the products produced and exported in the early stages of development are presumably labor intensive, while those imports not domestically produced are presumably those that would require the most capital intensive techniques of production. It follows that a satisfactory estimate of the factor intensity of trade can only be made if the question of how to treat non-competitive imports is answered. The third purpose of this paper is to argue that, in a developing country like Korea, the factor intensity differential between non-competitive (non-natural-resource-intensive) imports and exports will be greater than that between competitive imports and exports.

The paper is organized as follows. Chapter 1 gives an overview of growth and trade in Korea; Chapter 2 describes the theoretical framework of the empirical analysis; Chapter 3 and 4 investigate the changes in factor supply in Korea; Chapter 5 examines the changes in the wage/rental ratio and the share of labor in total national income; Chapter 6 presents a simple analysis of growth factors in Korea; Chapter 7 presents the core of the research, i.e., the investigation of changes in the factor intensity of Korea's trade over the period 1960–73; Chapter 8 examines the impact of capital-labor substitution on the factor intensity of trade; Chapter 9 investigates the factor intensity of non-competitive imports and its implications; Chapter 10 examines the skill intensity of trade; Chapter 11 gives a static estimate of gains from trade in Korea and analyzes its implications; and Chapter 12 summarizes our findings and presents concluding remarks.

Approximately a hundred pages of statistical tables on commodity trade and capital accumulation in Korea are attached as an appendix. The decision to include this material was based on the fact that the collection and organization of the basic trade data from the original sources required more than a hundred hours of computer time and several man-years of assistants' time, and their wider availability should be of considerable assistance to other scholars undertaking research work which makes use of such data.

This research project was jointly financed by the Korea Development Institute and the Council for Asian Manpower Studies. A preliminary and shortened version of my research work was published under the title of "Capital Accumulation, Factor Substitution, and the Changing Factor

Intensity of Trade: The Case of Korea," in *Trade and Development in Korea* (KDI Press, 1975) edited by myself and professor Anne Krueger of the University of Minnesota. I would like to take this opportunity to thank professor Krueger for her many helpful comments and suggestions. The chapter on a static estimate of gains from trade owes very much to professor Jagdish Bhagwati of M.I.T. Needless to say, any remaining errors are my own, and I hope to have the improved and revised edition of this paper completed in the near future. Finally, I wish to thank Messrs. Young Koo Lee, Chan Soo Park and Moon Jong Kim, and Miss Myung Soon Rho and Miss Hyun Mi Tai for their invaluable research assistance.

Wontack Hong

January, 1976

CHAPTER 1

GROWTH AND TRADE IN KOREA

1. Growth, Trade and Structural Changes

Korea was developed as a colonial economy by the Japanese during 1910–45, exporting rice and other primary products to Japan and importing all kinds of manufactures from it. In the later years of the colonial period, Japan tried to convert the Korean peninsula into a logistic base for the creation of the so-called Greater East Asian Coprosperity Sphere. As a result, some light and heavy industries as well as extended social overhead capital facilities began to be developed. The electric power resources, mineral deposits and heavy industries were mostly located in the northern part of Korea and the industries in the southern part consisted mainly of agriculture and light industries such as textiles and food manufacturing. However, the Korean economy, which was initially designed as a colonial economy dependent on Japan and then further crippled by the separation of the North from the South, had to industrialize out of the ruins left in the wake of the Korean War (1950–53).

In 1953, which was the year the Korean War ended in a ceasefire, the gross national product amounted to about $2.7 billion in 1970 dollar prices. About 46 percent of the GNP was generated by the agricultural sector and about 43 percent by such service sectors as construction, wholesale and retail trade, public administration and defense, ownership of dwellings, education, etc. The manufacturing sector contributed only about 6 percent of the GNP and the social overhead sectors such as electricity, water and sanitary services, transportation and communication contributed about 2 percent. Commodity exports amounted to less than $0.06 billion while imports amounted to $0.53 billion in 1953 (all in 1970 prices), and the difference was financed by foreign savings, mostly U.S. grants-in aid.[1]

The average annual growth rate of GNP during the nine year period following the war (1953–61) was approximately 4 percent, and the agricultural and service sectors together still contributed about 83 percent of the GNP in 1962. Commodity exports remained negligible throughout the period, usually amounting to less than 1 percent of GNP, while most of the imports, which averaged about 15 percent of GNP, were financed by U.S. grants-in aid. Persistently overvalued domestic currency effectively eliminated the export potential of the economy. (See Table A.4.) The industrialization policy pursued during this post-war period can be loosely characterized as a policy of import substitution of nondurable consumer goods with foreign aid funds under the protection of tariffs and quotas, but any kind of whole-hearted and systematic government effort for rapid economic growth was conspicuously absent during most of this era.

The military coup in mid-1961 provided a turning point. The military government started to make systematic efforts to achieve rapid economic growth, and its vigor was maintained by the formulation and energetic execution of a series of ambitious five-year economic development plans (1962–66; 1967–72; 1972–76). The average annual growth rate of GNP rose to about 9 percent during the decade 1962–71, and in 1973 the growth rate hit an all time high of 17 percent.

The initiation of the ambitious First Five-Year Plan (1962–66) necessitated the acquisition of a large amount of foreign exchange as well as increased domestic savings in order to finance various planned investment projects for import-substitution, social overhead capital formation, etc.[2]

---

[1] In this paper, we applied the exchange rate of 310.6 won per dollar in order to convert the (national income) figures in constant 1970 won values into those of 1970 dollar values, and also applied the GNP deflator of the United States to convert the (trade) figures in current dollar values during 1953–72 into those of 1970 constant dollar values. However, we applied the export or import unit value index constructed by the Bank of Korea to the trade data of 1973 and 1974 because of the extremely high rates of price inflation in tradable commodities since 1973. (See Tables A.4. and A.5.)

[2] The First Five-Year Plan emphasized investments for import substitution of cement, fertilizer, iron & steel and refined petroleum, and investments for electricity, coal mining, transportation and other social overhead capital formation. See the Government of Korea, *First Five Year Economic Development Plan (1962–66)*, Seoul, January 1962.

Table 1.1. *Growth and Changes in Industrial Structure: 1953, 1962 & 1973*

In 1970 Dollars & Percent

	1953	1962	1973
Agriculture & Forestry	46%	39%	20%
Fishery	2%	2%	3%
Mining & Quarrying	1%	2%	1%
Manufacturing	6%	12%	28%
Electricity, Water & Sanitary Services	0%	1%	2%
Transportation & Communication	2%	3%	7%
Construction	2%	3%	5%
Wholesale & Retail Trade	11%	15%	19%
Banking & Other Services	8%	9%	7%
Education & Public Administration	17%	12%	7%
Ownership of Dwellings	5%	4%	2%
Gross National Product	$2.7 billion	$3.9 billion	$11.3 billion
Per Capita GNP	$129	$150	$343

Source: Table A.22. and Table 5.1.

The inflow of U.S. aid funds which peaked in 1957 at nearly $0.4 billion had already started its irreversible decline. As a result the government had to turn to such alternative sources of foreign exchange as foreign loans and export expansion, along with increased taxation and higher interest rates on time and savings deposits to mobilize domestic investment funds.

The annual inflow of foreign loans increased from zero in 1961 to more than $0.1 billion in 1966 and to as high as $0.6 billion in 1973. The direct and indirect tax revenue of the government, which amounted to less than $0.4 billion before 1962, increased to about $0.6 billion in 1966 and to about $1.5 billion by 1973 (all in 1970 prices).[3] The existing interest rates on time and savings deposits and loans (except export credits) were almost doubled in 1965, and as a result the share of time and savings deposits in the rapidly expanding total loan funds of the deposit money banks increased from less than 20 percent before 1965 to nearly half in 1971.[4]

The government was able to achieve even more dramatic gains in the area of export expansion. Commodity exports which amounted to less than $0.1 billion prior to 1962 increased at the average annual rate of

---
[3] Data from the Bank of Korea, *National Income Statistics Yearbook*.
[4] Data from the Bank of Korea, *Monetary Statistics in Korea: 1960–73*.

Table 1.2. Exports, Imports and Foreign Aid & Loans
In Billion U.S. Dollars

	Imports		Exports		Official Aid	Foreign Loans
	Commodity	Service[1]	Commodity	Service[2]		
1953	0.35	0.01	0.04	0.12	0.19	—
1954	0.24	0.00	0.02	0.04	0.15	—
1955	0.34	0.01	0.02	0.06	0.23	—
1956	0.39	0.01	0.03	0.02	0.32	—
1957	0.44	0.01	0.02	0.04	0.37	—
1958	0.38	0.01	0.02	0.07	0.31	—
1959	0.30	0.02	0.02	0.07	0.21	—
1960	0.34	0.02	0.03	0.07	0.23	—
1961	0.32	0.02	0.04	0.09	0.20	—
1962	0.42	0.03	0.06	0.10	0.22	0.00
1963	0.56	0.04	0.09	0.07	0.23	0.05
1964	0.40	0.04	0.12	0.08	0.14	0.04
1965	0.46	0.04	0.18	0.09	0.14	0.03
1966	0.72	0.04	0.25	0.18	0.15	0.11
1967	1.00	0.08	0.32	0.30	0.15	0.17
1968	1.46	0.11	0.46	0.36	0.17	0.30
1969	1.82	0.12	0.62	0.41	0.16	0.48
1970	1.98	0.14	0.84	0.41	0.19	0.40
1971	2.39	0.17	1.07	0.41	0.13	0.54
1972	2.52	0.19	1.62	0.49	0.07	0.63
1973	4.24	0.28	3.23	0.77	0.02	0.63
1974	6.85	0.45	4.46	0.76	0.03	0.64

Source: Tables A.1., A.2. and A.3.
[1] Total invisible payments or receipts minus investment income and donations.
[2] Including imports financed by Properties and Claims funds from Japan.

about 40 percent during the period 1962–73, amounting to $0.3 billion in 1966 and $1.0 billion in 1971 (all in 1970 dollar prices). By efficient exploitation of the opportunity provided by the repeated yen appreciations during 1972-73, Korea further expanded its exports by about 50 percent in 1972 and 70 percent in 1973, mostly to Japan itself and to other markets in which Korean goods were in competition with those of Japan. Total commodity exports amounted to about $2.6 billion (in 1970 dollar prices) in 1973.

During 1953–61, non-commodity exports, which amounted to more than twice the value of commodity exports, were dominated by the sales of goods and services to the U.S. Army detachments stationed in Korea. The annual sales to the U.S. Army steadily increased from less than $0.1 billion during 1953–61 to more than $0.2 billion after 1967, but their magnitude started to decline after 1973. On the other hand, the receipts from exports of transportation, insurance, travel and miscellaneous services increased very rapidly from almost neglible amounts during 1953–61 to $0.25 billion by 1972. In 1973, these receipts from invisible trade amounted to $0.6 billion while sales to the U.S. Army amounted to less than $0.2 billion. The rapidly increasing tonnage of domestic vessels, tourist services, remittances of Korean workers abroad and revenues from overseas construction works made the greatest contribution to the remarkable increase in non-commodity exports. (See Table A.2. and A.3.)

In the late fifties, the government had increasingly relied on various quantitative import restrictions in order to offset the adverse effects of the progressive inflation on the balance of payments. A complex structure of multiple exchange rates was also developed, but on balance the structure of incentives during this period appears to have been biased against exports although there existed some export promotion schemes. The military governemnt completed the task of unifying the exchange rate which was initiated by the short-lived civilian government established after the 1960 Student Revolution.[5] There was a series of devaluations in the early sixties, and the one enforced in the mid-1964 was significant enough to effectively terminate the post-war era of overvalued domestic currency. (See Table A.4.) The Korean "won" was devaluated by almost 50 percent in May 1964, and the unitary floating exchange rate system was formally put into effect in March 1965. The "won" was stabilized at 270 won per dollar by the end of 1965, and floated slowly upward under continued intervention by the Bank of Korea.

---

[5] The transition to the unified exchange rate in 1961 did not immediately increase export earnings appreciably because the new rate was somewhat lower than the free market rate on export earnings had been. But it raised the unit cost of imports by more than 40 percent. Due to the decline in the U.S. aid, the government tightened import controls during this period by means of import licencing system and high tariffs. Trade controls were gradually relaxed after the 1964 devaluation, and further liberalized in 1967 when a switch was made from the so-called "positive" list system, under which only those commodities listed in the trade program could be imported, to the "negative" system, under which all commodities not listed are automatically approved to be imported. There were also decreases in the average rates of tariffs on imports. See K.S. Kim "Outward-Looking Industrialization Strategy: The Case of Korea, in *Trade and Development in Korea,* ed. by Wontack Hong and Anne O. Krueger, Seoul: KDI Press, 1975.

On the other hand, the government also increased the incentives given to exporters through the exemptions from tariffs and indirect taxes on imported materials used in export production, the provision of wastage allowances on (tariff-exempt) imported raw materials to be used for export production, direct tax preferences (50 percent exemption) on profits arising from export activities (not applied since 1973), preferential interest rates on loans related to export activities, and the establishment of the government-financed Korea Trade Promotion Corporation to promote exports and develop marketing networks.

In view of the backward state of financial institutions in Korea which contributed to the chronic shortage of domestic investment funds, the automatic award of low interest rate bank loans to direct export activities (three month loan of 200–350 won per dollar exported at an annual interest rate of 6 percent during 1965–73), and selective long-term bank loans to finance investments in various export production activities seem to have been effective in propelling the export-oriented growth during the sixties.

The export subsidy policies were not purposely designed to discriminate among industries. However, due to the limited export potential of the primary sector, the share of manufactured products in total commodity exports, which never exceeded 20 percent level during 1953–61, steadily increased to about 80 percent in 1966 and to about 95 percent of total commodity exports by 1973.[6] (See Tables A.11. and A.12.) We may say that, as one of the most densely populated country in the world, Korea possessed the strong potential for the production of labor intensive manufactures for export, and this latent potential has effectively realized by the positive government policies.

Korea started to intensify its promotion of import substitution systematically in the early sixties, but being faced by a balance of payments problem in financing the various investment projects it had to promote export expansions. The export promotion policies in turn started to gather momentum of their own as time passed, and as a result people started to identify the period after 1962 as the export-orinted growth phase in Korea's development. However, Korea also achieved a very significant level of import substitution in cement, fertilizers, refined petroleum, textile yarn & fabrics, etc. during this period, which in due course started to emerge as a new generation of exportables. Import substitution and export expansion seem to go side by side although understandably with some time lag.

Having enjoyed such positive effects of export-oriented growth as ex-

---

[6] The First Five-Year Plan (1962-66) set up the target of achieving 33 percent of total commodity exports ($138 million) to be manufactured goods by 1966.

panded market size and improved skills, technological transfers and the over-all spur to efficiency which results from international competition, it does not seem likely that Korea will abruptly reverse its "outward-looking" industrialization policy in the seventies.

In 1973, the modernized manufacturing sector contributed more than 28 percent of the GNP while the social overhead sectors contributed nearly 10 percent. The once dominant agricultural sector declined to merely 20 percent of GNP by 1973, and even the share of the service sectors was reduced to about 40 percent.

2. Changes in the Commodity Trade Pattern

Until early in the sixties, the major export items were such primary products as metal ores & concentrates, raw materials of vegetable or animal origin, fish, swine and raw silk. By mid-sixties, however, plywood, clothes and miscellaneous manufactures emerged as the principal export commodities. In 1973, electronic products (thermionic valves, tubes & transistors), footwear, plates & sheets of iron or steel, and woven fabrics of synthetic fibres joined the list of major export commodities.

In 1961, for example, the only manufactured goods which could be exported in sizable quantities were raw silk, plywood and cotton fabrics. Beginning in the seventies, however, Korea could list as important export commodities such diversified items as: clothes, thermionic valves, tubes & transistors, footwear, cotton yarn, synthetic fibre yarn, iron & steel plates, twines & ropes, synthetic fibre fabrics, silk fabrics, leather products, knitted fabrics, cement, TV sets, tape recorders, radio receivers, toys, trunks & suitcases, etc. (See Table A.6.)

Machinery and transport equipment made up roughly 10–15 percent of total imports during 1953–61, but their share steadily increased to the 30 percent level during the ten year period 1962–71. (See Tables A.13., A.14. and A.15.) Significant changes in the list of major manufactured imports resulting from import substitution and changing demand patterns can also be observed.

During 1953–61, large amounts of such manufactured products as chemical fertilizers, synthetic fibre yarns & thread, yarn of regenerated fibres, petroleum products, printing papers, cement, iron or steel plates, plastic materials, etc. were imported. By 1971, however, the progress in import

Table 1.3. Major Commodities Exported and Imported: 1961 & 1973

1961 Exports	Million Dollars	1973 Exports	Million Dollars
Metal Ores & Concentrates	8.9	Clothes	661.0
Raw Silk	2.9	Plywood	274.0
Fish, salted or dried	2.7	Thermionic, Valves & Tubes	179.7
Swine	2.5	Synthetic Yarn & Fabrics	134.6
Coal	2.2	Footwear	106.4
Vegetable Origin Materials	1.5	Steel Plates & Sheets	104.5
Fish, fresh or frozen	1.3	Misc. Manufactures	83.7
Plywood	1.2	Raw Silk	72.8
Animal Origin Materials	1.1	Silk Fabrics	67.3
Clay & Other Minerals	1.1	Fish, fresh or frozen	56.8
Plants for Medicine	1.0	Clothing Accessories	49.3
Vegetable Products	0.9	Crustacea & Mollusca	45.4
Cotton Fabrics	0.8	Cotton Fabrics, woven	43.8
Fluorspar, Felspar, etc.	0.7	Gramophones, Recorders	42.3
Misc. Manufactures	0.6	Radio Receivers & Parts	32.8
Subtotal (S)	29.4	Subtotal (S)	1,954.4
(S)/Total Exports	72%	(S)/Total Exports	61%

1961 Imports		1973 Imports	
Chemical Fertilizers	40.3	Crude Oil	277.4
Raw Cotton	29.4	Sawlogs & Veneer Logs	273.9
Wheat & Meslin	24.0	Wheat & Meslin	256.6
Fuel Oils, Motor Spirit	15.9	Synthetic Yarn & Fabrics	182.9
Electrical Power Machinery	7.2	Thermionic Valves & Tubes	162.0
Wool	7.1	Steel Coils for Re-rolling	148.2
Regenerated Fibre Yarn	6.6	Textile Machines	147.3
Raw Sugar	5.6	Raw Cotton	112.4
Barley	5.2	Aircraft	101.9
Sawlogs & Veneer Logs	5.2	Iron Scrap	74.3
Natural Rubber	5.2	Synthetic Fibres	73.3
Textile Machines	4.4	Mechanical Equipments	71.1
Coal	4.3	Rice	66.1
Synthetic Fibre Yarn	4.3	Beet or Cane Sugar	63.0
Internal Combustion Engines	3.8	Telecommunications Eq.	55.1
Subtotal (S)	168.5	Subtotal (S)	2,065.5
(S)/Total Imports	53%	(S)/Total Imports	49%

Source: Tables A.6. and A.7.

substitution eliminated all these items but synthetic fibre yarn & thread and plastic materials from the list of major import commodities. For instance, the remarkable progress of import substitution in the production of chemicals resulted in a sharp decrease in the share of chemical products in total commodity imports from more than 20 percent in 1962 to less than 10 percent by 1973. We can also observe the emergence of a new generation of manufactured imports such as woven fabrics of synthetic fibres, iron & steel coils, thermionic valves & transistors, chemical pulp, synthetic fibres, etc. which were mostly used as raw materials for export production. (See Table A.7.)

The major imported materials for export production were basic chemicals and other various chemical products, forestry products (timber), steel products, textile fabrics, fibres and miscellaneous textile proudcts, various agricultural products, and electronic products. The share of imports for export production in total commodity imports steadily increased from about 14 percent in 1966 to 38 percent in 1973. Their import value was equivalent to about 40–50 percent of the total value of commodity exports during 1966–73. This implies that the apparent value added content of exports was less than 60 percent, although the actual import content of exports might have been smaller due to the official wastage allowances which leaked out large amount of duty-free imported raw materials to domestic markets.

The most remarkable fact seems to be that about half of the imported materials for export production were those items classified by the Bank of Korea as "competitive" imports. This perhaps overlooks some intrinsic (quality) differences between the competitively imported products and the so-called "competing" domestic products. However, it still suggests the existence of large potential increases in the value added content of total commodity exports. (See Tables A.20. and A.21.)

Another notable fact is that during 1967–74 about 70 percent of Korea's total trade was conducted with the U.S. and Japan and 13 percent was with other developed countries. The share of developing countries in total trade was less than 20 percent. Most of the imports from developing countries consisted of crude oil, crude rubber and timber. Hence it appears that Korea had very little to offer other developing countries and *vice versa*, with the exception of natural-resource intensive goods.

Although the government started to promote export expansion early in the sixties in order to reduce the balance of payment deficit, this policy was developed in the absence of any concrete ideas about which industries had comparative advantages for export production. Subsidy policies did

Table 1.4. Commodity Trade by Countries

Annual Averages	Developed Countries			Developing Countries	
	U.S.A.	Japan	Others	East Asia	Others
Commodity Exports
1956–61	20%	52%	12%	13%	3%
1962–66	31%	31%	10%	23%	2%
1967–71	48%	25%	13%	11%	4%
1972–74	37%	32%	17%	9%	5%
Commodity Imports
1958–61	47%	17%	24%	8%	5%
1962–66	46%	32%	11%	8%	4%
1967–71	30%	42%	13%	10%	6%
1972–74	26%	40%	13%	10%	11%

Source: The Bank of Korea, *Economic Statistics Yearbook* (1956–59), Ministry of Finance, *Foreign Trade of Korea* (1960–68), and Office of Customs Administration, *Statistical Yearbook of Foreign Trade* (1969–74).
Note: East Asia represents Asian countries east of (including) Pakistan and India.

not directly discriminate among industries, and did not particularly favor any specific kind of industries. Neither did the government envision a major role for heavily labor-intensive manufactured exports. As export expansion arose along the lines of classical comparative advantage theory, the government quickly started to channel investments into such emerging export sectors as textiles, clothing, plywood, electronics, wigs, etc. While the government maintained a high effective exchange rate, it seems to have been the private entrepreneurs who led in the determination of resource allocations.

With the beginning of the seventies, the Korean government showed signs of having learned its lesson and started, though very crudely, to project expected future export patterns corresponding to the future state of comparative advantage at higher per capita income levels, and at the same time started to plan for future investments in such industries as shipbuilding, electronics, machineries, steel products, petro-chemicals, etc. That is, instead of following the lead of private enterprises in resource allocation, the government has tried to lead entrepreneurs according to the expected changing state of comparative advantage. The government seems to anticipate that Korea will soon lose its comparative advantage in relatively unskilled-labor intensive manufactures such as textiles and plywood, and will soon have comparative advantages in relatively skill intensive and also moderately capital intensive manufacturing, such as shipbuilding and the machinery industries.

Heavy investments in petrochemical industries might turn out to be a mistake, both because these industries are extremely capital intensive and because it is more likely that the U.S. and other oil producing countries will have a natural comparative advantage in petrochemical production. On the other hand, the investments in shipbuilding, electronics, machineries, and iron & steel products may well turn out to be successful. However, considering the existence of a large potential labor force, the simple unskilled labor intensive industries may have to continue to expand for the time being. Otherwise, Korea may face a serious unemployment problem, or at best the under-utilization of its full potential for growth.

CHAPTER 2

FACTOR SUPPLY AND FACTOR INTENSITY OF TRADE: A THEORETICAL FRAMEWORK

1. A Generalization of the Rybczynski Theorem

The proposition Leontief wanted to test was a static one: that exports from a country which is relatively abundantly endowed with, say, labor are relatively less capital intensive than that country's imports, provided that domestic demand is not heavily biased towards labor intensive goods. However, the main objective of this paper is to investigate the changing factor supply in Korea and the associated changes in the factor intensity of trade.

The Rybczynski-Stolper-Samuelson theorems can provide a basic theoretical framework for the empirical analysis.[1] Assuming a small country trading under a constant set of international commodity prices, the original two-good two-factor Rybczynski proposition may be stated as follows: with an increase in per capita capital stock, per capita production of the capital intensive good increases while per capita production of the labor intensive goods decreases. Should we assume less than infinitely elastic foreign demand and also assume that the country exports the labor intensive good, it follows that since the country's exports decrease, the external terms of trade must improve, and consequently, according to the Stolper-Samuelson theorem, the wage/rental ratio as well as the sectoral capital/

---

[1] T. N. Rybczynski, "Factor Endowments and Relative Commodity Prices," *Economica,* New Series, November 1955, and W. F. Stolper and P. A. Samuelson, "Protection and Real Wages," *Review of Economic Studies,* Novmeber 1941.

labor ratios must rise, provided of course that the changes in the domestic demand pattern do not more than offset the changing output pattern.

We consider first the problem of extending the Rybczynski theorem so that it copes with two factors (capital K, labor N) and any number of product. We begin by introducing notations:

X_j: amount of commodity j produced
C_j: amount of commodity j domestically demanded
a_{ij}: the amount of factor i $(i=k, n)$ used in the production of a unit of commodity $j(j=1, ..., m)$
f_i: the country's endowment of the ith factor of production
w_i: the money reward of the ith factor of production
p_j: the money price of jth product

In addition we employ the following vector notations:

$$a_j = (a_{kj}, a_{nj}) \qquad A = \begin{bmatrix} a_{k1} & \ldots & a_{km} \\ a_{n1} & \ldots & a_{nm} \end{bmatrix}$$

$$f = (f_k, f_n) = (K, N) \qquad w = (w_k, w_n)$$

$$X = (X_1, \ldots, X_m) \qquad p = (p_1, \ldots, p_m)$$

In terms of these notations, the jth production function can be written,

$$1 = F_j(a_j)$$

We may write the equilibrium full-employment and price-cost relation as (the prime indicates the transpose):

$$f' = AX'$$

$$p = wA$$

respectively. If $m=2$, we get

$$dw = A^{-1}(dp)$$

and if only the jth price changes

$$dw_i = \beta_{ji}(dp_j)$$

where β_{ji} is the (j, i)th component of A^{-1}. On the other hand, if commodity prices (and therefore factor prices and the input-output coefficients a_{ij}) are held constant,

$$df' = A(dX')$$

If $m=2$ *(i.e., $j=1, 2$)*, we get

$$dX' = A^{-1}(df')$$

Again, if only ith factor endowment changes

$$dX_j' = \beta_{ji}(df_i)$$

So far we have simply followed Kemp's exposition on the Rybczynski-Stolper-Samuelson theorems for the case of an equal number of products and factors.[2] However, since we are considering the multi-commodity case of $m>2$, we do not get the inverse of the A matrix. As far as output patterns are concerned, the only certainty under full-employment is that:

$$\begin{cases} K = \sum_{j=1}^{m} a_{kj}X_j \\ N = \sum_{j=1}^{m} a_{nj}X_j \end{cases} \text{ and } \begin{cases} dK = \sum_{j=1}^{m} a_{kj}dX_j \\ dN = \sum_{j=1}^{m} a_{nj}dX_j \end{cases}$$

We may list sectors from 1 to m in the order of factor intensities such that

$$\frac{a_{k1}}{a_{n1}} \geq \frac{a_{k2}}{a_{n2}} \geq \ldots \geq \frac{a_{km}}{a_{nm}}$$

If $\dfrac{dK}{dN} > \dfrac{K}{N}$, $dX=(dX_1, \ldots, dX_m)$ should be such that

$$\frac{dK}{dN} = \frac{\sum_{j=1}^{m} a_{kj}dX_j}{\sum_{j=1}^{m} a_{nj}dX_j} > \frac{\sum_{j=1}^{m} a_{kj}X_j}{\sum_{j=1}^{m} a_{nj}X_j}$$

i.e., the additional weights $(dX_j$'s$)$ should be more capital-intensive than the original weights $(X_j$'s$)$, such that the new weighted average factor intensity ratio of production

$$F_p = \frac{K+dK}{N+dN} = \frac{\sum_{j=1}^{m} a_{kj}X_j + \sum_{j=1}^{m} a_{kj}dX_j}{\sum_{j=1}^{m} a_{nj}X_j + \sum_{j=1}^{m} a_{nj}dX_j}$$

is larger than the old one, K/N. We will assume a small country exporting relatively labor intensive commodities and $dK/dN > K/N$ in the following section.

---

[2] M. C. Kemp, *The Pure Theory of International Trade and Investment*, New Jersey: Prentice-Hall, 1969, Chapter 1.

2. A Two-Sector Multi-Commodity Trade Pattern

In order to derive a proposition regarding the pattern of trade, we now have to introduce the demand side. Assuming a constant set of commodity prices and hence constant factor prices (w_k, w_n), an increase in the supply of capital and labor implies that income (Y) increases by $dY = w_k dK + w_n dN$. If we assume, tentatively, unitary income elasticities of demand for all commodities, there will occur a balanced growth of domestic demand for each good at the rate of dY/Y, and hence there will be no change in the weighted factor intensity ratio of domestic demand, F_c, where

$$F_c = \frac{\sum_{j=1}^{m} a_{kj}C_j + \sum_{j=1}^{m} a_{kj}dC_j}{\sum_{j=1}^{m} a_{nj}C_j + \sum_{j=1}^{m} a_{nj}dC_j}$$

Since F_p has increased and F_c has stayed constant, the weighted average factor intensity ratio of exports, F_e, should also increase, where

$$F_e = \frac{\sum_{j \varepsilon E} a_{kj} [(X_j + dX_j) - (C_j + dC_j)]}{\sum_{j \varepsilon E} a_{nj} [(X_j + dX_j) - (C_j + dC_j)]}$$

where E represents the set of export commodities. We expect the opposite result for the weighted average factor intensity ratio of imports.[3]

We know that every export commodity of the country need not be more N-intensive in relation to every import commodity of the country; the comparative advantage chain can be crisscrossed by the actual trade pattern.[4] Moreover we know that the (either relative or absolute) increase in production will not be restricted to the more K-intensive commodities, i.e., the production of some labor-intensive goods may also increase. The only certainty is that the country with $dK/dN > K/N$ must be producing a combination of commodities such that the new weighted average factor

---

[3] Cf. Wontack Hong, "The Heckscher-Ohlin Theory of Factor Price Equalization and the Indeterminacy in International Specialization," *International Economic Review*, June 1970 and "A Global Equilibrium Pattern of Specialization: A Model to Approximate Linder's World of Production and Trade," *The Swedish Journal of Economics*, December 1969.

[4] J. Bhagwati, "The Heckscher-Ohlin Theorem in the Multi-Commodity Case," *Journal of Political Economy*, September/October 1972.

intensity F_p is larger than the old ratio K/N, and that the country must be exporting a "bundle of exports" with a higher capital/labor ratio than before and importing a "bundle of imports" with a lower capital/labor ratio, unless there exist non-unitary income elasticities of demand and these elasticities are such that the changes in demand strongly favor capital intensive goods. This is the first part of our proposition regarding two-factor multi-commodity trade pattern.

3. Changes in the Wage/Rental Ratio and Sectoral Capital/Labor Ratios

If we do not assume infinitely elastic foreign demand, the increased exports and/or decreased imports of relatively capital-intensive commodities will lower the relative prices of capital intensive goods in varying degrees. After full price-output adjustments, however, the two-good two-factor original Stolper-Samuelson theorem will hold for any pair of relatively capital-intensive good (whose price has fallen) and labor-intensive good (whose price has risen). That is, we expect a higher wage/rental ratio and higher sectoral capital-labor ratios than before. Furthermore, since the origin of disturbance was the relative increase in the production of capital-intensive goods, the ex-post increase in sectoral capital intensities will not completely reverse the changes in the output pattern to a relative decrease in the production of capital intensive goods.[5]

If we assume a constant set of international prices and incomplete specialization, there is no room for changes in the wage/rental ratio and sectoral capital-labor ratios within the framework of the Rybczynski-Stolper-Samuelson theorems. However, if we presume a Lewis-type dual economy with large amounts of disguised unemployment in the rural sector, we may observe rising wage/rental ratios and rising sectoral capital-labor ratios in both the rural and industrial sectors as capital accumulates, even assuming a constant set of international commodity prices. That is, if the (per capita) capital accumulation of the economy is not limited to the industrial sectors, the average product of labor in agricultural sector will also increase, and as a result the wage rates and

---

[5] Cf. M. C. Kemp, *op. cit.*, Chapter 1.

sectoral capital-labor ratios in the industrial sectors will be driven upward.[6]

Assuming that the economy starts from an equilibrium state with a given set of international commodity prices, the rising wage/rental ratio would imply an increase in the relative profitability of producing capital intensive goods either for exports or for import substitution. Extra factor supplies available to the economy, if not the already invested capital stock and the associated workers, would naturally tend to flow into the relatively more capital intensive sectors.

The rising wage/rental ratio and the associated factor substitutions in both the capital and labor-intensive sectors would slow down the expansion of the capital intensive sectors. However, the greater the rate of increase in the wage/rental ratio and the higher the rate of per capita capital accumulation in the industrial sector, the faster will be the expansion of the capital intensive sectors producing for exports and/or for import-substitution.

A relative increase in the production of capital intensive goods implies the increased capital intensity of exports and the decreased capital intensity of imports (due to import substitution for capital intensive imports) unless changes in the domestic demand pattern more than offset changes in the output pattern. However, the substitution of capital for labor in every industry caused by the rising wage/rental ratio implies increased capital intensity of both export production and import substitution. That is, we expect increased capital intensity of exports due to both changes in output (and consequently the trade) pattern as well as factor substitution to accompany per capita capital stock increases in an economy. We may also expect a decline in the capital intensity of imports due to changes in output pattern (i.e., due to increased production of capital intensive goods) but the import competing industries themselves will become more capital intensive due to factor substitution. This somewhat loose description of a disequilibrium sequence constitutes the second part of our proposition on the changing factor intensity of trade.

---

[6] The wage which the growing industrial (capitalist) sector has to pay is determined in Lewis' model by what labor earns in the agricultural (subsistence) sector. Industrial wages, as a rule, will have to be somewhat higher than the agricultural earnings in order to compensate labor for the cost of transferring. Hence the rise in average product in agricultural sector due to agricultural capital formation will cause a rise in wage rate in the industrial sector, even if we assume a constant set of commodity prices. See A. Lewis, "Economic Development with Unlimited Supplies of Labor," *The Manchester School*, May 1954 and G. R. Ranis and J. H. Fei, "A Theory of Economic Development," *American Economic Review*, September 1961.

CHAPTER 3

DOMESTIC AND FOREIGN SAVINGS AND CAPITAL FORMATION

1. Savings and Investments

During the nine year period of 1953–61, domestic consumption expenditures in Korea averaged nearly 98 percent of GNP, and gross domestic capital formation could be maintained at the 10 percent level (of GNP) only through the inflow of large amounts of foreign savings, mostly U.S. grants-in aid. Annual domestic savings amounted to even less than the estimated annual consumption of fixed capital which amounted to about 4 percent of GNP during 1953–61.

Since 1962, however, the share of consumption expenditures in GNP has steadily fallen, and amounted to an average of 88 percent of GNP during 1962–71. Foreign savings continued to amount to about 9 percent of GNP during 1962–71 and due to increased domestic savings the share of gross investment increased to about 20 percent of GNP during this period. During 1972–73, the share of investment in GNP amounted to about 24 percent while that of foreign savings amounted to less than 5 percent.

The provisions for the consumption of fixed capital stock stood at around 4 percent of GNP during 1953–61, and steadily increased to more than 8 percent during 1972–73. If we can take the difference between gross investment and provisions for the consumption of fixed capital stock as net investment, net investment averaged about 6 percent of GNP during 1953–61, about 15 percent during 1962–71, and about 16 percent during

Table 3.1. Total Available Resources, Consumption and Investment

Percentage Ratio to GNP

Average Annual Ratios	Total Available Resources (GNP Plus Foreign Savings) Estimate I	Estimate II	Consumption Expenditures	Gross Investment
1953–61	107%	108%	98%	10%
1962–71	109%	109%	88%	20%
1972–73	105%	103%	81%	24%

Average Annual Ratios	Provisions for the Consumption of Fixed Capital Government	Private	Net Domestic Savings Government	Private
1953–61	0.5%	3.5%	–2.6%	1.1%
1962–66	0.5%	4.2%	0.1%	1.2%
1967–71	0.4%	5.6%	5.3%	3.1%
1972–73	0.5%	7.7%	—	—

Source: The Bank of Korea, *National Income Statistics Yearbook*.
Note: Estimate I computed the foreign savings by taking the differences between imports and exports at current market prices which were then deflated by the implicit price deflator for gross domestic capital formation. Estimate II computed the foreign savings by taking the differences between imports and exports at 1970 constant market prices which were constructed by the Bank of Korea.

1972–73. This increase in the magnitude of investment seems to have been reflected in the rapid GNP growth experienced during 1962–73.

According to the National Income Statistics of the Bank of Korea, the private sector contributed nearly 90 percent of the provisions for the consumption of fixed capital stock throughout the period 1953–73. However, the private sector contribution to "net" domestic saving was negligible (being less than two percent of GNP) during 1953–66, and did not increase very much (being about 3 percent of GNP) during 1966–71. On the other hand, while the contribution of the government sector to the provisions for the consumption of fixed capital stock was suspiciously small throughout the period of 1953–73, its contribution to "net" domestic saving increased from less than zero percent of GNP on the average during 1953–65 to more than 5 percent during 1966–71.

If we accept the BOK's national income statistics as they are, the following picture emerges. The private enterprises financed most of the ever-increasing provisions for the consumption of fixed capital. But neither private enterprises nor private households contributed any sizable amount to "net" domestic savings. Indeed, the contribution of household sector was negative during 1960–65, though its contribution increased after the interest rate adjustment. Therefore, it appears that it was the rapidly increasing contribution of government savings and the steady inflow of foreign savings which enabled Korea to achieve the very high rate of investment during the 1962–73 period. Moreover, it might be speculated that any further expansion of net investments and savings in Korea would be possible only through fuller realization of the savings potential of private enterprises and, especially, households.

2. Capital Formation

On the basis of the 1968 National Wealth Survey data, Professor K.C. Han has computed the fixed capital stock employed in industrial production, while including the ownership of dwellings as a form of fixed capital stock for industrial production.[1] Total gross (undepreciated) fixed capital stock in 1968 was estimated by Han to be 4,836.4 billion won, and the total average (gross) capital-output ratio of 1.60103 was derived for the 1968 Korean economy as a whole. He also estimated the same coefficient on a net (depreciated) basis to be 1.04721. We have adopted Han's estimate of 3,163.5 billion won as the net fixed capital stock in 1968. (See Table A.23.)

In order to measure the annual (sectoral) fixed capital stock for the period after 1953, we used Han's net fixed capital stock estimate for 1968 as a benchmark and subtracted (or added) the net annual fixed capital formation for successive years.[2] (See Tables A.24. through A.27.) In 1953, the total net fixed capital stock (including the ownership of dwellings) amounted to about $7.7 billion in 1970 dollar prices. It increased by an average annual rate of 1.8 percent during 1953–61, 4.1 percent during

---

[1] K. C. Han, *Estimates of Korean Capital and Inventory Coefficients in 1968*, Seoul: Yonsei University, 1970, and Economic Planning Board, *Report on National Wealth Survey (as of December 31, 1968)*, Seoul, 1972. According to the National Wealth Survey conducted by the Economic Planning Board, the total national wealth in the form of fixed capital in 1968 was estimated to be 4,819.8 billion won in gross terms (i.e., price-adjusted but undepreciated acquisition prices) and 2,469.1 billion won in net terms (i.e., depreciated). Excluding the household wealth in the form of dwellings, it also estimated the total fixed capital sotck employed in industrial production to be 3,028.3 billion won in gross terms and 1,875.3 billion won in net terms.

[2] We computed the annual net fixed capital formation by subtracting the provisions for the consumption of fixed capital stock from the gross value of fixed capital formation. Since these annual fixed capital formation data have been provided by the Bank of Korea, we will call our annual (sectoral) net capital stock data as "Han-BOK" data.

Table 3.2. Capital Formation in Korea: 1953–73

In Million 1970 Dollars & Percent

	Composition of Annual Gross Fixed Capital Formation				Total Net Fixed Capital Stock	
	Dwellings	Buildings & Structure	Machinery & Transport Eq.	Total	Including Dwellings	Excluding Dwellings
1953	23%	52%	25%	164	7,650	3,293
1954	30%	43%	27%	209	7,736	3,364
1955	18%	49%	33%	238	7,855	3,471
1956	18%	40%	42%(24%)	253	7,987	3,585
1957	14%	46%	40%(21%)	293	8,145	3,731
1958	14%	49%	37%(18%)	282	8,286	3,862
1959	17%	53%	30%(18%)	300	8,437	3,992
1960	24%	42%	34%(17%)	312	8,602	4,110
1961	18%	50%	32%(16%)	336	8,796	4,269
1962	14%	53%	33%(20%)	429	9,058	4,495
1963	13%	53%	34%(26%)	540	9,389	4,784
1964	15%	55%	30%(17%)	499	9,661	5,001
1965	14%	58%	28%(14%)	629	10,047	5,323
1966	12%	47%	41%(22%)	948	10,725	5,909
1967	12%	45%	43%(31%)	1,155	11,564	6,637
1968	13%	46%	41%(37%)	1,604	12,782	7,667
1969	11%	51%	38%(30%)	2,058	14,373	9,055
1970	14%	51%	35%(27%)	2,093	15,950	10,375
1971	14%	46%	40%(30%)	2,191	17,567	11,709
1972	14%	45%	41%(33%)	2,122	18,940	12,823
1973	14%	45%	41%(37%)	2,743	20,730	14,253

Source: Tables A. 28. and A. 29., and the Bank of Korea, *National Income Statistics Yearbook* and *Economic Statistics Yearbook*.
Note: The figures in the parentheses represent the portion of imported machineries and transport equipments.

1962–66, and a remarkable 9.9 percent annually during 1967–73, reaching a total of $20.7 billion in 1973.

If we exclude the ownership of dwellings, the total net fixed capital stock in 1953 amounted to only $3.3 billion. It increased by an average annual rate of 3.5 percent during 1953–61, 6.7 percent during 1962–66 and 13.4 percent annually during 1967–73, standing at $14.3 billion level in 1973. As will be shown throughout this paper, the remarkably high rates of capital accumulation in the recent period can not but had an enormous impact on the economic structure of the country.

About 20 percent of annual gross fixed capital formation was in the form of household dwellings during 1953–61, but the share of dwellings declined to less than 15 percent after 1962. Machinery and transportation equipment made up about 30 percent of total fixed capital formation during 1953–65, but this share increased to over 40 percent after 1966. Until 1966, about half of the machinery and transportation equipment used for capital formation were supplied by domestic producers. However, following the increase of this component in total investment, about 80–90 percent of new machinery and transportation equipment has been imported since 1967. We can also see that nearly half of gross fixed capital formation was in the form of non-residential buildings and structures.

The annual rate of aggregate capital depreciation was about 1–2 percent during 1953–61, but this rate subsequently increased to more than 4 percent.[3] (See Table A.28.) Applying these annual depreciation rates, the age structure of the fixed capital stock in Korea can be examined. In 1973 about 20 percent of the existing total fixed capital stock could be dated to the pre-1953 period while about 40 percent of it had been created after 1970.

If we exclude the ownership of dwellings from total fixed capital stock, the annual rate of aggregate capital depreciation becomes much higher, i.e., 2–3 percent during 1953–61, 3–5 percent during 1962–67, and 5–7 percent during 1968–73. Furthermore, it can also be observed that the industrial capital stock (which excludes household dwellings) in Korea is really quite new. In 1973 less than 10 percent of the total existing industrial capital stock could be dated to the pre-1953 period, while half of it could be dated to the 1970–73 period, and more than three-quarters of the entire fixed capital stock could be dated to the post-1966 period. (See Table A.29.) The relative youth and the high level of import content in machinery and transportation equipment seem to suggest that Korean industries have primarily been using new capital stock embodying the most up-to-date production technologies. We may also speculate that there must have been large amounts of embodied technical transference and diffusion during 1966–73, a period which exhibited remarkably high rates of capital accumulation and depreciation.

---

[3] We computed the annual rate of aggregate capital depreciation by taking the annual provision for the consumption of fixed capital stock as the real annual magnitude of fixed capital depreciation.

CHAPTER 4

SUPPLY OF LABOR AND EMPLOYMENT

1. Labor Force and Employment

A. Growth of Labor Supply and Employment

According to the population census data, the total population of Korea in 1949 was about 20.2 million and increased to 21.5 million by 1955, 25.0 million by 1960, 29.2 million by 1966 and to 31.4 million by 1970.[1] If we exclude the inter-war period, the population growth rates have been steadily falling, i.e., from an average annual growth rate of 3.1 percent during 1955–60 to 2.6 percent during 1960–66 and 1.9 percent during 1966–70. According to the sample survey conducted by the Economic Planning Board in 1974, the average annual population growth rate during 1970–74 was about 1.7 percent.

We may represent the age group 14–69 as the "potential labor force" which can be engaged either in industrial production, education or housekeeping. The potential labor force was about 10.7 million in 1949, 12.3 million in 1955, 14.4 million in 1960, 16.6 million in 1966 and 18.3 million in 1970. In contrast with the steadily decreasing rates of aggregate population growth, the supply of potential labor force has been growing at a fairly rapid rate: an average annual growth rate of 2.4 percent during 1949–55, 3.1 percent during 1955–60 and 2.5 percent during 1960–66 and

---

[1] The pre-1960 population census data were obtained from Economic Planning Board, *Korea Statistical Yearbook: 1973*.

Table 4.1. Total Population, Potential Labor Force and Effective Labor Supply: Population Census Data (1960, 1966 & 1970)

In Million Persons & Percent[1]

	Complete Enumeration		Economically Active Population in Age Group 14–69 (10% Sample)					
	Total Population[2]	Potential Labor Force[3]	Effective Labor Supply[4]			Labor Force Participation Rate[5]		
			Both Sex	Male	Female	Both Sex	Male	Female
1960	24.95	14.35	7.35[6]	5.26[6]	2.09[6]	51%[7]	74%[7]	29%[7]
	(2.6%)	(2.5%)	(2.7%)	(2.1%)	(4.2%)			
1966	29.16	16.61	8.61	5.94	2.67	52%	72%	32%
	(1.9%)	(2.5%)	(4.6%)	(3.1%)	(7.8%)			
1970	31.44	18.34	10.30	6.70	3.60	56%	74%	39%

Source: Economic Planning Board, *1960 Population and Housing Census of Korea*, Vol. 1, Complete Tabulation Report and Vol. 2, 20% Sample Tabulation Report; *1966 Population Census Report of Korea*; and *1970 Population and Housing Census Report*, Vol. 1, Complete Enumeration and Vol. 2, 10% Sample Survey, (4–1) Economic Activity.

[1] Percentage figures in the parentheses represent the average annual growth rates during the inter-census years.
[2] Excluding the foreigners.
[3] Represents the age group 14–69.
[4] Represents the sum of persons employed and unemployed.
[5] Labor force participation rates were obtained by dividing the economically active population figures (14–69 years old) from the 10% Sample Survey with the total number of population figures (14–69 years old) from the Complete Enumeration of Population Census. Military personnel residing inside of military bases were excluded from the economically active population figures while they were included in the population totals.
[6] Age group 15–69 by Korean traditional counting age.
[7] We obtained the male and female population of age group 15–70 exclusive of foreigners by applying those ratios inclusive of foreigners to the total population figure which excludes foreigners.

Table 4.2. *Potential Labor Force and Effective Labor Supply: Quarterly Sample Survey Data (1963–74)*

In Million Persons & Percent

Economically Active Population in Age Group 14 Years Old & Over (0.1% Sample)

	Population 14 Years Old & Over	Effective Labor Supply			Labor Force Participation Rate			Unemployment Rate		
		Both Sex	Male	Female	Both Sex	Male	Female	Both Sex	Male	Female
1963	15.1	8.3	5.5	2.9	55%	76%	36%	8.2%	8.7%	7.2%
1964	15.5	8.5	5.6	2.9	55%	76%	35%	7.7%	8.8%	5.6%
1965	15.9	8.9	5.8	3.1	56%	77%	37%	7.4%	8.4%	5.5%
1966	16.4	9.1	6.0	3.1	55%	77%	36%	7.1%	8.1%	5.3%
1967	16.8	9.3	6.1	3.2	55%	76%	37%	6.2%	6.6%	5.4%
1968	17.2	9.7	6.2	3.4	56%	76%	38%	5.1%	5.6%	4.2%
1969	17.6	9.9	6.4	3.5	56%	77%	38%	4.8%	5.1%	4.3%
1970	18.3	10.2	6.5	3.7	56%	75%	39%	4.5%	5.4%	2.9%
1971	19.0	10.5	6.7	3.8	56%	74%	39%	4.5%	5.2%	3.2%
1972	19.7	11.1	7.1	4.0	56%	75%	39%	4.5%	5.6%	2.5%
1973	20.4	11.6	7.3	4.3	57%	74%	41%	4.0%	5.0%	2.3%
1974	21.2	12.1	..	..	57%	..	..	4.1%	..	..

Source: Economic Planning Board, *Annual Report on the Economically Active Population: 1974.*
Note: Foreigners, soldiers and prisoners are excluded from the survey.

1966–70.

We may now define the "effective labor supply" as the sum of total employed and unemployed persons, i.e., the so-called economically active population. According to the (10 percent) sample surveys conducted together with the 1960, 1966 and 1970 population censuses, the effective labor supply was about 7.4 million in 1960 (5.3 million males and 2.1 million females), about 8.6 million in 1966 (5.9 million males and 2.7 million females), and about 10.3 million in 1970 (6.7 million males and 3.6 million females). Female labor engaged in industrial production grew more than twice as fast as the male industrial labor force during 1960–66 and 1966–70. As a result, the labor force participation rate of women increased from about 29 percent in 1960 to 32 percent in 1966, and to about 39 percent in 1970, while among males the economic participation rate fluctuated around 74 percent.

According to the Economic Planning Board's method of classifying employed and unemployed persons (counting everyone who did "any" work during the week immediately preceding the census date as employed) the employment rates increased from about 91 percent during 1960–66 to 95 percent in 1970 for men and from 94–95 percent during 1960–66 to about 98 percent in 1970 for among women.[2]

We have two different sources of employment data. One is the 10 percent sample survey conducted during the population census (20 percent sample in 1960) and the other is the quarterly 0.1 percent sample survey carried out since 1963. Both of them are surveyed by the Economic Planning Board but there are significant differences between them. For instance, according to the census data, the average annual growth rate of employment was 2.3 percent during 1960–66 and 6.3 percent during 1966–70. But according to the quarterly sample data, the growth rate was 3.7 percent during 1966–70, and it is generally believed that the latter data underestimated the increase in employment during the period.

According to the census data, total employed persons in the manufacturing sector amounted to only about 7 percent of total employed persons (i.e., about 0.5 million) in 1960, which was increased to 12 percent (about 1 million) in 1966 and to more than 14 percent (about 1.5 million) in 1970. The number of persons employed in the agricultural sector was nearly 64 percent of all employed persons in 1960, but declined to 55 percent in 1966 and to 49 percent in 1970. On the other hand, the number of persons

---

[2] The employed include persons who had a job or business but did not work temporarily due to vacations, bad weather, illness, labor disputes or personal reasons. The statistics exclude military personnel who resided "inside" military bases.

Table 4.3. Employed Persons by Industry (14 Years & Over): 1960–73

[In Million Persons

	Agriculture, Fishery & Mining Male Female	Manufacturing Male Female	Social Overhead & Service Male Female	Total Employed Persons Male Female
1960	*3.27 1.41*	*0.35 0.13*	*1.39 0.49*	*4.95 1.98*
1963	3.05 1.84	0.43 0.18	1.51 0.65	4.99 2.67
1964	3.04 1.83	0.44 0.20	1.60 0.68	5.08 2.72
1965	3.04 1.85	0.54 0.24	1.74 0.80	5.32 2.88
1966	3.06 1.90	0.57 0.26	1.86 0.78	5.48 2.94
1966	*3.08 1.57*	*0.64 0.32*	*1.71 0.65*	*5.43 2.54*
1967	3.01 1.90	0.68 0.34	1.96 0.83	5.66 3.06
1968	2.97 1.94	0.77 0.40	2.11 0.96	5.86 3.30
1969	3.05 1.89	0.80 0.43	2.24 1.00	6.09 3.33
1970	2.97 2.06	0.86 0.42	2.34 1.10	6.17 3.58
1970	*3.11 2.14*	*0.93 0.52*	*2.54 0.91*	*6.58 3.58*
1971	2.92 2.05	0.87 0.47	2.58 1.18	6.37 3.70
1972	3.10 2.30	0.96 0.49	2.61 1.10	6.67 3.89
1973	3.27 2.35	1.09 0.68	2.57 1.18	6.92 4.22

Source: The same as Table 4.1. and Table 4.2.
Note: *Italic* figures are 10% sample figures collected during the population census. The remainder are 0.1% quarterly sample figures. 1960 employment figures include the age group 12–13. (Total number of employed persons excluding the 12–13 age group amounted to 6,933 thousand in 1960. Farm workers belonging to the age group 12–13 totalled 70,495 in 1960.)

employed in the social overhead and service sectors steadily increased from about 27 percent of total employed persons in 1960 to about 30 percent in 1966 and about 34 percent in 1970.

It is noteworthy that while the total number of female workers employed in the primary and tertiary sectors increased by 65 percent during 1960-70, the number of female workers employed in manufacturing sector more than quadrupled. There was a 50 percent increase in female labor employed in primary sectors (agriculture, forestry, fishery and mining sectors) during 1960-70, while the number of male workers employed in the primary sector *decreased* by 5 percent. It seems that an ever increasing portion of the labor in both the manufacturing sector and the traditional primary sectors is being provided by the female work force. On the other hand, there was about 80 percent increase in both male and female labor employed in the social overhead and service sectors during 1960-70. Such rapid increases in female employment during 1960-70 elevated the female labor force participation rate to about 40 percent from less than 30 percent at the beginning of the period.

B. Disguised Unemployment in the Agricultural Sector

According to the census data, the total number of employed persons (14 & over) amounted to about 6.93 million in 1960, 7.96 million in 1966 and 10.15 million in 1970. Among these, 4.39 million in 1960, 4.39 million in 1966 and 4.86 million in 1970 were employed in agricultural sectors. Agricultural employment figures are well-known to be biased in the upward direction because of extensive disguised unemployment.[3] The problem is aggravated by the practice of the Economic Planning Board which defines as employed persons "all persons fourteen years and over who did *any* work during the reference period before census date for pay or profit, including unpaid family worker and persons who had a job but did not work temporarily".

Since 1962, the Ministry of Agriculture & Forestry (now "Fishery" instead of "Forestry") has conducted annual sample surveys on 1,200 farm households spread over 80 enumeration districts throughout the country covering 124 questions concerning the farm household economy. "The Report on the Results of Farm Household Economy Survey and Production Cost Survey of Agricultural Products" (which will be simply called the "Farm Household Survey" in this paper) is regarded as the most reliable source of information on the agricultural sector in Korea.

The Farm Household Survey provides estimates of annual labor input on a man-hour basis. If we multiply the average labor input per farm household by the total number of farm households, and if we assume an eight hour working day and 280 working days a year, we get 2.90 million man-years employed in the agricultural sector in 1966 and 2.39 million

---

[3] The strict interpretation of disguised unemployment is that the marginal productivity of labor, over a wide range, is zero. The disguised unemployment may take the form of a smaller than "normal" number of working hours per head per year. Seasonal underemployment is not regarded as disguised unemployment. However, since it can become a temporary migrant labor in the industrial sector, we use the term "disguised unemployment" loosely here to include the seasonal underemployment also. See A. Lewis, "Economic Development with Unlimited Supplies of Labor" *The Manchester School*, May 1954, and G. R. Ranis and J. H. Fei, "A Theory of Economic Development," *American Economic Review*, September 1961.

Table 4.4. Total Number of Employed Persons Adjusted: 1960, 1966 & 1970

In Million Persons or Man-Year

	Total Employed Persons		Employed Persons in Agricultural Sector				Adjusted Total Employed Persons	
	Census 10% Sample (A)	Quarterly 0.1% Sample (Annual Av.)	Census 10% Sample (B)	Quarterly 0.1% Sample[1] (Annual Av.)	Farm Household Survey (C)	Farm Household & I-O Output (D)	A-(B-C)	A-(B-D)
1960	6.93	—	4.39	—	—	—	—	—
	(2.3%)[2]		(0.0%)					
1966	7.96	8.42	4.39	4.70	2.90[3]	3.42[4]	6.47	6.99
	(6.3%)	(3.7%)	(2.6%)	(0.7%)	(-4.9%)	(-4.9%)	(-4.4%)	(-3.7%)
1970	10.15	9.75	4.86	4.83	2.39[3]	2.80[4]	7.68	8.09

Source: Ministry of Agriculture & Fisheries, *Reports on the Results of Farm Household Economy Survey: 1974*, The Bank of Korea, *Economic Statistics Yearbook: 1974* and Economic Planning Board, *Annual Report on the Economically Active Population: 1973* and *Population and Housing Census Report: 1960, 1966 & 1970*.

[1] Includes persons employed in forestry.
[2] Figures in the parentheses represent the constant average annual growth rates during the intercensus periods.
[3] Represents total labor input (in man-years) in the agricultural sector including non-agricultural work, which amounted to 0.56 million man-years in 1966 and 0.38 million in 1970.
[4] Estimated by applying the labor-output ratios of agricultural sectors obtained from the Farm Household Economy Survey to the agricultural output values presented in the input-output tables.

man-years in 1970, which are less than two-thirds the census agricultural employment figures.[4]

Possibly due to sampling bias, there were substantial differences between the estimates of agricultural outputs based on the Farm Household Survey and those presented in the input-output tables. If we apply the labor-output ratios obtained from the Farm Household Survey to the agricultural output values presented in the input-output tables, we get 3.42 million man-years in 1966 and 2.80 million man-years in 1970, which are still 20–40 percent less than the census employment figures.

It is possible to consider the difference between the Census (10% Sample) agricultural employment figures and the estimated man-year figure based on the Farm Household Survey or on labor coefficients from the Farm Household Survey and output values from the input-output table as a measure of disguised unemployment in the Korean agricultural sector. This amounted to about 1.5 million persons (or one million persons according to the latter approach) in 1966 and about 2.5 million persons (or two million persons) in 1970. If we subtract disguised unemployment, the total number of employed persons in 1970, for instance, becomes 7.7 million persons (or 8.1 million persons by the latter estimate.)

According to the 1960 population census data, each household in rural areas included an average of 0.26 dependent parents, which was 73 percent larger than in urban areas, and an average of 0.45 relatives, which was 25 percent larger than that in urban areas.[5] On the other hand, according to the EPB's quarterly 0.1 percent sample survey, the average number of hours worked per week in the manufacturing and service sectors was about 30 percent greater than that in the agricultural sector during 1963–72. The 1970 Population Census (10% Sample) also classifies the employed persons according to the duration of work. When we convert the employment data into man-years, we get an estimate about 8 million for 1970. Hence we may safely assume that, overall, disguised unemployment in Korea in 1970 was equivalent to at least two million man-years.

The average annual growth rate of the population during 1970–73 was about 1.7 percent, and the female labor force participation ratio stood at only about 40 percent in 1973. It seems, therefore, that Korea still possesses a vast reservoir of potential labor in the forms of natural population

---

[4] It is generally regarded reasonable to assume 280 working days a year in the agricultural sector. See Y. S. Cho, *Disguised Unemployment in Underdeveloped Areas, with Special Reference to South Korean Agriculture*, Berkely, 1963.

[5] On the other hand, each household in the urban areas included 0.32 non-relatives who seem to have been chiefly household maids.

growth, increases in female labor force participation, and disguised unemployment in agricultural sector and possibly also in service sector.

2. Educational Level of the Labor Force

A. Changes in Labor Force Distribution by Amount of Education

Educational background is a crucial determinant of the quality of labor. It conditions both the type of work an individual is able to do and his efficiency in doing it.[6]

Table 4.5. Population 14 Years Old & Over by Level of Education: 1960 & 1970

In Million Persons & Percent

	Total	\newline Years of School Completed				
		0	1–6	7–9	10–12	13 & over
Male						
1960	7.30	2.32	2.76	1.00	0.85	0.33
1970	9.31	1.47	3.25	2.01	1.75	0.83
Net Change	(28%)	(−37%)	(18%)	(101%)	(106%)	(152%)
Female						
1960	7.53	4.15	2.58	0.43	0.28	0.05
1970	9.63	2.97	4.18	1.39	0.87	0.22
Net Change	(28%)	(−28%)	(62%)	(223%)	(211%)	(340%)

Source: The same as Table 4.1.

The total potential labor force (age group 14 & over) increased by 33 percent during 1960–70, while that of employed persons increased by 47 percent. Not only was there a relative increase in the number of productively employed persons in the potential labor force, there has also been a significant upward movement of the distribution of Korea's potential labor force by amount of formal education during 1960–70.

In 1960, about 44 percent of age group 14 & over had no formal education. However, the percentage of the potential labor force without formal education declined to about 24 percent by 1970. The potential

[6] E. F. Denison, *Why Growth Rates Differ*, Washington D. C.: The Brooking Institution, 1967, Chapter 8.

labor force with a college education amounted to about 2.6 percent of the total in 1960, but was 5.5 percent in 1970. Furthermore, the potential female labor force with at least a senior high school education (10 or more years of education) amounted to only about 4.4 percent of the total potential female labor force in 1960, but rose to 11.3 percent by 1970. The potential male labor force with at least a senior high school education increased from about 16 percent in 1960 to about 28 percent in 1970.

There was about an 80 percent increase in the total number of employed females during 1960-70. At the same time, the number of women with a (junior & senior) high school or college education more than tripled. On the other hand, the number of men with a (junior & senior) high school or college education more than doubled during 1960-70, while the total number of employed males increased by 33 percent.

B. Increases in the Educational Level of the Labor Force by Industry and Occupation

A better educated work force will be better able to learn about and utilize the most efficient production practices available. According to the sample surveys on employed persons by occupation (20 percent sample in 1960 and 10 percent sample in 1970), about 45 percent of all employed persons in 1960 had no formal education and only 15 percent had a high school or college education. However, the proportion of employed persons without any formal education declined to about 24 percent by 1970, and about 32 percent of all employed persons had a high school or college education in 1970. In particular, the proportion of employed persons with a college education increased from about 2 percent of the total in 1960 to about 6 percent in 1970.

In 1960, only one quarter of the professional, technical and administrative workers had a college education. By 1970, however, more than half had a college level education. Nearly 30 percent of sales and service workers in 1960 lacked formal education, but this proportion was reduced to about 10 percent by 1970, while the proportion of sales and service workers with a high school or college level education nearly doubled. About 80 percent of production process workers had no more than an elementary education in 1960, but in 1970 nearly half enjoyed a high school level education.

According to the (10 percent) sample surveys on employed persons by industry which were conducted together with the population censuses in 1966 and 1970, there was a significant decrease in the proportion of em-

Table 4.6. Employed Persons by Occupation and Level of Education: 1960 & 1970

In Million Persons & Percent

	Professional Technical & Admin.	Clerical Workers	Sales & Service Workers	Production Process Workers	Farmers & Fishermen	Total[1]
1960						
Total Employed	0.26	0.18	0.99	0.93	4.61	6.93
0 y.e.[2]	7%	1%	29%	26%	55%	45%
1–6 y.e.	20%	21%	45%	54%	37%	39%
7–12 y.e.	48%	58%	22%	18%	7%	13%
13 & over y.e.	25%	20%	3%	2%	0%	2%
1970						
Total Employed	0.42	0.59	1.71	2.20	5.15	10.15
0 y.e.	1%	0%	12%	9%	39%	24%
1–6 y.e.	7%	9%	44%	48%	49%	44%
7–12 y.e.	39%	59%	38%	40%	11%	26%
13 & over y.e.	52%	32%	6%	3%	1%	6%

Source: The same as Table 4.1.

[1] Total includes unclassifiable and unknown workers. Employed persons by occupation and those by industry do not agree each other.

[2] "y.e." stands for "years of education".

Table 4.7. Employed Persons by Industry and Level of Education: 1966 & 1970

In Million Persons & Percent

	Agriculture, Fishery & Mining	Manufacturing	Service	Total
1966				
Total Employed	4.64	0.96	2.36	7.96
0 y.e.	43%	14%	15%	31%
1–6 y.e.	44%	46%	39%	43%
7–12 y.e.	12%	34%	35%	21%
13 & over y.e.	1%	6%	11%	5%
1970				
Total Employed	5.26	1.45	3.45	10.15
0 y.e.	38%	6%	9%	24%
1–6 y.e.	49%	44%	35%	44%
7–12 y.e.	12%	42%	42%	26%
13 & over y.e.	1%	8%	14%	6%

Source: The same as Table. 4.1.

ployed persons without any formal education in the primary sectors. That is, in 1966, about 43 percent of employed persons in the primary sectors had no formal education and about 44 percent had elementary school education, but in 1970 about 39 percent did not have any formal education and 49 percent had an elementary school education. However, this still means that nearly 90 percent of those employed in the primary sectors in 1970 had less than a junior high school education.

In the manufacturing and service sectors, the proportion of employed persons with only an elementary school education and those without formal education also declined significantly during 1966-70, while the proportion of those with a high school or college education greatly increased. Nonetheless, nearly half of those employed in the manufacturing and service sectors in 1970 had only an elementary school education or no formal education.

Although there is still much room for further improvement, it is clear that the level of formal education of the Korean labor force increased fairly rapidly during 1960-70. As a result, there has been a general upgrading of the educational level of the labor force in all occupational categories and in all industrial sectors. The educational level of the female labor force has been rising at an especially rapid rate. One may speculate that this improvement in the educational level of the labor force served to significantly improve the average quality of Korean labor and contributed to the growth of national income.

CHAPTER 5

CAPITAL ACCUMULATION, CAPITAL DEEPENING AND THE RISING WAGE/RENTAL RATIO

1. The Rising Wage/Rental Ratio

The "per capita" capital stock in Korea (excluding the ownership of dwellings) increased by only 30 percent during the fourteen year period 1953–66 (from $156 to $203) and it was only after 1966 that per capita capital stock started to increase very rapidly. The "per capita" capital stock more than doubled during 1966–73, but due to rapidly increasing employment (about a 30 percent increase), the fixed capital stock "per employed person" increased by around 80 percent. However, this still implies that significant overall capital deepening occurred in Korea during 1966–73.

In order to examine the association between capital deepening and wage rates, we computed the average wage rate (and per worker value added) in the manufacturing sector on the basis of the manufacturing census data. We then computed the per worker fixed capital stock in the manufacturing sector on the basis of the Han-BOK capital stock data and the employment data obtained from the population census as well as from the EPB's quarterly sample survey. This revealed a close association between the average wage rates (as well as the per worker value added) and the fixed capital stock per worker in the manufacturing sector. For instance, the per worker capital stock did not increase during 1960–66 and nor did the average wage rate; the former increased significantly during 1967–72 and so did the latter.

Table 5.1. Per Capita and Per Worker Fixed Capital Stock: 1953–74

	Total Fixed Capital Stock (billion 1970 $)[1]	Total Population (million persons)[2]	Total Employed Persons (14 & Over) (million persons)[3]	Per Capita Capital Stock (1970 $)	Capital Per Employed Person (1970 $)
1953	3.29	21.05		156	
1954	3.36	21.27		158	
1955	3.47	21.50		161	
1956	3.59	22.15		162	
1957	3.73	22.82		164	
1958	3.86	23.51		164	
1959	3.99	24.22		165	
1960	4.11	24.95		165	
1961	4.27	25.61		167	
1962	4.50	26.28		171	
1963	4.78	26.98	7.66	177	624
1964	5.00	27.69	7.80	181	641
1965	5.32	28.41	8.21	187	649
1966	5.91	29.16	8.42	203	702
1967	6.64	29.71	8.72	224	761
1968	7.67	30.28	9.16	253	837
1969	9.06	30.85	9.41	294	962
1970	10.38	31.44	9.75	330	1,065
1971	11.71	31.97	10.07	366	1,163
1972	12.82	32.51	10.56	394	1,214
1973	14.25	33.07	11.14	431	1,280
1974	15.73	33.63	11.59	468	1,357

Sources: The same as Tables 4.1., 4.2., A.27. and Economic Planning Board, *Korea Statistical Yearbook: 1973* for pre-1960 population figures.

[1] Excluding the ownership of dwellings.

[2] Population figures for inter-census years were obtained by applying constant average annual growth rates. That is, we applied 1.075% for 1949-55, 3.02% for 1955–60, 2.63% for 1960–66, and 1.90% for 1966–70 population growth. We applied 1.7% for the 1971–74 population growth rate, which was based on the result of the EPB's monthly 0.2% sample survey of population in 1973.

[3] Based on the quarterly 0.1% sample survey of the Economic Planning Board.

Table 5.2. Capital Stock per Worker and Average Wage Rates: Agricultural and Manufacturing Sectors

In Thousand 1970 Dollars

	Agricultural Sector					Manufacturing Sector		
	Per Worker (Population Census Data)	Capital Stock* (EPB Sample Survey Data)	Per Worker Farm Income	Wage for Farm Employee		Per Worker (Population Census Data)	Capital Stock (EPB Sample Survey Data)	Wage Rate for Employee	Per Worker Value Added
1960	0.09	—	—	—		1.62	—	—	0.97
1961	0.10	—	—	—		1.52	—	—	0.71
1962	0.10	—	0.23	0.22		1.44	—	—	0.92
1963	0.11	0.11	0.26	0.21		1.38	1.53	0.33	1.19
1964	0.12	0.12	0.26	0.25		1.30	1.55	—	0.91
1965	0.13	0.13	0.22	0.19		1.26	1.39	—	1.06
1966	0.15	0.14	0.22	0.17		1.33	1.53	0.29	1.16
1967	0.16	0.16	0.23	0.20		1.37	1.43	0.36	1.32
1968	0.17	0.18	0.25	0.23		1.43	1.44	0.41	1.54
1969	0.19	0.19	0.27	0.26		1.47	1.56	0.47	1.82
1970	0.20	0.21	0.28	0.27		1.48	1.67	0.53	2.06
1971	—	0.24	0.35	0.30		—	1.76	0.61	2.53
1972	—	0.25	0.36	0.30		—	1.70	0.61	2.52
1973	—	0.27	0.40	0.35		—	1.58	0.63	2.82

Source: Capital stock data are from Table A.29. Employment data are from the 10 percent sample surveys conducted together with the population census of 1960, 1966 and 1970 (figures for inter-census years being the interpolated ones) and the EPB's quarterly 0.1 percent sample surveys. (See Table 4.3.) Per worker farm income and wage for farm employee data are from the *Reports on the Results of Farm Household Economy Survey* of the Ministry of Agriculture and Fisheries. The data on wage rate for employee and per worker value added of manufacturing sector are from the *Report on Mining and Manufacturing Census (or Survey)* of Economic Planning Board.

* Includes forestry and fishery.

During 1967-72, the per worker capital stock in the manufacturing sector increased by about 19 percent (at an average annual growth rate, r, of 3.6 percent), while the average wage rate for employees increased by about 70 percent (r = 11%) and the value added per worker by about 90 percent (r = 14%).[1] Hence it seems that, in addition to the increase in per worker capital, there have been very significant increases in labor productivity due to technical progress and improved labor quality. However, the fact that per worker value added increased at an average annual growth rate of 14 percent while the wage rate increased by 11 percent implies that a relatively large share of the increased value added was retained as the return for enterpreneurship, which may have been conducive to increased reinvestment and the higher growth rate in the manufacturing sector during 1967-72.

The fixed capital stock per employed person in agriculture, forestry and fishery sector steadily increased throughout the period of 1960-73. However, perhaps reflecting the rapid increase in the social overhead capital stock in Korea since 1966, farm household income per worker as well as the average wage rate for farm household employees started to rise significantly only after 1966.

The capital stock per worker in the agricultural sector has increased by about 56 percent (r = 9.6%) during 1967-72, while the average wage rate for farm employees as well as per worker farm income increased by about 50 percent (r = 8.0%).[2] Although the per worker capital stock in the agricultural sector (excluding land) was still less than one-sixth of that in manufacturing in 1972, the increase in per capita capital stock in agricultural sector was very rapid. However, the rate of increase in farm income was almost identical to that of capital per worker and hence there does not seem to have been a very significant increase in labor productivity in agricultural sector.

Although the per worker capital stock in the agricultural sector has been rising since 1960, and the increase in per worker capital stock in manufacturing during 1967-72 was a moderate 19 percent, wage rates in both

---

[1] As we can see in Table 5.2., there was a 7 percent fall in the per worker fixed capital stock in manufacturing sector in 1973. It seems that the drastic increase in Korea's total (manufactured) exports during the year of 1973 (about 70 percent increase in real terms) caused an unusually high rate of utilization of the production capacities in manufacturing sector. The capital stock in manufacturing increased by 14 percent while the number of workers increased by 23 percent in 1973.

[2] If we examine the Tables 7.1. and 7.3., we can see that the capital-labor ratio for the agricultural sector increased by 65 percent during 1966-70, i.e., from 0.23 in 1966 to 0.38 in 1970.

manufacturing and agricultural sectors only started to rise significantly after 1967. It is tempting, therefore, to associate the rising wage rates in agriculture and manufacturing since 1967 to the rapid accumulation of social overhead capital during 1967-72. The total fixed captial stock in social overhead and other service sectors increased by only 36 percent during 1960-66. However, it grew by 260 percent during 1966-73 and this must have contributed significantly to the over-all efficiency of the Korean economy. (See Tables 7.1. and 7.3.)

Since per worker farm income started to rise significantly after 1967 as did the wage rate for employees in the manufacturing sector, while the increase in per worker capital stock in the manufacturing sector was rather moderate in the 1967-72 period, we may also try to relate these sectoral wage movements in terms of the Lewis model.[3] The wage which the growing industrial (capitalist) sector has to pay is determined in Lewis' model by what labor earns in the agricultural (subsistence) sector. Rural labor will not leave the family farm for industrial employment unless the real wage is at least equal to the average product on the land. Industrial wages will have to be somewhat higher than agricultural earnings in order to compensate labor for transfer costs and to induce labor to abandon the traditional life style. Lewis suggested that a difference of 30 percent or more is required. In Korea, the difference amounted to approximately 40 percent throughout the period 1967-72. (See Table 5.2.) We may have to add the unavoidable extra costs of urban living such as commuting costs, public service fees, etc., and also returns to worker-financed investment in the elementary skill training which is necessary to transform a rural laborer into an industrial worker. Furthermore, there may develop shortages in specific skill groups, and at best there will be a time lag due to the time consuming skill training process. The significant capital accumulation and rise in per worker income in agricultural sector after 1967 and the associated rise in the manufacturing wage rate seem to be consistent with Lewis' hypothesis.

Before 1965 the real interest rates on savings and time deposits were very low and frequently negative. In september 1965, the government drastically raised the nominal interest rates on savings and time deposits in order to increase the absolute magnitude of domestic savings. With inflation more or less under control, the real interest rates on savings reached their peak in 1967, and then both the nominal and real rates were gradually lowered thereafter.

---

[3] A. Lewis, *op. cit.* and G. R. Ranis and J. H. Fei, *op. cit.*

Table 5.3. *Weighted-Average Interest Rates of Total Domestic Loans and the Interest Rate on Time Deposits*

In Billion Won & Percent (%)

	Total Domestic Loans	(Loans by Deposit Money Banks)	Weighted-Average Interest Rates of Total Loans (Nominal)	(Real)	Time & Savings Deposits	Interest Rates on Time Deposits (Over 1 Year) (Nominal)	(Real)
1961	—	—	—	—	5	15.0%	1.8%
1962	—	—	—	—	12	15.0%	5.6%
1963	101	(49)	18.9%	−1.7%	13	15.0%	−5.6%
1964	121	(53)	23.2%	−11.4%	15	51.0%	−19.6%
1965	161	(73)	27.3%	17.3%	31	26.4%	16.4%
1966	229	(103)	30.1%	21.2%	70	26.4%	17.5%
1967	395	(207)	29.1%	22.7%	129	2.64%	20.0%
1968	604	(351)	26.9%	18.8%	256	25.2%	17.1%
1969	946	(597)	25.3%	18.5%	452	22.8%	16.0%
1970	1,282	(808)	24.8%	15.6%	576	22.8%	13.6%
1971	1,652	(1,058)	22.7%	14.1%	709	20.4%	11.8%
1972	—	—	—	—	912	12.0%	−2.0%
1973	—	—	—	—	1,214	12.0%	5.1%

Source: B. K. Shim, et al., *A Study of Preferential Interest Rate Structure: The Korean Experience (1961–71)*, Seoul: Seoul National University, 1972 (mimeographed), and The Bank of Korea, *Monthly Economic Statistics*.

Note: The real rates of interest were computed by subtracting the rates of increase in wholesale price index from the nominal interest rates.

On the other hand, the interest rates on bank loans were also raised in proportion to the increase in interest rates on savings. However, after reaching a peak in 1967, the real interest rates on loans by commercial banks and specialized banks were gradually lowered. Furthermore, the weighted average real interest rate on all types of loans supplied by monetary and non-monetary financial institutions as well as the curb markets also peaked in 1967 and decreased gradually thereafter.[4] This suggests, therefore, that rapid and significant capital accumulation and capital deepening has occurred in Korea since 1966 and has been accompanied by increases in the wage/rental ratio.

2. The Share of Labor in Total National Income

This section estimates labor's share in total income, which will be used in the subsequent chapter to determine the contribution of labor, capital and technical progress to growth.

According to the BOK's national income statistics, the share of compensation of employees in total national income fluctuated around 30 percent throughout the period 1953–66. However, presumably reflecting the rising wage/rental ratio, this share increased to nearly 40 percent during 1967–73, though the growth rate of national income was much higher than the growth rate of the labor supply during this period.

The share of property and other income, such as the income of government enterprises, corporate savings and direct taxes, corporate transfer payments, etc., amounted to about 15 percent of total national income during 1953–64. Presumably due to the rapid capital accumulation and expanded business activities since 1966, this share increased to nearly 20 percent in 1967–73.

The share of agricultural income decreased substantially: from more than 40 percent of total national income during 1953–57 to about 25 percent in 1968–73. The share of the income of unincorporated enterprises did not change greatly.

Since the income of the agricultural sector and unincorporated enterprises include large amounts of implicit return to unpaid family workers and proprietors, the share of compensation of employees can not be re-

---

[4] B. K. Shim, et. al., *op. cit,*

Table 5.4. Distribution of National Income: 1953-73

In Percent

	Compensation of Employees	Agricultural Income	Unincorporated Enterprises	Property & Other Income
1953	25%	43%	16%	16%
1954	31%	36%	18%	15%
1955	30%	41%	18%	11%
1956	28%	43%	18%	11%
1957	30%	43%	16%	11%
1958	34%	38%	15%	13%
1959	38%	31%	17%	14%
1960	37%	34%	14%	15%
1961	34%	38%	13%	15%
1962	37%	34%	13%	16%
1963	31%	40%	14%	15%
1964	28%	43%	15%	14%
1965	31%	35%	18%	16%
1966	33%	32%	18%	17%
1967	37%	28%	16%	19%
1968	38%	25%	16%	21%
1969	39%	26%	17%	18%
1970	39%	26%	16%	19%
1971	39%	27%	16%	18%
1972	39%	27%	17%	18%
1973	37%	24%	21%	19%

Source: The Bank of Korea, *National Income Statistics Yearbook*.

garded as the total return to labor.

The fact that the share of compensation of employees in total national income increased significantly during the 1953-73 period might suggest that the elasticity of substitution between factors is somewhat less than unity. However, the drastic fall in the share of agricultural income during this period suggests that we can get no clear picture of actual changes in labor's share on the basis of the BOK's national income statistics alone.

According to the 1970 input-output table, the share of labor (the so-called compensation of employees) was about 37 percent of total value added (which includes indirect taxes but excludes the consumption of fixed capital). The compensation of employees apparently did not include imputed wages for family workers and other unpaid workers, which are abundant in the agricultural sector and such service industries as wholesale and retail trade.

The Bank of Korea provides data on sectoral paid and unpaid workers in its *Report on the 1970 Input-Output Table*. When we include imputed wages (applying the sectoral average wage rates to unpaid workers), labor's share increases to 71 percent of total value added.

However, since there are substantial differences between the BOK's employment data for the agricultural sector and those from the Farm Household Survey, we decided to compute labor income in agricultural sector using the latter data. That is, we computed the labor-output ratios (on a man-year basis) and average wage rates for paid workers in the agricultural sector using the latter data and then applied these estimates to the agricultural output data as presented in input-output table in order to get total labor employed in the agricultural sector on a man-year basis and to compute total (actual and imputed) labor income in the agricultural sector. In effect, we excluded disguised unemployment in the agricultural sector from the computation of labor income based on the average wage rate of hired labor in agriculture. With this modification for the agricultural sector, a figure of 60 percent is obtained for labor's share of total value added as of 1970.

CHAPTER 6

ANALYSIS OF GROWTH FACTORS

1. Factor Share Approach

This section will adopt the factor share approach in order to calculate the contribution of increases in labor, capital and other residual factors to growth. We will presume a simple neo-classical growth model in which
$$y = Uk + Qn + r$$
where y, k and n represent growth rates of output, capital and labor respectively, and U and Q represent the share of capital income and labor income respectively, *a la* the Cobb-Douglas production function.[1]

This factor share approach will indicate the approximate percentage increase in national income that is expected from increase in each type of factor if the economy were operating under constant returns to scale. If there is technical progress or changes that would improve or worsen factor allocations, the effects will be included in the residual term, r.

The factor share approach provides an accurate estimate if the earnings (prices) of factors of production are proportional to the value of their marginal products. So long as economic units seek to minimize costs, the existence of factor market distortions will not destroy this proportionality, but may prevent utilization of the full potential supply of a given factor.

Since the tendency toward proportionality of factor prices and marginal

---

[1] J. E. Meade, *A Neo-Classical Theory of Economic Growth*, London: Allen & Unwin, 1962, and E. F. Denison, *Why Growth Rates Differ*, Washington D. C.: The Brookings Institution, 1967, Chapter 4.

products is likely to be weaker in developing countries, an analysis of distributive shares may not provide an adequate basis for assessing the relative contributions of factors to growth. Once we get out of the neoclassical trance, we may discover that factor share distributions are affected more seriously by other determinants such as the unionization of the labor force than by the relative quantities of the factors.

On the other hand, the inability to isolate pure profits from returns to capital leads to an overestimate of the effect of a change in capital input. The shifting of corporate income taxes will also lead to an understatement of labor's share. Furthermore, profits arising from imperfect competition in product markets are counted statistically as returns to capital which may cause overweighting of the role of capital. However, with a nod to these major shortcomings of the factor share approach, we will proceed with our analysis.

In the preceding chapter, the share of labor in total value added in Korea was estimated to be about 60 percent in 1970. Employing this 60 percent figure as the aggregate labor share Q, we can observe the following facts from the analytical exercise. During 1960–66, the average annual growth rate of GNP was 6.5 percent. Since the average annual growth rates of capital (excluding the ownership of dwellings) and labor (employment) were 5.8 percent and 2.3 percent respectively during the same period, about 35 percent of the growth in GNP could be attributed to capital accumulation and 22 percent to the growth of labor. The contribution of unexplained residual factors which include technical progress amounted to 43 percent.

During 1967–73, which was the period of most rapid capital accumulation in Korea, the average annual growth rate of GNP was 10.9 percent. Since the average annual growth rates of capital and labor were 13.4 percent and 4.1 percent respectively during the same period, 50 percent of the growth in GNP could be attributed to capital accumulation and 23 percent to labor growth. The contribution of unexplained residual factors amounted to 28 percent.

It is noteworthy that GNP growth due to residual factors amounted to about 3 percent per annum on the average during both 1960–66 and 1967–73. However, due to the low rates of GNP growth during 1960–66, the relative contribution of these residual factors amounted to 43 percent of the total growth.

The relative decrease in the share of residual factors during 1967–73 can not simply be interpreted as the relatively slower rate of technical progress during the 1967–73 period. During 1967–73, annual net capital

Table 6.1. Analysis of Growth Factors

		Whole Industry		
Average Annual Growth Rates	GNP (y)	Capital[1] (k)	Labor[2] (n)	Residual (r)
1960–66	6.5%	5.8%	2.3%[3]	
1967–73	10.9%	13.4%	4.1%[4]	
1960–73	8.7%	9.6%	3.2%	
	y =	$0.4k$ +	$0.6n$ +	r
1960–66	0.065 =	0.023 (35%) +	0.014 (22%) +	0.028 (43%)
1967–73	0.109 =	0.054 (50%) +	0.025 (23%) +	0.030 (28%)
1960–73	0.087 =	0.038 (44%) +	0.019 (22%) +	0.030 (34%)

		Manufacturing Sector		
Average Annual Growth Rates	Value Added (y)	Capital (k)	Labor (n)	Residual (r)
1960–66	12.2%	8.3%	12.3%[3]	
1967–73	22.0%	12.0%	11.7%[4]	
1960–73	17.1%	10.2%	12.0%	
	y =	$0.6k$ +	$0.4n$ +	r
1960–66	0.122 =	0.050 (41%) +	0.049 (40%) +	0.023 (19%)
1967–73	0.220 =	0.072 (33%) +	0.047 (21%) +	0.101 (46%)
1960–73	0.171 =	0.061 (36%) +	0.048 (28%) +	0.062 (36%)

Source: Table 4.3., Table A.28. and the Bank of Korea, *National Income Statistics Yearbook*.
[1] Excluding the ownership of dwellings.
[2] Number of employed persons.
[3] Applying the census employment data.
[4] Applying the EPB's quarterly sample survey data.

accumulation averaged more than 13 percent of the total capital stock and the replacement of depreciated capital stock amounted to about 6 percent. Therefore, common sense suggests higher rates of embodied technical progress during 1967–73 than in earlier period. On the other hand, better utilization of existing excess capacity and improvement in the quality of labor may have contributed to the larger share of residual factors during 1960–66.

For the period of 1960–73 as a whole, about 44 percent of the growth in Korea can be attributed to increases in fixed capital stock, while about 22 and 34 percent of the growth can be attributed to the growth of labor and residual factors, respectively.

During 1960–73, the value added of manufacturing sector increased at an average annual rate of 17 percent. Our estimate of labor's share in manufacturing sector income in 1970 was considerably lower than the national average, i.e., we estimated that labor contributed 42 percent of total value added in manufacturing.[2]

During 1960–66, the rates of capital accumulation in manufacturing sector were very high, but the rates of growth in value added and employment were even higher. As a result, about 41 percent of the growth can be attributed to capital accumulation while about 40 percent of the growth can be attributed to the increased labor inputs. On the other hand, less than 20 percent can be attributed to the residual factors. However, the share of residual factors in explaining total growth in manufacturing more than doubled from 19 percent in 1960–66 to 46 percent in 1967–73. This trend was exactly the opposite of that for the economy as a whole, which may imply much greater technical progress in the manufacturing sector since 1967 than in other sectors. During 1967–73, about 33 percent of the growth in manufacturing can be attributed to capital accumulation and about 21 percent to labor.

The total amount of net fixed capital stock in the manufacturing sector in 1973 was estimated to be $2.81 billion (in 1970 prices). The most remarkable fact is that during 1968–73 the total amount of net fixed capital formation in the manufacturing sector and that of provisions for the consumption of fixed capital amounted to $1.35 billion and $1.43 billion, respectively. That is, most of the existing capital stock in the manufacturing sector in 1973 could be dated to the post-1968 period. We can speculate, therefore, that the apparent high rate of technical progress in the manufacturing sector may have occurred mostly through so-called "embodied" technical progress which arises from the process of expanding and/or replacing old capital stock with new capital stock. (See Tables A.24. through A.27.)

---

[2] Our estimate of labor share in manufacturing sector was also based on the sectoral paid and unpaid workers data of the Bank of Korea, *Report on 1970 Input-Output Table* (in Korean).

2. Aggregate Factor/Value-Added Ratios

The concept of the capital-output ratio has played an indispensable role in projecting capital requirements and future growth rates and in selecting investment criteria, notwithstanding numerous theoretical objections. Based on the accepted proposition that wage rates tend to be higher and the cost of capital lower as an economy attains a higher level of development, each industry in the economy is assumed to undergo a process of factor substitution so as to raise the capital coefficient.[3]

The aggregate capital/GNP ratio of Korea has steadily decreased from 2.8 in 1953 to 1.8 in 1973, which confounds our expectation. However, if we exclude the ownership of dwellings from industrial capital stock, the capital/GNP ratio stayed constant at around 1.1–1.2 throughout 1953–70 and has increased slightly since 1971, which is more consistent with the conventional proposition.

But these observations are very partial, with limited implications. If we examine the employment/GNP ratio, we can see a consistent and significant fall in the ratio from 1.8 person per $1,000 of output in 1963 to 1.0 in 1973, implying very significant increases in labor productivity which might be attributable either to increased capital-intensity, technical progress, or both.

If we examine the manufacturing sector, we can observe that both the capital/value-added ratio and the employment/value-added ratio fell steadily during 1960–73. This seems to suggest that very rapid technical progress in manufacturing sector prevented any increase in the capital/value-added ratio. However, there still seems to have been a relative increase in the capital intensity (capital/labor ratio) of manufacturing during 1968–72, though quite moderate compared to the increase in the aggregate capital-labor ratio of the whole economy.

In the case of the agricultural sector, there was a steady increase in the capital/value-added ratio and slight fall in the employment/value-added ratio during 1953–73, which indicates a significant increase in the capital intensity of agricultural production and somewhat rising labor productivi-

---

[3] See Y. C. Kim, "Sectoral Output-Capital Ratios and Levels of Economic Development, "*The Review of Economics and Statistics*, November 1969. Kim found surprisingly large number of cases substantiating a negative relationship between the capital-output ratio and the level of income, contradicting the conventional proposition.

Table 6.2. Capital-Stock/GNP and Employment/GNP Ratios: 1953-73

	Capital/GNP		Sectoral-Capital/GNP Ratios					Employment/GNP
	(Whole Industry)	(Excluding Dwellings)	Agriculture & Mining	Manu-facturing	Social Overhead	Services	Ownership of Dwellings	Whole Industry (per $1,000)
1953	2.8	1.2	0.1	0.2	0.2	0.7	1.6	
1954	2.7	1.2	0.1	0.2	0.2	0.7	1.5	
1955	2.6	1.2	0.1	0.2	0.2	0.7	1.5	
1956	2.6	1.2	0.1	0.2	0.2	0.7	1.5	
1957	2.5	1.1	0.1	0.2	0.2	0.6	1.4	
1958	2.4	1.1	0.1	0.2	0.2	0.6	1.3	
1959	2.4	1.1	0.1	0.2	0.2	0.6	1.3	
1960	2.4	1.1	0.1	0.2	0.2	0.6	1.2	
1961	2.3	1.1	0.1	0.2	0.2	0.5	1.2	
1962	2.3	1.1	0.1	0.2	0.3	0.5	1.2	
1963	2.2	1.1	0.1	0.2	0.3	0.5	1.1	
1964	2.1	1.1	0.1	0.2	0.3	0.5	1.0	1.8
1965	2.0	1.1	0.1	0.2	0.3	0.5	1.0	1.7
1966	1.9	1.1	0.1	0.2	0.3	0.4	0.9	1.7
1967	1.9	1.1	0.1	0.2	0.3	0.4	0.8	1.5
1968	1.9	1.1	0.1	0.3	0.4	0.4	0.8	1.5
1969	1.9	1.2	0.1	0.3	0.4	0.4	0.7	1.4
1970	1.9	1.2	0.1	0.3	0.5	0.4	0.7	1.2
1971	1.9	1.3	0.1	0.3	0.5	0.4	0.6	1.2
1972	1.9	1.3	0.1	0.3	0.5	0.4	0.6	1.1
1973	1.8	1.3	0.1	0.3	0.5	0.4	0.6	1.0

Source: The Bank of Korea, *National Income Statistics Yearbook*, Table A.27. and Table 4.3.

Table 6.3. Capital/Value-Added and Employment/Value-Added Ratios in the Agricultural and Manufacturing Sectors: 1960–73

	Manufacturing Sector			Agricultural Sector		
	Capital/ Value- Added	Employment/ Value- Added	Capital/ Labor	Capital/ Value- Added*	Employment/ Value- Added	Capital/ Labor
1960	1.97			0.28		
1961	2.01			0.27		
1962	1.90			0.30		
1963	1.74	1.13	1.53	0.30	2.83	0.11
1964	1.72	1.11	1.55	0.28	2.46	0.11
1965	1.56	1.12	1.39	0.31	2.49	0.12
1966	1.58	1.04	1.53	0.32	2.29	0.14
1967	1.47	1.03	1.43	0.37	2.38	0.16
1968	1.34	0.93	1.44	0.40	2.33	0.17
1969	1.26	0.81	1.56	0.39	2.11	0.18
1970	1.19	0.71	1.67	0.45	2.21	0.20
1971	1.11	0.63	1.76	0.48	2.13	0.23
1972	1.00	0.59	1.70	0.54	2.31	0.23
1973	0.87	0.55	1.58	0.58	2.31	0.25

Source: The same as Table 6.2.
* Including fishery.

ty. However, such a small fall in the employment/value-added ratio in agriculture may imply the absence of any significant technical progress.

The amount of social overhead capital stock may significantly influence the overall efficiency of an economy. In Korea, the ratio of capital stock in social overhead sectors (electricity, water, transportation and communication) to GNP increased from 0.2 during 1953–61 to 0.5 during 1970–73. However, the ratio of capital stock in service sectors to GNP has steadily decreased from 0.7 to 0.4.

The ratio of capital stock in manufacturing to GNP stayed constant during 1953–67, but increased by 50 percent during 1968–73, reflecting the rapidly expanding share of manufacturing output in GNP. The ratio of capital stock in agriculture and mining to GNP stayed constant throughout the period 1953–73, which seems to be remarkable if we consider their rapidly decreasing weight in GNP.

3. Contribution of Export Expansion to GNP Growth

We can now try to analyze the contribution of commodity export expansion to the economic growth of Korea. During 1953–59, the annual amount of commodity exports fluctuated around $20 million, and it was only after 1960 that sustained high rates of growth in exports can be observed.

The magnitude of "annual increases" in GNP rose from $0.07 billion in 1960 to $0.61 billion in 1966, and to $1.61 billion in 1973 (all in 1970 prices). The percentage ratio of the annual increase in gross exports to the annual increase in GNP amounted to less than 20 percent until 1969, but the ratio started to increase drastically in 1970, reaching as high as 75 percent in 1972.

The increase in primary exports was negligible in absolute terms. On the other hand, the rapid expansion of manufactured exports necessitated the importation of large amounts of raw (and processed) materials for export production, amounting to about 40–50 percent of total export value during 1966–73. Nonetheless, the ratio of "net increase" in export value (the increase in the difference between gross exports and imported materials for export production) to the increase in GNP steadily grew from 7 percent in 1966 to 12 percent in 1971. This "net" direct contribution of export expansion to the growth of GNP amounted to as much as 55 percent in 1972, and 29 percent in 1973.

The increases in the value added of the manufacturing sector has typically contributed about 40–50 percent of net annual increases in GNP. As a result, the share of the manufacturing sector in GNP, which amounted to only 11 percent in 1960, rose to 28 percent by 1973. Furthermore, the share of manufactures in total commodity exports (based on I-O type classification) rose to 80 percent in 1966 and to 95 percent in 1973. As a result, in 1972 for example about half of the increase in the value added of manufacturing could be attributed to the increase in manufactured exports. However, in terms of value added, the direct contribution of manufactured exports to GNP growth amounted to only 27 percent in 1972 according to both the type II estimate and the type III estimate. This seems to be due to the relatively low rates of value added in the manufacturing sector, which usually amounts to about one-third of gross output value. It is necessary to keep this fact in mind when we make such state-

Table 6.4. *Direct Contribution of Export Expansion to GNP Growth*

In Billion 1970 Dollars & Percent

	Gross Value of Commodity Exports			Increase in GNP	Ratio of Increase in Exports to GNP Increase
	Manu-factures (A)	Primary Goods (B)	Total (C)	(D)	(dC/D)
1963	0.08	0.03	0.11	0.35	11%
1964	0.11	0.04	0.15	0.36	11%
1965	0.16	0.05	0.21	0.29	21%
1966	0.24	0.06	0.30	0.61	15%
1967	0.31	0.06	0.37	0.43	16%
1968	0.43	0.07	0.50	0.75	17%
1969	0.57	0.09	0.66	1.01	16%
1970	0.74	0.10	0.84	0.61	30%
1971	0.93	0.09	1.02	0.76	24%
1972	1.41	0.09	1.50	0.64	75%
1973	2.42	0.13	2.55	1.61	65%

	Imports for Export Production (E)	Net Value of Com-modity Exports (F = C-E)	Net Value of Manu-factures Exports (G = A-E)	Direct Contribution of Net Export Expansion to GNP Increase (Type I)	
				All Commodities (dF/D)	Manufactures (dG/D)
1963	0.00	0.11	0.08	—	—
1964	0.00	0.15	0.11	11%	8%
1965	0.01	0.20	0.15	17%	14%
1966	0.12	0.18	0.12	-3%	-5%
1967	0.16	0.21	0.15	7%	7%
1968	0.24	0.26	0.19	7%	5%
1969	0.31	0.35	0.26	9%	7%
1970	0.39	0.45	0.35	16%	15%
1971	0.48	0.54	0.45	12%	13%
1972	0.61	0.89	0.80	55%	55%
1973	1.20	1.35	1.22	29%	26%

Table 6.4. (Continued)

In Billion 1970 Dollars & Percent

	Gross Value of Manufactured Outputs (H)	Share of Exports in Manufactured Outputs Type II (I = A/H)	Type III (J = dA/dH)	Value Added of Manufacturing Sector (K)	Contribution of Manufacturing Sector to GNP Increase (dK/D)
1963	1.77	5%	—	0.54	23%
1964	1.85	6%	38%	0.57	8%
1965	2.18	7%	15%	0.69	41%
1966	2.54	10%	22%	0.81	20%
1967	3.10	10%	13%	0.99	42%
1968	3.92	11%	15%	1.26	36%
1969	4.75	12%	17%	1.52	26%
1970	5.58	13%	21%	1.80	46%
1971	6.57	14%	19%	2.12	42%
1972	7.56	19%	49%	2.46	53%
1973	10.42	23%	35%	3.22	47%

	Estimated Value Added of Manufactures Exports (L = IxK)	Increase in Value Added of Manufactures Exports Type II (dL)	Type III (M = JxdK)	Contribution of Increase in Value Added of Manufactures Exports to GNP Growth Type II (dL/D)	Type III (M/D)
1963	0.02	—	—	—	—
1964	0.03	0.01	0.01	3%	3%
1965	0.05	0.02	0.02	7%	7%
1966	0.08	0.03	0.03	5%	5%
1967	0.10	0.02	0.02	5%	5%
1968	0.14	0.04	0.04	5%	5%
1969	0.18	0.04	0.04	4%	4%
1970	0.23	0.05	0.06	8%	10%
1971	0.30	0.06	0.06	8%	8%
1972	0.47	0.17	0.17	27%	27%
1973	0.74	0.27	0.27	17%	17%

Source: Tables A.12., A.20., A.21. and A.22. The gross output values of the manufacturing sector were obtained from the Bank of Korea, *National Income Statistics Yearbook*.

Note: "d" is the first difference operator.

Table 6.5. Contribution of Export Expansion and Import Substitution to GNP Growth

	Total Gross Output X	Domestic Demand D	Exports E	Imports for Exports M^e	Imports for Domestic Demand M^d	(M^d/D) m^d	Net Exports $E-M^e$
	(In Billion Current Won)						
1960	350	383	10	0	43	0.11	10
1963	739	808	21	0	90	0.11	21
1966	1,747	1,861	114	22	206	0.11	92
1968	2,869	3,118	217	57	409	0.13	160
1970	5,027	5,341	376	121	569	0.11	255
	(In Billion 1970 Dollars)						
1960	5.17	5.66	0.15	0.00	0.64	0.11	0.15
1963	6.47	7.07	0.18	0.00	0.79	0.11	0.18
1966	9.36	9.97	0.61	0.12	1.10	0.11	0.49
1968	12.06	13.11	0.91	0.24	1.72	0.13	0.67
1970	16.19	17.20	1.21	0.39	1.83	0.11	0.82
	dX	dD	$(1-m^d)dD$	$d(E-M^e)$	m^dD-M^d	$d(E-M^e)/dX$	$(m^dD-M^d)/dX$
1960–63	1.30	1.41	1.26	0.03	0.00	2%	0%
1963–66	2.89	2.90	2.58	0.31	0.00	11%	0%
1966–68	2.70	3.14	2.80	0.18	−0.28	7%	−10%
1968–70	4.13	4.09	3.56	0.15	0.41	4%	10%
1966–70	6.83	7.23	6.44	0.33	0.00	5%	0%

Notes: [1] All data except those of "imports for exports" were obtained from I-O tables.
[2] Domestic demand includes "statistical discrepancies."
[3] In (m^dD-M^d), m^d is for base period and D and M^d are for final period.
[4] We applied the GNP deflator and the exchange rate of 310.6 won per dollar to get 1970 dollar values.
[5] Imports for exports data are from Table A.20 and A.21.

ments as "manufactured exports and consequently manufacturing production was the engine of rapid economic growth in Korea during 1963–73."

We can also estimate the direct relative contributions of domestic demand, exports and import substitution to output growth in the following fashion.

Let
$$X = D + E - M^e - M^d$$
where
  X = gross output,
  D = domestic (intermediate and final) demand,
  E = export demand,
  M^e = imported material used in export production, and
  M^d = imports for domestic demand.

Then, with simple manipulation, we get
$$dX = [(1 - m^d)dD] + d(E - M^e) + [m^d D - M^e]$$
where m^d ($= M^d/D$) is the import propensity in the base period, and D and M^d in $[m^d D - M^d]$ are domestic demand and imports for domestic demand in the final period, respectively. "d" is the first difference operator. One may interpret the first righthand term as the contribution of domestic demand increase, the second term as the contribution of export expansion, and the last term as the contribution of import subsitution.

According to this method of estimation, about 2 percent of output growth during 1960–63, about 11 percent during 1963–66, about 7 percent during 1966–68 and about 4 percent during 1968–70 could be attributed to (net) export expanison. Interestingly, according to this method the contribution of import substitution to output growth was zero during 1960–63 and 1963–66, minus 10 percent during 1966–68, 10 percent during 1968–70, and zero during 1966–70. The rest of the growth in output is attributed to the increase in domestic demand.[4]

This method of computing growth contributions may give a misleading impression to unwary readers. For instance, while there was significant import subsitution in many sectors, there were also significant increases in imports for domestic demand in other sectors during 1960–70. The net result came out as zero import substitution which should not be interpreted to imply the absence of any import substitution in Korea during 1960–

---

[4] The growth of intermediate demand may be traced back to final demand growth, export expansion and import substitution respectively. The total (direct plus indirect) contributions can be calculated by using the input-output matrix.

70. Furthermore, as the rates of − 10 percent and 10 percent respectively during 1966–68 and 1968–70 suggest, the selection of the period strongly affects the calculation of the rates. However, if we keep in mind the limitations and defects of this method, it is still possible to get some rough idea on the relative importance of export expansion in output growth, say, less than a 10 percent contribution to total output growth during the 1966–70 period.[5]

On the other hand, one may argue that the really important contributions of rapid expansion in (manufactured) exports are the elimination of the balance of payment constraint on growth potential and other indirect and external effects *a la* Keesing.[6] Unfortunately, these are the aspects which can not be easily quantified.

---

[5] K. S. Kim also estimated the direct (and indirect) contribution of exports to the growth of aggregate commodity output during 1955–68. However, his estimates overstated the contribution of export expansion and understated the contribution of import substitution because he does not take account of the import-content of exports. See his "Outward-Looking Industrialization Strategy: The Case of Korea," in Hong and Krueger, *op. cit.*

[6] D. B. Keesing, "Outward-Looking Policies and Economic Development," *Economic Journal*, June 1967.

CHAPTER 7

FACTOR INTENSITY OF TRADE

1. Computational Procedures

This chapter investigates the main issue of our research project, i.e., the factor intensity of Korea's trade and changes in factor intensity over the period 1960–73.

Two approaches to this problem are possible. One may either obtain data from exporting or import-competing firms regarding their labor, capital stock and input purchases and estimate the total employment of labor and capital attributable to exports or import substitution.[1] Or one may employ input-ouput data and average sectoral factor-output coefficients to estimate direct and indirect employment generated by exports or import substitution. The first approach runs into difficulties when tracing through the multiple indirect effects, while the second generally fails to take account of any special characteristics of production for exports.[2] Here we follow the second aproach to estimate the amount of labor and capital

---

[1] Cf. S. Watanabe, "Exports and Employment: The Case of the Republic of Korea," *International Labor Review*, December 1972.

[2] D. C. Cole and L.E. Westphal, "The Contribution of Exports to Employment in Korea," in Hong and Krueger, *op. cit.* They estimated the employment generated from exports in Korea in 1960, 1963, 1966 and 1970 using the BOK data of labor coefficients (43 sector) and input-output tables. The major differences between their and our approach are that we constructed our own sectoral factor coefficients on the basis of a more detailed sectoral classification (117 sectors) and also estimated the amount of capital used for exports.

required for export production or import substitution. We have tried to bypass the basic limitations of this approach by adopting a fairly detailed 117 sector classification.

The balance equations of the Leontief type system can be written as:[3]

$$\begin{bmatrix} I-A & -e \\ -r' & e \end{bmatrix} \begin{bmatrix} x \\ 1 \end{bmatrix} + \begin{bmatrix} m \\ -m \end{bmatrix} = \begin{bmatrix} q \\ q \end{bmatrix}$$

where I is a unit matrix, A the matrix of domestic and competitive import input coefficients, r a column vector of non-competitive import input coefficients, e a column vector of exports in thousand dollars, e the value of total exports, x a column vector of outputs, m a column vector of competitive imports, m the value of total competitive imports, q a column vector of final demands, and q the value of non-competitive imports which is allocated to final demand.[4] If the balance of trade equation is omitted, the system is reduced to

$$[I - A]x = e - m + q$$

Solving the above equation for x and premultiplying x by the row vectors of capital and labor coefficients (defined as the amounts of capital and labor directly required by each sector per thousand dollar of its output), we obtain;

$$k'x = k'[I - A]^{-1}(e - m + q)$$
$$n'x = n'[I - A]^{-1}(e - m + q)$$

where k and n represent capital and labor coefficients respectively. Here, the expression $k'[I - A]^{-1}e$ may be interpreted as the amount of capital directly and indirectly required for exports while $k'[I - A]^{-1}m$ may be interpreted as the amount of capital directly and indirectly required to replace competitive imports by domestic production; $n'[I - A]^{-1}e$ and $n'[I - A]^{-1}m$ may be interpreted in a similar way.

In computing domestic factor requirements for exports or import replacements, the demand for non-competitive imports is assumed to be completely satisfied by foreign sources. For competitive imports, stepped-up domestic production can be an alternative to imports and vice versa. The final demand which arises from the process of replacing imports or

---

[3] W. Leontief, *op. cit.* (1953 & 1956)

[4] Each of the first (n − 1) equations of the system states that the output of a sector i plus competitive imports into that sector, i.e., its total supply, is distributed to other sectors (including itself), to exports, and to the final demand. The last equation describes the balance of trade relationship; it states that total exports are equal to total competitive imports plus total non-compttitive imports.

expanding exports can not be assumed to result in an unavoidable demand for additional competitive imports since domestic production is an alternative. In particular when we want to compute the domestic factors required to "replace" current competitive imports, we logically must assume that whatever the demand for competitive imports (which arises from the process of replacing competitive imports themselves), this will be satisfied entirely by domestic output. Hence for the computation of the domestic capital and labor required to replace competitive imports, the use of A matrix is justified.

However, when we want to compute the "domestic" factor requirements for current exports, we cannot arbitrarily assume that current export production does not use competitively imported inputs. Therefore, we have to use A^d, the matrix of domestic input coefficients, instead of A, the matrix of domestic and competitive import input coefficients, when we compute "domestic" capital and labor requirements for current exports.[5]

By using A matrix instead of A^d matrix in computation of factor requirements for exports, Leontief assumes that export production uses noncompetitive imports but does not use competitive imports. However, A is the matrix of average sectoral input coefficients for the country as a whole which includes the actual use of competitive imports in each industry. It is clearly not appropriate to use average coefficients in order to compute the "domestic" capital and labor requirements as if the exported portion of production does not use competitive imports. This misconception arose in Leontief's work because he was thinking in terms of "reducing or increasing" exports by a million dollars and seeing the amount of capital and labor which would be "released or required" as a result, while what is required in such an exercise is, as Bhagwati states, a computation of the total capital and labor requirements of current exports or import replacements.[6] Following Bhagwati's argument, we use the A^d matrix to estimate the labor and capital requirements for exports.

One of the most serious problems in this research is the treatment of non-competitive imports. The Bank of Korea (BOK) has classified commodities whose domestic production was either absent or negligible (and

---

[5] If we let A^m represent the matrix of competitive import input coefficients, we obtain a separate balance equation for domestic output and competitive imports, i.e.,
$A^m x + q^m = m$
$A^d x + (q^d + e) = x \quad [I-A^d]^{-1}(q^d + e) = x$
where q^d is a column vector of final demand for domestic products, and q^m is a column vector of final demand for competitive imports.

[6] J. Bhagwati, "The Pure Theory of International Trade: A Survey," *Economic Journal*, March 1964.

was expected to stay negligible in the foreseeable future) as non-compe titive imports, and grouped them as one input item in its pre-1970 input-output tables. As a result, some 1,600 out of about 4,500 imported items (according to the seven-digit SITC classification) including various kind of machinery and chemical products were classified as non-competitive imports. If we follow Leontief's method of computing factor requirements to replace imports, we have to exclude all such non-competitive imports from the computation.

It appears that Leontief treated natural resource intensive goods which the U.S. does not produce as non-competitive goods.[7] Since he assumed that such imports could not be replaced by domestic production, he excluded them from his computation of the capital and labor required to replace imports.

In the U.S. there are very few things which can not be produced because of a scarcity of capital, and hence we may safely assume that anything not produced in the U.S. is a non-competitive natural-resource (which the U.S. does not possess) intensive imports. However, there are many things which are not produced in Korea because of a scarcity of capital, and hence are imported non-competitively. Since Korea is likely to be saving a large amount of capital by importing rather than producing these goods, they should not be excluded from the computation of factor requirements to replace imports.

We divide "non-competitive imports" into two groups, i.e., "non-competitive non-natural-resource intensive imports" and "noncompetitive natural-resource-intensive imports." The total factor intensity of imports is obtained by adding the factors required to replace "non-competitive non-natural-resource-intensive imports" to the factors required to replace "competitive imports".

The factor requirements needed to replace competitive imports can be computed by using the A matrix and sectoral capital- and labor-output ratios. Ideally, the factor requirements needed to replace non-competitive non-natural-resource intensive imports should be computed on the basis of "blue-prints" for actual domestic production. However, since we do

---

[7] Leontief himself defined the non-competitive imports in the following fashion: "With its present technology and a given endowment of labor, capital and natural resources, this country finds it advantageous to satisfy its entire demand for commodities such as coffee and other tropical products as well as certain minerals by imports from abroad. These are identified for purpose of the present study as non-competitive imports." He then defined the competitive imports as following: "The competitive imports comprise all other goods which, although imported, are also produced in relatively substantial quantities at home." W. Leontief, *op. cit.* (1953)

not have the necessary information to take this approach, and since Korea has imported most of the "non-competitive non-natural-resource-intensive commodities" from the U.S. and Japan, we have approximated their factor requirements by using U.S. and Japanese sectoral factor requirements.[8]

About 40 percent of total commodity imports in 1968, for instance, were "non-competitive imports" according to the BOK's classification. We have designated crude oil, crude rubber, raw cotton, raw sugar, timber and wool, which made up about 15 percent of total commodity imports in 1968, as "non-competitive natural-resource intensive" goods.[9] We have classified the remaining 25 percent (out of 40 percent) of what the BOK has defined as non-competitive imports as "non-competitive non-natural-resource intensive" goods. Hereafter we will refer to "non-competitive non-natural-resource intensive" imports simply as "non-competitive" imports and to "non-competitive natural-resource intensive" imports as "natural-resource intensive" imports.

Commodity trade statistics for the 1966–74 period were obtained from the original taped data of the Office of Customs Administration. The trade statistics in SITC code (6 or 7 digit) were converted into I-O sectoral classifications according to the BOK's (mimeographed) manual of SITC codes vs. I–O sector classification. The trade statistics for 1964 and 1965 were obtained from *Foreign Trade of Korea* published by the Ministry of Finance. Trade statistics for 1960–63 and the pre-1960 period were obtained from *Monthly Foreign Exchange Statsitics* and *External Trade Statistics* published by the Bank of Korea. Since these BOK data employ a fairly aggregated SITC classification, our I-O sectoral classification of competitive and non-competitive imports is somewhat arbitrary in many cases. Moreover, some commodity exports or imports will be included in

---

[8] So long as we are concerned with the "relative" factor intensity of "non-competitive non-natural-resource intensive" imports as a separate group, the use of the U.S. or Japanese factor input coefficients will not give us a very distorted picture. Only in the unlikely event of large-scale factor intensity reversals would the conclusion based upon analysis using U.S. or Japanese factor input coefficients be grossly in error. However, if we add the absolute amount of capital and labor required to replace "non-competitive non-natural-resource intensive" imports to those required to replace "competitive" imports, we may be adding very heterogeneous factors of production.

[9] In the case of these and similar goods, even a very drastic change in the domestic supply of capital and labor would not lead to any significant amount of domestic production.That is, by "non-competitive natural-resource intensive" goods we imply those goods which use intensively those natural resources which Korea does not possess or has in only very limited supply. There may be many other items with similar characteristics, but since there are difficulties in identification and classification and since their magnitude is rather small, we decided to limit the so classified items to the six listed above.

the service sectors. For example, sensitized plates and film, cinematograph film, etc. are classified as commodity imports by the Office of Customs Administration, but they were classified as imports of service sectors (educational, business or entertainment services) in BOK's I-O sector classification.

2. Sectoral Direct Labor Requirements

There are three different sources of employment data for the agriculture and hunting, forestry and fishery sectors in 1966 and 1970 (i.e., the 10% Sample Survey conducted in conjunction with population census; the EPB's quarterly sample survey on the economically active population; and the BOK's estimation in conjunction with its I-O tables), each differing widely the other.

In order to check the relative reliability of these different data, we examined the 1970 figures. The total number of employed persons in fishery sector was 234,311 according to the Census (10% Sample), 90,000 according to the EPB's Survey, and 178,000 according to the BOK's estimation. Fortunately, the Office of Fisheries conducted the First Fishery Census on December 1, 1970. According to this Fishery Census, the total number of employed persons in the fishery sector was 367,645, but when we converted this into man-years using as weights the number of days worked, we got 175,000 for 1970 which is very close to the BOK's estimation. We decided to use the I-O output data and the employment data from the First Fishery Census (adjusted to man-years) when we computed the labor coefficient of the fishery sector for 1970, and due to the lack of reliability of other data we decided to apply the 1970 coefficient (0.8396) in other years as well.

On the other hand, the total number of employed persons in the forestry sector was 63,943 according to the 1970 Census and 283,400 according to the BOK's estimation. If we apply the census employment figure to the 1970 I-O forestry output value, we get a labor coefficient of 0.3036 for the forestry sector and if we apply the BOK's employment estimation, we get a coefficient of 1.3457.

Industrial occupation of an employed person in the 10% Sample Survey conducted in conjunction with the population census refers to the kind of work actually done during the reference week. For the persons "with a job but not at work," the occupation refers to the kind of work they had been doing. If a person was engaged in more than two jobs, the kind of work was decided by the work in which he (thought he) was mainly engaged. However, the total forestry products in the BOK's Input-Output Table includes branches and leaves, miscellaneous charcoal and firewood, green manure, and forage.[10] Since a farmer who produces such items is likely to identify himself as a person employed in agriculture rather than in forestry, we decided to exclude the above listed items from total forestry products when we computed the labor coefficient of forestry sector in 1970 applying the census employment data to the I-O forestry output value. We got 0.7363 for the labor coefficient of forestry sector in 1970, which was employed for other years as well.

In order to compute the labor coefficients of agricultural subsectors in 1963, 1966, 1968 and 1970, we utilized the data on agricultural outputs and monthly labor hours of farm household by the type of work (average per household) in the Farm Household Survey. We first computed the twelve-months sum of monthly labor hours by the type of works, converted this into work-days by assuming eight hours per day, and then calculated man-years by assuming 280 work-days per year. The 280 work-days per year figure is regarded as a reasonable approximation for the agricultural sector. For 1960 the 1963 coefficients were used. (See Table A.30.)

Labor coefficients for the mining and manufacturing sectors were computed using output and number of workers data from the *Report on the Mining and Manufacturing Census* (or *Survey*) published by the Economic Planning Board. The mining and manufacturing census covers only those establishments operating with five or more workers.

We computed the 1960, 1966 and 1970 labor coefficients for non-commodity sectors using the employment data from the 1960, 1966 and 1970 population censuses (10% Sample Survey) and output data from input-output tables. We obtained the 1963 and 1968 employment figures by assuming constant average annual gorwth rates of sectoral employment during the inter-census years, i.e., during 1960-66 and 1966-70. We then applied the output data from the input-output tables in order to compute the 1963 and 1968 labor coefficients for non-commodity sectors.

---

[10] According to the BOK's 1970 Input-Output Table, the forestry products consisted mainly of fruit-culture (23%), forest planting (7%) and logs (6%) on the one hand, and green manure (36%), forest fuel (17%), and forage (6%) on the other. It seems that more than 60 percent of forestry production is conducted largely as subsidiary activities in conjunction with other agricultural productions without any clear distinction.

Table 7.1. Aggregated Sectoral Labor/Output Ratios
Per Thousand Dollars (1970 Price) of Outputs

	1960	1963	1966	1968	1970
Agriculture	—	1.15	1.23	1.19	1.08
Manufacturing	0.39	0.33	0.32	0.25	0.20
SOC & Services	0.89	0.81	0.67	0.59	0.50
Whole Industry*	1.34	—	0.85	—	0.66
	(—)	(—)	(0.75)	(—)	(0.52)

Source: See text.
* Total census employment figures divided by total I-O output values. Figures in the parentheses represent the ratios excluding the underemployments in agricultural sector. (See Table 4.4.)

Since the only employment figure available for the "agricultural service sector" was that in the 1960 population census, we had to use the 1960 labor coefficient for other years as well.

When we examine the aggregate sectoral labor-output ratios, we can observe a relatively small decrease in labor requirements in the agricultural sector, compared to a nearly 50 percent fall in labor requirements in the manufacturing and non-commodity sectors (social overhead and service sectors) during 1960–70. This is consistent with what we have already observed: a relatively small decrease in the employment/value-added ratio of the agricultural sector and a 50 percent fall in that of the manufacturing sector during 1963–73. (See Table 6.3.)

We computed sectoral labor requirements on the basis of our 117 sectoral labor coefficients and the 117 I-O sectoral output values and then compared them with the sectoral employment figures of the population census (10% Sample Survey). Since labor inputs for the agricultural sector were computed on a man-year basis, it was in this sector that the largest absolute discrepancies were observed. On the other hand, since we computed the labor input for non-commodity sector on the basis of the census employment data, only slight differences were observed in this sector, mainly due to rounding errors.

The census employment figures for the forestry sector are very erratic, suggesting that our fixed coefficient (1970) estimations may be more reliable. Since we computed the labor-input for fishery sector on a man-year basis, our fishery employment figures are much smaller than those indicated in the censuses.

The estimated labor requirements for the mining and manufacturing sectors are somewhat smaller than the population census employment

Table 7.2. Comparison of Estimated and Census Sectoral Employments

	In Thousand Persons		
	1960	1966	1970
Agriculture			
Estimated	1,916	3,421	2,797
Population Census	4,468	4,389	4,858
Forestry			
Estimated	84	119	155
Population Census	39	9	64
Fishery			
Estimated	53	121	178
Population Census	125	154	234
Mining			
Estimated	56	79	96
Population Census	48	91	100
Manufacturing			
Estimated	470	884	1,258
Population Census	477	958	1,448
Non-Commodity Sector			
Estimated	1,583	2,137	3,145
Population Census*	1,574	2,126	3,134
Total Employed Persons			
Estimated	4,162	6,762	7,629
Population Census*	6,792	7,728	9,845

Source: See text.

* Excluding persons employed in government service sector and persons unknown: 297 thousand in 1960, 236 thousand in 1966 and 315 thousand in 1970.

figures. This may be due to the fact that we used average labor coefficients based only on those establishments employing five or more workers. Apart from the probability of scale economies, such firms may be characterized by relatively less underemployment.

3. Sectoral Direct Capital Requirements

We will first describe how we constructed a complete set of 1968 sectoral capital coefficients. On the basis of the national wealth survey conducted by the Economic Planning Board in 1968, professor Han has estimated the sectoral capital coefficients. Since national wealth is a heterogeneous collection of assets purchased at various times and prices, the survey adopted the adjusted replacement cost method for the valuation of net fixed capital assets.[11] Han, however, uses gross (undepreciated) capital stock in his computation of the capital coefficients of 117 sectors (I-O industrial classification), arguing that it is difficult to estimate correctly the actual depreciation cost and hence gross stock data are more reliable than estimates of net stock. Perhaps he is correct in questioning the validity of the simple depreciation procedure adopted in the national wealth survey. However, if we ignore wear and tear, not to mention technical progress and the related obsolescence of capital stock, we end up with exaggerated capital coefficients for old industries. These coefficients may indicate the upper limit for capital requirements needed to replace imports or to export, but they have very limited implications for our study.

In fact, Han also attempted to compute the net values of fixed capital stock for a more aggregated sectoral classification (27 sectors instead of 117) in order to compare Korean capital coefficients and those of Japan. Using his gross-to-net conversion rates for these aggregated 27 sectors, we can convert Han's 117 sectoral gross capital coefficients into corresponding net coefficients.

There is another source of data for calculating capital coefficients in the mining and manufacturing sectors. *The Report on Mining and Manufacturing Census* provides data on fixed capital stock for establishments operating with five or more workers. In the census fixed assets were evaluated on the basis of "book value". Although the law requires periodic revaluation of book values, whenever the book value looked too unreasonable to represent the current value of an asset, such assets were evaluated at their current market price, and hence the census estimation is close to a net value estimation of fixed capital stock.

Comparing Han's deflated (net) capital coefficients with those derived from the mining and manufacturing census data, we found that in 44 sectors the (net) capital coefficients computed from Han's data were larger than those computed from the census data, while in 40 sectors Han's coefficients were smaller than those computed from the census data. We decided to use the 1968 Mining and Manufacturing Census data for these

---

[11] Replacement cost was deduced by multiplying the "acquisition price", price ratio (price inflator) and the residual cost ratio (depreciation factor). In estimating depreciation, the fixed rate method was used. When the replacement cost was not available, the assets were valued at current market prices.

84 sectors, on the grounds that while it is very difficult to judge which data are more accurate, the Mining and Manufacturing Census had already been conducted many times, while the National Wealth Survey was the first of its kind. Furthermore, the latter survey is based on ownership and does not report sectoral output values, whereas the former census data are based on establishment units and contains sectoral output values and hence are more relevant for the estimation of sectoral capital-output ratios. In any case, we have to use the former census data to determine labor coefficients in the mining and manufacturing sectors, and hence it is more consistent to use the same data in calculating capital coefficients as well.

Among the capital coefficients estimated by Han, those in the agricultural sectors seem most unreliable. For instance, according to Han, $576 worth of fixed capital is used per $1,000 worth of rice, barley and wheat production. On the other hand, only $13, $26 and $42 worth of fixed capital are used per $1,000 worth of other cereals, vegetables, and livestock & sericulture production respectively.[12]

Since it is generally acknowledged that the annual sample survey of 1,200 farm households conducted by the Ministry of Agriculture and Fishery is the most reliable source of agricultural data, we decided to compute the 1968 capital coefficients of each agricultural subsector on the basis of the "Report on the Results of Farm Household Economy Survey and Production Cost Survey of Agricultural Products."[13]

The Farm Household Survey provides "beginning of the year" fixed capital stock data. In order to obtain fixed capital stock data for the agricultural sectors in 1968, we took the average of the 1968 and 1969 "beginning of the year" figures. What we obtained represents, approximately, the capital stock figures as of mid-1968, and hence takes account of any possible inflationary trend between the beginning of 1968 and the beginning of 1969 period.[14]

---

[12] The lack of consistency in Han's results seems partly due to the fact that he utilized the results of Farm Household Economy Survey (1968) for the rice, barley & wheat sector while he used the national wealth survey data for other agricultural subsectors.

[13] In the Survey Report, the by-products of crops are not broken into five different groups of crops (i.e., rice, barley & wheat, other cereals, vegetables, fruit, and special crops). However, according to the 1963 input-output table, total value of by-products of crops was 16,476,495 won in 1963, and their sectoral distribution was 75.13 percent for rice, 8.96 percent for barley & wheat, 4.09 percent for other cereals, 0.69 percent for potatoes, 5.83 percent for vegetables, 4.50 percent for fruits and 0.80 percent for special crops. We applied these distribution rates to 1968 by-products of crops.

[14] We assigned animal house to the fixed capital for livestock and sericulture only. Other buildings were allocated to each sector in proportion to its output value. Mul-

Our capital coefficients for rice, barley & wheat (0.3252), other cereals (0.3450), and vegetables (0.2835) do not show the extreme differences that are shown by Han's coefficients (0.5669, 0.0125 and 0.0260). Furthermore, the value of fixed capital used for $1,000 worth of livestock & sericulture production is $747 by our computation, while Han places it at $42. We believe, therefore, that our results are more reasonable than those of Han.[15]

We computed the capital coefficients for the forestry sector (0.1778) and the fishery sector (1.5933) using the output values in the 1968 input-output table and net capital values from the National Wealth Survey.

We utilized Hans' capital coefficients for all "non-commodity subsectors", but converted his gross capital values into net (depreciated) values by applying the uniform gross-to-net conversion rate of 0.6448, except in the case of the electricity, water & sanitary service sector, where we applied the rate of 0.9558.

For most non-manufacturing sectors Han converted his sectoral capital coefficients based on gross values into those of net value coefficients using

---

berry trees were treated as fixed capital for sericulture, and other trees as fixed capital for fruit production.

According to the 1968 Survey Report, animal power hours were distributed to each type of work in the following way: 79.65 percent for rice, barley & wheat, 5.73 percent for other cereals, 8.14 percent for vegetables, 3.31 percent for fruit and special crops, and 3.17 percent for livestock & sericulture. We distributed the value of cattle and horse accordingly. Then we assigned other large animal such as pig, goat, honey beehives, etc., to the fixed capital for livestock.

We assigned treading, weeder, thresher, and winnower to rice, barley & wheat sector. Then we assigned sprayer, and duster to rice, barley & wheat, vegetables, and fruit sectors; and engine, plough, cart and other large equipments to rice, barley & wheat, other cereals, vegetables, fruit and special crop sectors in proportion to each sector's output value.

[15] The Farm Household Economy Survey data covers only privately accumulated capital stock, and public investments in the field of irrigation, paddy rearrangements, soil improvements, etc., are excluded from our (as well as Han's) computation of capital coefficients in agriculture. According to the Korean Standard Industrial Classification (KSIC), the agricultural service sector is included in the agricultural sector as an agricultural subsidiary service industry. However, it is treated as one of the other service sectors in the I-O industry classification (sector 110). This sector includes the activities of the Land Improvement Association which undertakes the irrigation and drainage work, the rural guidance activities of Agricultural & Fishery Cooperative Unions, and veterinarian services. The total fixed capital stock of the agricultural service sector was estimated by Han to be 50 billion won in 1968 which was close to the magnitude of capital stock in the communication sector (48 billion won) or about 40 percent of that in the electricity sector (120 billion won). The value of land as well as the improvements made on the existing farm land were completely excluded from our computation of fixed capital stock. The original national wealth survey did not include estimates of such values.

a conversion ratio of 0.665. The only exception was in the case of the construction sector for which a conversion ratio of 0.229 was employed. The conversion ratios of the manufacturing sectors deviated from each other around a mean value of 0.68, but the deviations were less than 12 percent of the mean value. However, the gross-to-net conversion ratios computed on the basis of gross and net fixed capital stock values in the *Report on the National Wealth Survey* were more significantly different from each other. The extreme values were 0.331 for dwellings on the one hand and 0.999 for electricity on the other.

Since we could not determine, *a priori*, the best method for generating a consistent set of sectoral net fixed capital stock data, we first decided to apply, in principle, the conversion rate of 0.6541 to every sectoral (gross) capital coefficient of Han. This is the ratio of net fixed capital stock to gross fixed capital stock for the country as a whole in 1968. We obtained the ratio 0.6541 by dividing Han's average net capital coefficient for all industries (based on total net fixed captial stock and actual total value of outputs) by his average gross capital coefficient for all industries (based on total gross fixed capital stock and actual total value of outputs) for the 1968 Korean economy, i.e., 1.04721/1.60103.

There was one exception from this approach: according to Han, the amount of gross fixed capital stock for the electricity, water & sanitary service sector was 145,448 million won in 1968, which was very similar to the amount estimated in the *Report on the National Wealth Survey* (146, 181 million won). However, Han applied 0.6649 as the conversion ratio (from gross to net value) while the national wealth survey applied 0.9558 (0.9994 for electricity and 0.7580 for water & sewerage). We first applied the uniform conversion rate of 0.6541 which is very close to 0.6649. However, based on the 1968 net capital stock obtained by applying this rate, we got negative capital stock for this sector during 1953–62. On the other hand, when the national wealth survey conversion rate of 0.9958 was applied, we obtained a capital stock series for this sector which did not appear unreasonable. On these grounds, we decided to use the latter conversion rate of 0.9558 for the electricity, water & sanitary service sector in 1968. As a result, we had to use a gross-to-net cnoversion ratio of 0.6448 for other sectors in order that the weighted average ratio for the whole industry equal 0.6541. In the factor requirement computations, only the net capital coefficients of the "non-commodity sectors" are derived from Han's estimates of gross sectoral coefficients. (See Table A.23.)

So far we have described how the 1968 sectoral capital coefficients were computed. We estimated the sectoral capital coefficients for other years

(1960, 1963, 1966 and 1970) in the same fashion. For instance, the capital coefficients of the agricultural, mining and manufacturing sectors were determined from Farm Household Survey and the Mining and Manufacturing Census. However, there were some exceptional procedures. First, since the only available set of capital coefficients for "non-commodity" sectors was that for 1968 derived from Han's (gross) estimates, we simply modified the 1968 coefficients by "actual/required" ratio to obtain the capital coefficients in non-commodity sectors for other years.[16] Second, since the mining and manufacturing censuses have not collected data on total fixed capital stock since 1968, we added net sectoral capital formation in 1969 and 1970 to the 1968 capital stock data in order to compute the 1970 capital coefficients of the mining and manufacturing sectors.[17] We computed the 1966 capital coefficients of the mining and manufacturing sectors in a similar fashion, i.e., by subtracting the net capital formation in 1968 and 1967 from the 1968 coefficients. This procedure was followed even though the *Report on the 1966 Mining and Manufacturing Census* was available because somehow, the 1966 Census grossly underestimated sectoral fixed capital stock in 1966. We will discuss this problem further at the end of this section.

When we examined the aggregate sectoral capital-output ratios, we could observe a significant increase in capital requirements in the agricultural sector, while there seems to have been a slight fall in capital requirements in manufacturing and non-commodity sectors (excluding the ownership of dwellings) during 1966–70. These findings are consistent with what we have already observed: a significant increase in the capital-value-added ratio in the agricultural sector and a significant fall in that of the manufacturing sector during 1960–73. (See Table 6.3.)

The 1960 Census covered all mining and manufacturing establishments operating with "three' or more workers, but excluded the establishments of the government monopoly enterprises (such as tobacco products and salt) and other establishments operated through the government budget. The 1962 Census also excluded government monopoly enterprises and other establishments operating through the government budget (e.g., locomotive and coach manufacturing and the repair facilities of the Min-

---

[16] Applying the 1968 capital coefficients and the I-O sectoral output values of 1960, 1963, 1966 and 1970, we can compute the "required" capital stock for each non-commodity sector in 1960, 1963, 1966 and 1970. The "actual" capital stock implies the annual capital stock data derived from the Han-BOK data for each non-commodity sector.

[17] We applied the 1968 sectoral rates of capital depreciation in order to get net sectoral capital formation figures for other years.

Table 7.3. Aggregated Sectoral Capital/Output Ratios

	1960	1963	1966	1968	1970
Agriculture[1]	—	—	0.29	0.38	0.41
Manufacturing	0.39	0.33	0.56[2]	0.43	0.39
SOC & Services[3]	3.89	3.29	2.56	2.20	1.97
	(1.63)	(1.47)	(1.22)	(1.15)	(1.16)
Whole Industry[4]	1.67	1.45	1.15	1.06	1.03
	(0.82)	(0.76)	(0.65)	(0.65)	(0.69)

Source: See text.

[1] Land/Output ratio in the agricultural sector was 3.48 in 1963, 3.28 in 1966, 3.16 in 1968 and 2.75 in 1970.

[2] Capital stock estimated by subtracting the (census) net capital formation in 1967 and 1968 from the 1968 (census) fixed capital stock. If we use the 1966 mining and manufacturing census itself, we get 0.33.

[3] Figures in the parentheses are the ratios excluding ownership of dwellings.

Table 7.4. The Coverage of Manufacturing Census

	Number of Workers (persons)	Fixed Capital Stock (million 1970 $)	Gross Output (million won)
1960			
A. M & M Census	275,254	274.5	59,735
B. All Establishments	476,975	772.0	111,484
(A/B)	58%	36%	54%
1963			
A. M & M Census	401,981	409.4	166,858
B. All Establishments	(676,000)[1]	935.7	237,475
(A/B)	60%	44%	70%
1966			
A. M & M Census	566,665	573.4[2]	417,370
B. All Establishments	958,030	1,273.2	595,338
(A/B)	59%	45%[2]	70%
1968			
A. M & M Census	748,184	1,204.4	769,060
B. All Establishments	(1,178,000)[1]	1,681.6	1,077,340
(A/B)	64%	72%	71%
1970			
A. M & M Census	861,041	1,678.0	1,334,515
B. All Establishments	1,447,519	2,137.8	1,732,653
(A/B)	60%	79%	77%

Source: See text.

[1] Interpolated figures.

[2] If we estimate the 1966 capital stock by subtracting net capital formation in 1967 and 1968 from the 1968 fixed capital stock, we get $979.2 million and 77% respectively.

istry of Transportation.) The 1963 Census also excluded establishments operating with government funds but included railroad workshops and tobacco manufacturing factories as exceptions.

The mining and manufacturing censuses, except that of 1960, cover establishments operating with five or more workers.[18] As a result, the total output of establishments covered in the 1970 census, for example, amounted to 77 percent of the total output of all manufacturing establishments, and included about 60 percent of the total workers and 79 percent of the total capital stock. We can see that a slightly more than proportionate amount of capital and much less than a proportionate amount of labor were employed by those establishments covered in the census. The coverage of the 1968 census was very similar to that of 1970.

However, we got very different results for 1960, 1963 and 1966. In 1966, for example, about 70 percent of total manufactured output was produced by those establishments covered in the census, while the amount of capital estimated to be employed by these establishments was only 44 percent of the total capital stock in the manufacturing sector (derived from the Han-BOK data). Such an underestimation of capital stock may be attributed to the lack of proper revaluation of capital assets in each establishment before 1966. Hence the capital coefficients of manufacturing sectors derived from the 1966, 1963 and 1960 censuses do not seem to be very reliable.

We computed the aggregate sectoral capital requirements on the basis of our 117 sectoral capital coefficients and the 117 I-O sectoral output values and then compared them with the sectoral capital stock figures of Han-BOK data. The largest absolute differences could be observed in agricultural (and fishery) sector. This seems to be due to the fact that we computed the sectoral capital coefficients on the basis of the Farm Household Survey but applied the I-O sectoral output values which were about 50 percent larger than those derived from the Farm Household Survey.

On the other hand, since we adjusted the (1968) capital coefficients for the non-commodity sectors on the basis of the (annual) Han-BOK capital stock data, we naturally could not observe any differences between our

---

[18] The Census (or Survey) of Mining and Manufacturing covers all mining and manufacturing establishments which are operating with five or more workers as of December 31 and those operated with five or more workers on the average during December as well as those operated for more than three months with an average of five or more workers. It excludes those establishments which are under construction as of December 31, establishments directly operated by the armed forces, workshops operated by public occupational guidance centers and experimental facilities in laboratories.

Table 7.5. *Comparison of Estimated and Han-BOK Capital Stock Data*

In Million 1970 Dollars

	1960	1966	1970
Agriculture & Fishery			
Estimated Capital Stock[1]	680	1,262	1,669
Han-BOK Capital Stock Data	417	695	1,047
Mining			
Estimated Capital Stock	18	68	96
Han-BOK Capital Stock Data	96	82	79
Manufacturing			
Estimated Capital Stock	448	1,118[2]	2,274
Han-BOK Capital Stock Data	772	1,273	2,138
Non-Commodity Sectors			
Estimated Capital Stock[3]	6,791	8,127	12,023
Han-BOK Capital Stock Data[4]	6,791	8,127	12,023
Total Capital Stock			
Estimated Capital Stock	7,937	10,575	16,063
Han-BOK Capital Stock Data[4]	8,077	10,177	15,286

[1] Includes the capital requirements of the agricultural service sector: $95 million in 1960, $134 million in 1966 and $152 million in 1970.

[2] 1966 M & M Census coefficients were obtained by subtracting the net sectoral capital formation in 1968 and 1967 from the 1968 sectoral capital stock, instead of using the 1966 Census capital stock data. (We used the 1966 Census output data.)

[3] Excludes the capital requirements of the agricultural service sector.

[4] Excludes the capital stock of the public administration sector: $526 million in 1960, $549 million in 1966 and $664 million in 1970.

estimates and the Han-BOK data. Neither did the manufacturing sectors show any significant differences, except in 1960 (and 1963). It seems that the undervaluation of fixed assets in the manufacturing sectors, which was evidenced by the less than proportionate coverage of capital stock in the mining and manufacturing censuses of 1960 and 1963, resulted in a significant underestimation of the sectoral capital coefficients of the manufacturing sectors for these years.

4. Factor Intensity of Trade

A. Employment Generated by Exports

We estimated the factor requirements for exports in 1960, 1963, 1966, 1968, 1970 and 1973 by applying the (117) sectoral factor coefficients and A^d matrix of each year. Commodity exports increased about 20 times (in 1970 constant prices) and the number of employed persons in export production increased by about 8 times during 1960–70, implying average annual growth rates of about 35 percent and 24 percent respectively and an export expansion elasticity of employment of 0.7.

If we take the period of 1963–73, commodity exports increased about 23 times and the number of employed persons in export production increased about 7 times, implying average annual growth rates of about 37 percent and 21 percent respectively and an employment elasticity of about 0.6.

The employment elasticity of 0.6–0.7, which is significantly less than unity, seems to be due partly to the changing composition of commodity exports towards less labor intensive goods and partly to changing input coefficients caused by technical progress, factor substitution and economies of scale. This aspect will be analyzed in the following chapter.

According to the census employment data, the total number of employed persons increased by about 3.2 million in the period 1960–70. During the same period, the total number of directly and indirectly employed persons in export production increased by about 0.5 million, which implies that about 15 percent of the increase in total employment was due to export expansion.

According to the EPB's quarterly sample survey, the total number of employed persons increased by about 3.5 million during the period 1963–73. During the same years, total employed persons in export production increased by about 0.9 million owing to the extreme rapid growth of exports in 1972 and 1973. This implies that nearly a quarter of the increase in total employment during 1963–73 was due to export expansion. As a result, about 9 percent of all employed persons in 1973 were engaged in export production.

On the average, about 60 percent of all employed persons in export production have been directly employed, and 40 percent indirectly employed. On the other hand, the labor content of competitively imported inputs used in export production has steadily increased from an amount

Table 7.6. Exports and Employment: 1960–73

In Thousand Persons

	1960	1963	1966	1968	1970	1973
Total Employed Person						
Population Census (10% Sample)	6,933	—	7,963[1]	—	10,153[2]	—
EPB Survey (0.1% Sample)	—	7,662	8,423	9,155	9,745	11,139
Employed Persons in Manufacturing						
Population Census (10% Sample)	477	—	958	—	1,448	—
EPB Survey (0.1% Sample)	—	610	833	1,176	1,284	1,774
Total Commodity Exports (Million 1970 $)	*(42)*	*(110)*	*(294)*	*(503)*	*(835)*	*(2,550)*
Total Employed Persons in Export Production[3]	66[4]	150[4]	286	410	549	1,015
Directly Employed Persons[5]	44	72	174	248	327	589
Indirectly Employed Persons	21[4]	78[4]	112	162	222	426
(Labor Content of Imported Inputs)[6]	( )	(—)	(21)	(43)	(64)	(248)
Employed Persons Per $100 Million Exports	157[4]	136[4]	97	82	66	40
Directly Employed Persons	105	65	59	49	39	23
Indirectly Employed Persons	50[4]	71[4]	38	32	27	17
(Labor Content of Imported Inputs)	(—)	(—)	(7)	(9)	(8)	(10)

[1] 6,990 thousand if we exclude underemployed persons in agricultural sector.
[2] 8,090 thousand if we exclude underemployed persons in agricultural sector.
[3] Obtained by using the A^d matrix.
[4] Includes the labor content of imported inputs, which seems to have been negligible.
[5] Applying the direct labor coefficients.
[6] Obtained by using the A^m matrix.

which was equivalent to 7 percent of all employed persons in export production in 1966 to 24 percent in 1973.

The amount of labor required to produce $100 million worth of exports (in 1970 prices) has steadily decreased from about 157 thousand man-years in 1960, to 97 thousand in 1966 and about 40 thousand in 1973. This trend seems to reflect the rapidly increasing productivity of labor in export production due to technical progress, factor substitution and increasing returns to scale, and the changing composition of the export commodity bundle towards less labor intensive commodities. However, the estimated labor content of competitively imported inputs used in export production has increased somewhat.

We may now analyze the direct and indirect impact of export expansion on sectoral employment. In 1960, only about 3 percent of all employed persons in the manufacturing sector worked for export production. However the proportion of employed persons directly or indirectly working for export production increased to about 22 percent of the total in manufacturing in 1970, and to around 33 percent in 1973.

The proportion of employed persons in the social overhead and other service sectors who contributed "indirectly" to commodity exports was negligible in 1960, but increased to about 2 percent of all employed persons in these sectors in 1970 and to about 5 percent in 1973.

The proportion of employed persons in the primary sector who worked directly or indirectly for export production also grew from 1 percent in 1960 to 3 percent in 1970 and 5 percent in 1973.

According to the population census data, the number of employed persons in the manufacturing sector increased by about 1 million (from 0.48 million to 1.45 million persons) during 1960–70, and, according to our estimate, 30 percent of the increase was due to the growth of export production. According to the quarterly sample survey of the Economic Planning Board, the employed persons in the manufacturing sector increased by about 0.94 million (from 0.83 million to 1.77 million) during 1966–73, and, according to our estimate, the net increase in the number of persons directly and indirectly working for export production was about 0.44 million. That is, about half of the increase in employment in manufacturing during 1966–73 was due to export expansion.

About three-quarters of the increased employment in manufacturing sector attributable to export expansion occurred as "direct" employment. In the primary sector, there was no such significant difference between direct and indirect employment effects. Of course, increased employment in SOC and service sectors caused by commodity export expansion was

Table 7.7. Contribution of Exports to Sectoral Employment: 1960–73

In Thousand Persons

	1960	1963	1966	1970	1973[1]
Primary Sector					
(A) Total Employment	4,680.0[2]	4,894.0[3]	4,644.0	5,257.0	5,616.0[3]
(B) Directly Employed for Exports	33.4	40.1	66.1	85.7	118.1
(C) Indirectly Employed for Exports	13.6	45.7	48.5	71.3	144.1
(B+C)/(A)	(1%)	(2%)	(2%)	(3%)	(5%)
Manufacturing Sector					
(A) Total Employment	477.0[2]	610.0[3]	958.0	1,448.0	1,774.0[3]
(B) Directly Employed for Exports	10.8	32.0	107.4	241.2	471.2
(C) Indirectly Employed for Exports	3.7	15.8	30.2	71.1	107.6
(B+C)/(A)	(3%)	(8%)	(14%)	(22%)	(33%)
SOC & Service Sector					
(A) Total Employment	1,871.0[2]	2,158.0[3]	2,362.0	3,449.0	3,749.0[3]
(B) Directly Employed for Exports	0.0	0.0	0.1	0.2	0.1
(C) Indirectly Employed for Exports	4.0	16.3	33.5	79.7	174.3
(B+C)/(A)	(0%)	(1%)	(1%)	(2%)	(5%)
Whole Industry					
(A) Total Employment	7,028.0[2]	7,662.0[3]	7,963.0	10,153.0	11,139.0[3]
(B) Directly Employed for Exports	44.3	72.2	173.6	327.1	589.4
(C) Indirectly Employed for Exports	21.3	77.8	112.3	222.0	426.0
(B+C)/(A)	(1%)	(2%)	(4%)	(5%)	(9%)

[1] The BOK's export unit value index (1970 = 100) was applied instead of the U.S. GNP deflator due to the wide deviation of the former from the latter index in 1973.
[2] Including age group 12–13.
[3] 0.1% Sample Survey of the Economic Planning Board.

entirely due to the "indirect" employment effect.[19]

B. Capital Stock Used for Export Production

The fixed capital stock directly and indirectly employed for export production increased about 21-fold during 1960–70 and 18-fold during 1963–73 implying an average annual growth rate of 33–36 percent for either period and an export expansion elasticity of capital absorption of 0.9–1.0. Apparently, the capital elasticity was greater than the employment elasticity, which may be attributed partly to a changing export pattern towards more capital intensive commodities and partly to increased capital-output ratios caused by factor substitutions, changes in inter-industrial relations, etc. It is notable that more than half of the capital used for export production was indirectly employed, which is opposite to the labor employment pattern.

For all industries in Korea, the proportion of persons directly and indirectly working for export production in total employment increased from 1 percent in 1960 to 5 percent in 1970 and to 9 percent in 1973. The proportion of capital stock employed for export production in total fixed capital stock increased from 1 percent in 1960 to 8 percent in 1970 and to 16 percent in 1973. Accordingly, the proportion of labor working for export production would appear to have been smaller than the proportion of capital. However, if we exclude disguised unemployment in the agricultural sector from total employment, the proportions of labor and capital working for export production become quite similar to each other.

The net increase in fixed capital stock (excluding the dwellings) during 1960–73 was equivalent to about 10.1 billion dollars, while the amount of capital used for export production increased by about $2.2 billion. That is, more than 20 percent of the increase in total fixed capital stock was absorbed by export production.

Unlike the case of labor inputs to export production, there was no significant change in the amount of fixed capital stock used per $100 million worth of exports which remained at around $90 million during the period 1960–73. Taking account of possible technical progress, this constancy of capital requirements may be explained in terms of the changing

---

[19] A comprehensive statistical presentation of various estimates of factor requirements can be found in my *Statistical Data on Korea's Trade and Growth*, Seoul: Korea Development Institute, 1975. (mimeographed) Anyone interested in the detailed procedures underlying our estimates should refer to this work.

Table 7.8. *Capital Requirements for Export Production: 1960–73*

In Million 1970 Dollars

	1960	1963	1966	1968	1970	1973
Total Fixed Capital Stock[1]	4,110	4,784	5,909	7,667	10,375	14,253
Capital Stock in Manufacturing	772	936	1,273	1,682	2,138	2,809
Total Commodity Exports	*(42)*	*(110)*	*(294)*	*(503)*	*(835)*	*(2,550)*
Total Capital Employed in Export Production[2]	39[5]	128[5]	266	462	821	2,240
Capital Directly Employed[3]	18	53	121	208	340	1,123
Capital Indirectly Employed	21[5]	75[5]	145	254	481	1,116
(Capital Content of Imported Inputs)[4]	—	—	(30)	(103)	(186)	(802)
Capital Used Per $100 Million Exports	93[5]	116[5]	90	92	98	88
Capital Directly Employed	43	48	41	41	41	44
Capital Indirectly Employed	50[5]	68[5]	49	50	58	44
(Capital Content of Imported Inputs)	—	—	(10)	(20)	(22)	(31)

[1] Excluding the ownerships of dwelling.
[2] Obtained by using A^d matrix.
[3] Applying the direct capital coefficients.
[4] Obtained by using A^m matrix.
[5] Including the capital content of imported inputs, which seems to have been negligible amount.

Table 7.9. Exports and Sectoral Capital Use: 1960–73

In Million 1970 Dollars

	1960	1963	1966	1970	1973[1]
Primary Sector					
(A) Total Fixed Capital Stock	513.1	600.9	776.8	1,125.2	1,567.9
(B) Directly Employed for Exports	12.9	26.5	41.7	76.4	140.4
(C) Indirectly Employed for Exports	7.4	19.9	33.6	52.0	130.2
(B+C)/(A)	(4%)	(8%)	(10%)	(11%)	(17%)
Manufacturing Sector					
(A) Total Fixed Capital Stock	772.0	935.7	1,273.2	2,137.8	2,808.5
(B) Directly Employed for Exports	5.3	26.0	79.0	263.0	982.4
(C) Indirectly Employed for Exports	4.3	20.7	50.8	212.2	432.8
(B+C)/(A)	(1%)	(5%)	(10%)	(22%)	(50%)
SOC & Service Sector					
(A) Total Fixed Capital Stock	2,824.5	3,247.1	3,859.3	7,111.6	9,876.5
(B) Directly Employed for Exports	0.0	0.0	0.1	0.4	0.3
(C) Indirectly Employed for Exports	9.7	34.8	60.5	216.5	553.4
(B+C)/(A)	(0%)	(1%)	(2%)	(3%)	(6%)
Whole Industry					
(A) Total Fixed Capital Stock	4,109.6	4,783.7	5,909.3	10,374.6	14,252.9
(B) Directly Employed for Exports	18.2	52.5	120.7	339.8	1,123.1
(C) Indirectly Employed for Exports	21.4	75.3	144.9	480.7	1,116.4
(B+C)/(A)	(1%)	(3%)	(4%)	(8%)	(16%)

[1] The BOK's export unit value index (1970 = 100) was applied instead of the U.S. GNP deflator due to the wide deviation of the former from the latter index in 1973

composition of the export commodity bundle and factor substitutions.

In the manufacturing sector, the proportion of capital stock used for export production increased from about 1 percent of the sector total in 1960 to about 10 percent in 1966, about 22 percent in 1970, and around 50 percent in 1973.[20]

In the primary sector, the proportion of persons working for export production increased from about 1 percent of the total employed in the primary sector in 1960 to about 5 percent in 1973. The proportion of capital stock employed for export production in the primary sector increased from about 4 percent of all fixed capital stock in the primary sector in 1960 to about 11 percent in 1970 and to around 17 percent in 1973. The more than proportionate absorption of capital for export production in the primary sector seems to have been due to the dominance of fishery products in primary exports which tend to be relatively high in capital intensity.

C. Factor Intensity of Trade

We also estimated the factor requirements for import replacement in 1960, 1963, 1966, 1968, 1970 and 1973 applying the (117) sectoral factor coefficients and the A matrix for each year. With these estimates we examined the factor intensity of Korea's exports and that of import replacements. In this paper the factor intensity of exports (or import replacements) is defined as the ratio of the amount of capital required for export production (or import replacements) to the amount of labor required for export production (or import replacements), and we use the terms "capital intensity" and "factor intensity" interchangeably.

In 1968 the direct and indirect capital requirements needed to produce $100 million (in 1970 prices) worth of exports were $41 million and $50 million, respectively. The corresponding direct and indirect labor requirements were 49 thousand man-years and 32 thousand man-years respectively. As a result, the direct factor intensity of Korea's exports was 0.84 and the total (direct plus indirect) factor intensity was 1.12 in 1968.

On the other hand, the amounts of directly and indirectly utilized capital required to replace $100 million worth of competitive imports were $49 million and $45 million respectively in 1968, and the amounts of labor

---

[20] The capital requirements for export production in 1973 seem to have been overestimated because fairly large portion of the drastic export increase in 1973 must have been produced by the increased rate of capital utilization. (Cf. p. 38 ff.)

Table 7.10. *Changing Factor Intensity of Trade: 1960–73 (Per $100 Million Commodity Exports or Import Replacements)*

In Million 1970 Dollars & Thousand Persons

	1960	1963	1966	1968	1970	1973
I. Direct Factor Intensity of Exports	(0.41)	(0.74)	(0.69)	(0.84)	(1.05)	(1.91)
Capital Directly Employed	43	48	41	41	41	44
Labor Directly Employed	105	65	59	49	39	23
II. Indirect Factor Intensity of Exports	(1.00)[1]	(0.96)[1]	(1.29)	(1.56)	(2.15)	(2.59)
Capital Indirectly Employed	50[1]	68[1]	49	50	58	44
Labor Indirectly Employed	50[1]	71[1]	38	32	27	17
III. Factor Intensity of Imported Inputs	—	—	(1.43)	(2.22)	(2.75)	(3.10)
Capital Content of Imported Inputs	—	—	10	20	22	31
Labor Content of Imported Inputs	—	—	7	9	8	10
IV. Aggregate Factor Intensity of Exports	(0.59)	(0.85)	(0.93)	(1.12)	(1.48)	(2.20)
Total Capital Employed (I plus II)	93	116	90	91	98	88
Total Labor Employed (I plus II)	157	136	97	81	66	40
I. Direct Factor Intensity of Imports[2]	(1.07)	(0.76)	(1.45)	(1.20)	(1.05)	(1.29)
Capital Directly Required	48	41	58	49	45	44
Labor Directly Required	45	54	40	41	43	34
II. Indirect Factor Intensity of Imports	(1.26)[1]	(1.29)[1]	(2.18)	(1.80)	(2.60)	(3.75)
Capital Indirectly Required	59[1]	58[1]	61	45	52	45
Labor Indirectly Required	47[1]	45[1]	28	25	20	12
III. Factor Intensity of Imported Inputs	—	—	(2.00)	(2.00)	(2.25)	(3.56)
Capital Content of Imported Inputs	—	—	22	24	18	32
Labor Content of Imported Inputs	—	—	11	12	8	9
IV. Aggregate Factor Intensity of Imports[2]	(1.16)	(1.00)	(1.78)	(1.51)	(1.62)	(2.20)
Total Capital Required (I+II+III)	107	99	141	118	115	121
Total Labor Required (I+II+III)	92	99	79	78	71	55

[1] Includes the capital or labor content of imported inputs required for exports or import substitution.
[2] Import substitution of competitive imports (competitive as of 1968), i.e., replacements of imports with domestic production.

directly and indirectly required were 41 thousand workers and 25 thousand workers respectively. The factor content of (competitively) imported inputs required to replace $100 million worth of competitive imports amounted to $24 million in capital and 12 thousand workers in 1968. Hence, the direct factor intensity of import replacements was 1.20 and the total factor intensity was 1.51 in 1968.

It can be seen that competitive imports were more capital intensive than exports in 1968 in terms of either direct or total factor content. Therefore, the trade pattern of Korea in 1968 appears to have been consistent with the Heckscher-Ohlin theorem. We may now examine the changing pattern of factor intensity in Korea's trade during the period 1960-73.

The direct factor intensity of exports became more capital intensive during 1960-73, as did the indirect factor intensity of exports. Consequently, the total direct and indirect factor requirements for exports increased greatly in capital intensity during 1960-73: the capital/labor ratio of the export commodity bundle increased from 0.59 in 1960 to 2.20 in 1973. There was also some increase in the capital intensity of imported inputs used for export production. However, it should be noted that the capital intensity of imported inputs used for export production was much higher than that of the domestic factor content of exports.

On the other hand, the total (direct plus indirect) factor intensity of competitive import replacements did not change consistently in any one direction. Consequently, although competitive imports were much more capital intensive than exports before 1968, the difference became smaller and there seems to have been little difference between their factor intensities after 1970. We may argue, therefore, that comparative advantage *a la* Heckscher-Ohlin no longer dominates Korea's trade in terms of the relationship of exports and competitive imports. However, we still have to examine the factor intensity of the remaining 40 percent of Korea's imports which have been excluded from our consideration so far, i.e., the factor intensity of non-competitive imports. This will be investigated in Chapter 9.

The findings of this chapter indicate that with significantly increasing per capita capital stock and a rising wage/rental ratio in Korea, not only did there occur capital deepening in domestic production but the export commodity bundle also became more capital intensive. On the other hand, the (competitive) import commodity bundle did not become less capital intensive, although on a theoretical level some decrease in capital intensity was expected. Taking into account the possible bias in the changing demand pattern, however, what we observed can still be fitted into the basic framework of our comparative static proposition on the two-factor multi-commodity trade pattern. However, in the process of estimating factor intensity, very biased changes in sectoral capital- and labor-output ratios were observed, which seem to have been caused by factor-substitution, technical progress, economies of scale, and changing inter-industry relationships. The extent of capital-labor substitutions and its implication for the factor intensity of trade will be examined in the following chapter.

CHAPTER 8

THE IMPACT OF CAPITAL-LABOR SUBSTITUTION ON THE FACTOR INTENSITY OF TRADE

This chapter investigates the impact of capital-labor substitutions in production processes on the direct and total factor intensity of trade.

To examine this phenomenon we first computed the direct plus indirect factor requirements per $100 million worth of commodity exports during 1960–72 using the 1966 and 1970 A^d matrices and sectoral factor coefficients. As we can see from Table 8.1., there was a significant decrease in the amount of labor required for ($100 million worth of) export production due to the changes in the "commodity composition" of exports towards less labor intensive goods during 1960–72. However, a more significant amount of the decrease in labor requirements was caused by changes in the sectoral labor-output ratios.

The direct and indirect labor requirements to produce $100 million worth of exports decreased by about 10 percent during 1966–72 due to changes in the composition of the export commodity bundle, and decreased by nearly 30 percent during 1966–70 due to changes in sectoral labor-output ratios. That is, the amount of employment generated by export expansion in the period of 1966–72 could have been about 10 percent larger if there were no change in the composition of commodity exports but more than 30 percent larger if there had been no change in the sectoral labor-output ratios. The labor requirements decreased a little due also to changes in input-output relationships, but the effect of interaction was negligible.[1]

---

[1] The interaction component in Table 8.1. is a residual term under the given set of weights, i.e., given export pattern of each year. Cf. L. A. Weiser, "Changing Factor Requirements of United States Foreign Trade," *Review of Economics and Statistics* (August 1968).

Table 8.1. *Changes in Industrial Structure and Total Factor Requirements Per $100 Million of Export Production (Applying the A^d Matrix)*

	Estimated Capital Requirements Applying				Impact of Changes In[1]			
	1966 Capital-Output Ratios & 1966 I-O	1966 Capital-Output Ratios & 1970 I-O	1970 Capital-Output Ratios & 1966 I-O	1970 Capital-Output Ratios & 1970 I-O	Input-Output Relationships	Capital-Output Ratios	Inter-action	All Coefficients
1960	90.5	97.6	97.6	102.4	8%	8%	3%	13%
1963	103.6	100.9	106.4	106.4	-3%	3%	3%	3%
1966	90.5	91.8	95.9	99.7	1%	6%	3%	10%
1968	92.4	91.7	98.2	100.4	-1%	6%	4%	9%
1970	95.3	92.8	98.0	98.3	-3%	3%	3%	3%
1972	98.7	95.0	102.1	100.9	-4%	3%	3%	2%

	Estimated Labor Requirements Applying				Impact of Changes In[1]			
	1966 Labor-Output Ratios & 1966 I-O	1966 Labor-Output Ratios & 1970 I-O	1970 Labor-Output Ratios & 1966 I-O	1970 Labor-Output Ratios & 1970 I-O	Input-Output Relationships	Labor-Output Ratios	Inter-action	All Coefficients
1960	107.1	107.1	78.6	81.0	0%	-27%	3%	-24%
1963	94.5	92.7	67.3	65.5	-2%	-29%	0%	-31%
1966	97.3	96.3	70.4	68.7	-1%	-28%	0%	-29%
1968	96.8	95.0	68.8	66.4	-2%	-29%	0%	-31%
1970	97.5	94.7	68.9	65.7	-3%	-29%	-1%	-33%
1972	89.3	86.3	63.9	60.6	-3%	-28%	-1%	-32%

In Thousand Persons & Percent

[1] Estimates of percentage changes in factor requirements (per $100 million of export production) during 1966-70 applying six different sets of weights, i.e., applying the export pattern of 1960, 1963, 1966, 1968, 1970 and 1972. These estimates exclude the effect of shifts in export composition.

Table 8.2. Changes in Sectoral Factor-Output Ratios, Export Pattern and Direct Factor Requirements Per $100 Million (in 1970 Prices) Exports

In Million 1970 Dollars or Thousand Persons

	Direct Capital Requirements Per $100 Million Exports Applying the Sectoral Capital-Output Ratios of			Percentage Changes in Capital Requirements Due to Changes in Capital Coefficients		Direct Labor Requirements Per $100 Million Exports Applying the Sectoral Labor-Output Ratios of			Percentage Changes in Labor Requirements Due to Changes in Labor Coefficients	
	1966	1968	1970	1966–70	1968–70	1966	1968	1970	1966–70	1968–70
1960	44.4	52.8	48.2	9%	-9%	73.1	65.2	53.2	-27%	-18%
1961	46.2	51.0	46.8	1%	-8%	70.8	63.8	50.2	-29%	-21%
1962	49.1	54.4	51.4	5%	-6%	67.6	61.6	50.5	-25%	-18%
1963	44.1	49.0	45.8	4%	-7%	52.7	44.3	35.3	-33%	-20%
1964	43.7	48.3	46.0	5%	-7%	57.3	50.2	40.4	-30%	-20%
1965	43.2	45.1	44.8	4%	-1%	55.3	48.4	39.0	-30%	-19%
1966	41.1	42.9	42.6	4%	-1%	59.1	51.4	41.8	-29%	-19%
1967	43.6	43.9	44.3	2%	1%	58.8	49.9	40.9	-30%	-18%
1968	42.6	41.3	42.6	0%	3%	57.5	49.2	39.9	-31%	-19%
1969	43.9	41.2	41.7	-5%	1%	57.5	49.3	40.1	-30%	-19%
1970	42.9	40.6	40.7	-5%	0%	57.0	48.4	39.2	-31%	-19%
1971	43.4	41.1	41.8	-4%	2%	53.6	45.9	37.2	-31%	-19%
1972	44.1	40.4	41.1	-6%	3%	50.0	44.1	34.9	-30%	-21%
Average	44.0[1]	45.5[1]	44.5[1]	1.1%	-2.2%	59.3[1]	51.7[1]	41.7[1]	-29%	-19%
Annual Av. 0%[2]		-2%[2]	-1%[2]	0.3%	-1.1%	-3%[2]	-3%[2]	-3%[2]	-8%	-10%

[1] Average amount of capital or labor required per $100 million exports during 1960–72.
[2] Average annual rate of changes in the amount of capital or labor required per $100 million exports due to changes in the commodity composition of exports during 1960–72.

On the other hand, there was a notable increase in the capital requirements for ($100 million worth of) export production after 1966, which can be attributed to the changes in the export pattern towards more capital intensive goods. Further, there was also a notable increase in the capital requirements (per $100 million of exports) during 1966–70 due to increased sectoral captial-output ratios, which may be attributed to factor substitutions in production processes.

We can also see from Table 8.2. that, during 1960–72, the direct labor requirements for export production decreased at an average annual rate of about 3 percent due to changes in the composition of exports while these direct labor requirements decreased by an average of more than 7 percent annually during 1966–70 due to changes in sectoral labor output ratios.

As far as the direct capital requirements for export production were concerned, one can observe a slight decrease due to the changes in export commodity composition as well as changes in sectoral capital-output ratios. Therefore, the absolute increase in total capital requirements for export production seems to have resulted from the increased "indirect" use of capital.

Since the direct plus indirect labor requirements for ($100 million worth of) exports decreased significantly while the direct plus indirect capital requirements for exports increased slightly (especially after 1966), the capital intensity of Korea's commodity exports rose substantially during 1960–72.

Applying the direct or total sectoral factor-output ratios for 1960, 1963, 1966, 1968 and 1970 to the trade data for 1960–72, we estimated five different sets of estimates of direct or total factor intensity of exports and competitive import replacements in the period of 1960–72.

As can be seen in Table 8.3. and Table 8.4., we obtained a different series of factor intensity estimates for exports or import replacements applying different sectoral factor-output ratios to the trade data for 1960–72. We can observe that the estimated increase in the direct capital intensity of exports due to shifts in the export pattern alone never exceeded 54 percent on the one hand, while on the other the decrease in the estimates of direct capital intensity of competitive import replacements due to shifts in the import pattern alone amounted more than 44 percent during 1960–72, regardless of the set of direct factor coefficients applied. However, the direct capital intensity of exports actually increased by about 150 percent during 1960–70 while that of competitive imports decreased by only 2 percent, apparently reflecting significant capital-labor substitutions in production processes.

Table 8.3. Impact of Capital-Labor Substitution on Direct Factor Intensity of Trade

(Factor Intensity = Capital/Labor)

	1960	1963	1966	1968	1970	1972
Direct Factor Intensity of Exports, Applying						
1960 Factor Coefficients	**0.41**	0.59	0.54	0.56	0.56	0.63
1963 Factor Coefficients	0.55	**0.73**	0.65	0.64	0.62	0.72
1966 Factor Coefficients	0.61	0.84	**0.70**	0.74	0.75	0.88
1968 Factor Coefficients	0.81	1.11	0.84	**0.84**	0.84	0.92
1970 Factor Coefficients	0.91	1.30	1.02	1.07	**1.04**	1.19
Direct Factor Intensity of Competitive Import Replacements,* Applying						
1960 Factor Coefficients	**1.07**	0.69	1.15	0.73	0.57	0.59
1963 Factor Coefficients	1.19	**0.76**	1.30	0.83	0.65	0.67
1966 Factor Coefficients	1.48	0.85	**1.45**	0.86	0.65	0.70
1968 Factor Coefficients	2.09	1.13	2.00	**1.20**	0.84	0.82
1970 Factor Coefficients	2.16	1.25	2.26	1.41	**1.05**	1.02

*Competitive as of 1968.

Table 8.4. Impact of Capital-Labor Substitution on Total Factor Intensity of Trade

(Factor Intensity = Capital/Labor)

	1960	1963	1966	1968	1970	1972
Total Factor Intensity of Exports, Applying						
1960 A Matrix & Factor Coefficients	**0.60**	0.77	0.70	0.69	0.69	0.74
1963 A Matrix & Factor Coefficients	0.71	**0.85**	0.77	0.75	0.74	0.81
1966 A^d Matrix & Factor Coefficients	0.86	1.09	**0.93**	0.96	0.98	1.11
1968 A^d Matrix & Factor Coefficients	1.07	1.34	1.11	**1.13**	1.14	1.25
1970 A^d Matrix & Factor Coefficients	1.28	1.62	1.45	1.51	**1.49**	1.66
Total Factor Intensity of Competitive Import Replacements, Applying						
1960 A Matrix & Factor Coefficients	**1.16**	0.87	1.18	0.89	0.77	0.78
1963 A Matrix & Factor Coefficients	1.16	**0.99**	1.39	1.02	0.88	0.88
1966 A Matrix & Factor Coefficients	1.59	1.25	**1.78**	1.23	1.03	1.07
1968 A Matrix & Factor Coefficients	1.97	1.48	2.14	**1.52**	1.24	1.23
1970 A Matrix & Factor Coefficients	2.24	1.77	2.53	1.90	**1.61**	1.60

Note: Due to the limited data available, the A matrix was applied to compute the direct plus indirect factor requirements of export production in 1960 and 1963. Imports are competitive as of 1968.

Table 8.5. *Changes in the Factor Intensity of Commodity Exports Due to Factor Substitutions and Shifts in the Composition of Exports: 1966–72*

		1966	1968	1970	1972	Changes Due to Shifts in Composition		
						1966–68	1968–70	1970–72
Direct Factor Intensity of Exports (Capital/Labor Ratios)
Applying 1966 Coefficients		**0.70**	0.74	0.75	0.88	5.7%	1.4%	17.3%
Applying 1968 Coefficients		0.84	**0.84**	0.84	0.92	0.0%	0.0%	9.5%
Applying 1970 Coefficients		1.02	1.07	**1.04**	1.19	4.9%	2.8%	14.4%
Changes
Due to Factor	1966–68	20.0%	13.5%	12.0%	4.5%	20.0%*	—	—
Substitutions	1968–70	21.4%	27.4%	23.8%	29.3%	—	23.8%*	—
Direct plus Indirect Factor Intensity of Export (Capital/Labor Ratios)
Applying 1966 Coefficients		**0.93**	0.96	0.98	1.11	3.2%	2.1%	13.3%
Applying 1968 Coefficients		1.11	**1.13**	1.14	1.25	1.8%	0.9%	9.6%
Applying 1970 Coefficients		1.45	1.51	**1.49**	1.66	4.1%	−1.3%	11.4%
Changes
Due to Factor	1966–68	19.4%	17.7%	16.3%	12.6%	21.5%*	—	—
Substitutions	1968–70	30.6%	33.6%	30.7%	32.8%	—	31.9%*	—

* Total changes, i.e., sum of changes due to shifts in export composition, those due to factor substitutions and those due to interactions (which were not presented in this table as separate items).

On the other hand, the "increase" in the estimated total factor intensity of exports due to shifts in the export pattern (obtained by holding the sectoral factor coefficients constant) never exceeded 30 percent and the estimated "decrease" of the total factor intensity of competitive imports due to shifts in the import pattern alone amounted to more than 24 percent during 1960–72. The fact that Korea's export bundle became more capital intensive while the bundle of imports to Korea became less capital intensive under the "fixed coefficient assumption" is perfectly consistent with our comparative static proposition on the two-factor multi-commodity trade pattern based on the Rybczynski theorem as presented in Chapter 2.

However, the total factor intensity of exports actually (i.e., if we take account of changes in factor coefficients) increased by about 150 percent during 1960–70, and that of competitive imports, instead of decreasing, increased by about 40 percent during 1960–70. If we take the time period 1966–70, the total factor intensity of exports actually increased by about 60 percent and that of competitive imports decreased by only 10 percent which, in any case, seems to reflect significant factor substitutions in production processes towards greater capital intensity. Again, this observation is consistent with our proposition on the disequilibrium sequence associated with the changing wage/rental ratio as presented in Chapter 2.

Since the sectoral capital coefficient data for 1960 and 1963 are not very reliable, we may restrict our investigation to the 1966–72 period. As can be seen in Table 8.5., during 1966–68 the direct capital intensity of exports increased by about 4 percent due to changes in the commodity export composition but rose by about 13 percent due to capital-labor substitutions. In sum, the direct factor intensity of exports increased by 20 percent during 1966–68. The direct plus indirect capital intensity of commodity exports increased by about 1 percent due to changes in export composition but increased by about 32 percent due to capital-labor substitutions during 1968–70. As a result, the total factor intensity of exports increased by 32 percent during 1968–70.[2]

Although a quite significant increase in the capital intensity of Korea's commodity exports occurred due to changes in the export bundle during the period of 1970–72, the overall impression is that it is the factor substitution which has dominated the changes in the factor intensity of Korea's exports during the period 1966–72. It seems reasonable to attribute such changes to the rapidly increasing per capita capital stock and associated

---

[2] Since we did not separate out the "interaction term" in Table 8.5., the sum of changes in capital intensity of exports due to shifts in export pattern and changes due to factor substitution does not exactly add up to the actual aggregate rate of change.

rising wage/rental ratio.

We may argue that the factor intensity of Korea's exports became more capital intensive partly due to shifts in the export pattern but more significantly due to capital-labor substitution in production processes. On the other hand, although the factor intensity of Korea's competitive import replacements became less capital intensive due to shifts in the import pattern, we could not observe any consistent decrease in the estimates of the capital intensity of competitive import replacements during 1966–70 due to the offsetting increases in sectoral capital-labor substitutions.

So far we have tried to identify the portion of the change in the factor intensity of trade which can be attributed to the shift in the commodity composition of trade and that attributable to changes in factor coefficients, and found that the latter was much more important than the former. However, it is still possible that the latter portion might have been smaller had we employed more detailed sectoral breakdown (say, 340 sector classification) rather than the 117-sector classification. That is, the increased capital-output ratio of a sector might have been the result of changes in the output composition of that sector rather than factor substitutions in the production process. But more detailed sectoral classification may not be desirable even if possible, because the reliability of sectoral factor coefficients seems to be inversely related to the extent of sectoral breakdown beyond certain point due to defects in the basic raw data on sectoral capital stock.

In Chapter 2, the factor substitution in each sector was explained in terms of the changing wage/rental ratio only. However, the actual changes in the sectoral factor coefficients observed in this chapter may have been caused by factor saving technical progresses and economies of scale as well.

CHAPTER 9

FACTOR INTENSITY OF NON-COMPETITIVE IMPORTS

In Chapter 7, we found that competitive imports were much more capital intensive than exports before 1968 but that the difference became insignificant after 1970, and hence that comparative advantage *a la* Heckscher-Ohlin no longer dominated Korea's trade of exports vs. competitive imports.

This chapter investigates the factor intensity of non-competitive imports. We will estimate the capital and labor requirements to replace non-competitive imports on the basis of the U.S. and Japanese sectoral (direct plus indirect) factor coefficients.

There are two sets of sectoral (direct plus indirect) factor coefficients available for the U.S. One is the set for 1947 used by Leontief in his original investigation of the factor proportions of American trade.[1] The other is the set for 1958 used by Baldwin in his re-examination of the commodity structure of U.S. trade.[2] Baldwin updated the factor coefficients of commodity sectors on the basis of the U.S. manufacturing census, etc., but he relied on Leontief's data for most of the non-commodity sectors.

For Japan, we calculated the (117) sectoral direct plus indirect factor coefficients for 1965 and 1970. We first estimated the direct capital and labor coefficients of Japanese manufacturing industries on the basis of the manufacturing censuses of 1965 and 1970. For the rest of the sectors we applied the 1960 capital coefficients which were estimated on the basis

---
[1] Leontief *op. cit.* (1953 & 1956).
[2] R. E. Baldwin, "Determinants of the Commodity Structure of U.S. Trade," *American Economic Review*, March 1971.

Table 9.1. Progress of Import Substitution and the Changing Composition of Imports

In Million 1970 Dollars

	Competitive Imports				Non-Competitive Imports				Natural Resource Intensive Imports
	1970 Basis	1968 Basis[1]	1966 Basis[2]	1963 Basis[3]	1970 Basis	1968 Basis	1966 Basis	1963 Basis	
1960	305	−12	n.a.	n.a.	47	59	n.a.	n.a.	79
1961	262	−12	—	—	54	66	—	—	72
1962	353	−25	—	—	104	129	—	—	85
1963	489	−25	—	—	128	153	—	—	91
1964	339	−32	−6	−61	67	99	105	166	96
1965	362	−41	−11	−46	86	127	138	184	117
1966	617	−79	−14	−89	79	157	171	260	156
1967	823	−212	−15	−117	129	251	266	383	194
1968	1,174	−212	−13	−163	198	410	423	586	247
1969	1,323	−206	−16	−139	284	491	507	646	319
1970	1,314	−204	−31	−143	313	517	548	691	358
1971	1,447	−224	−27	−178	400	623	650	828	441
1972	1,409	−246	−32	−145	460	706	738	883	465
1973	1,854	−321	−36	−183	662	983	1,019	1,202	621

Source: Tables A.9., A.18. and A.19.

[1] Differences between 1970 basis figures and 1968 basis figures.
[2] Differences between 1968 basis figures and 1966 basis figures. The small differences between 1966 and 1968 do not seem to be due to small progress in import substitution but rather due to the fact that 1968 input-output table was a simplified extension of 1966 table and as a result the import substitution could not have been adequately covered.
[3] Differences between 1966 basis figures and 1963 basis figures.

of the Japanese National Wealth Survey of 1960 and the 1965 labor coefficients which accompanied the 1965 Japanese input-output table. In computing the so-called 1965 and 1970 sectoral factor coefficients, we employed the 1965 Japanese input-output table.

The factor intensity of natural resource intensive imports which made up 15–20 percent of total commodity imports during 1960–74 could not be estimated in any meaningful way. These were simply treated as commodities intensive in non-labor and non-capital factors which Korea does not possess, and hence Korea has an extreme comparative disadvantage in production and trade.

In 1968, about 60 percent of total commodity imports were competitive imports and about 25 percent of them were non-competitive imports while about 15 percent were what we call natural-resource intensive imports. If we classify imports as competitive or noncompetitive on the 1968 basis, we can not observe any significant change in the import pattern in 1970. However, due to significant import substitution in the period of 1968–70, when the 1970 classification is employed only about 16 percent of total imports (instead of 26 percent on the 1968 basis) can be classified as non-competitive and about 66 percent of them as competitive. Similarly, about 21 percent of total imports in 1973 were non-competitive imports based on the 1970 classification, but this share would be substantially smaller were we to employ the 1973 basis of classification.

Although the relative share of non-competitive imports in total commodity imports has been steadily decreasing since 1968 owing to progress in import substitution, the absolute amount of non-competitive imports significantly increased each year.

We first classified the commodity imports as competitive or non-competitive on the 1968 basis and then estimated the (direct plus indirect) capital and labor requirements to replace non-competitive imports during 1966–72 applying the U.S. and Japanese factor coefficients.

According to the 1947 U.S. coefficients, the total amount of capital required to replace Korea's non-competitive imports (non-competitive as of 1968) increased from about $0.3 billion in 1966 (in 1970 prices) to about $1.3 billion in 1972, and the total amount of labor required increased from 16 thousand man-years to 72 thousand man-years. According to the 1965 Japanese coefficients, the total amount of capital required to replace non-competitive imports increased from about $0.25 billion in 1966 to about $1.1 billion in 1972, and the total amount of labor required increased from 53 thousand to 234 thousand man-years.

In 1970, the amount of capital required to replace $100 million worth of non-competitive imports was about $146 million if we apply the 1965 Japanese coefficients, about $139 million if we apply the 1970 Japanese coefficients, about $174 million if we apply the 1947 U.S. coefficients and about $146 million if we apply the 1958 U.S. coefficients. The amount of labor required to replace $100 million worth of non-competitive imports in 1970 was about 33 thousand man-years if we apply the 1965 Japanese coefficients, about 26 thousand if we apply the 1970 Japanese coefficients, about 10 thousand if we apply the 1947 U.S. coefficients and about 8 thousand if we apply the 1958 U.S. coefficients. As can be seen in Table 9.3., we get very similar results when we classify the commodity imports as competitive or non-competitive on the 1970 basis.

The remarkable fact is that the amount of both capital and labor required per $100 million worth of non-competitive imports decreases significantly when we apply the more recent set of coefficients of either the U.S. or Japan. This seems to indicate that significant technological progress occurred in both the U.S. and Japan, and a consequent decrease in factor requirements per unit of output. Another notable fact is that while the capital requirements per unit of output did not differ greatly between the U.S. and Japan, Japan required about four times more labor than the U.S. per unit of output. There was not much change in this pattern during the period of 1966–72, although there were significant changes in the composition of Korea's non-commodity imports which were used as sectoral weights in computing aggregate factor requirements.

The above results are summarized in Table 9.4. The factor intensity of Korea's non-competitive imports was about $18,500/worker in 1970 if we apply the U.S. coefficients (1947 or 1958), but was less than $5,000/worker if we apply the Japanese coefficients (1965 or 1970). In either case, the capital intensity of Korea's non-competitive imports was much higher than that of her competitive imports (or exports) in 1970. The results confirm our expectation that trade based on the comparative advantage doctrine of Heckscher-Ohlin held primarily for exports vs. non-competitive imports, as well as for exports vs. natural resource intensive imports.

Another interesting fact is that the capital intensity of Korea's trade in 1970 (both exports and competitive imports) seems to have been higher than that of Japan's trade in 1951 as estimated by Ichimura and Tatemoto.[3] Furthermore, Japan required more of both capital and labor to produce $100 million worth of exports or competitive imports in 1951 than did Korea in 1970. In 1965, however, Japan required about 25–50 percent

---

[3] See S. Ichimura and M. Tatemoto, "Factor Proportions and Foreign Trade: The Case of Japan," *Review of Economics and Statistics*, November 1957.

Table 9.2. Estimates of Capital and Labor Requirements to Replace Non-Competitive Imports: 1968 Basis

In Million 1970 Dollars or 1,000 Persons

	1947 U.S. Coefficients (Leontief's Data) Capital	Labor	1958 U.S. Coefficients (Baldwin's Data) Capital	Labor	1965 Japanese Coefficients (Manufacturing Census & I-O Data) Capital	Labor	1970 Japanese Coefficients (Manufacturing Census & I-O Data) Capital	Labor	Total Non-competitive Imports
				Total Requirements					
1966	284	16	243	13	250	53	241	42	157
1967	428	26	371	21	379	83	362	65	251
1968	695	41	597	34	612	131	580	100	410
1969	832	50	714	41	725	158	686	120	491
1970	901	51	756	43	756	171	717	132	517
1971	1,103	64	913	53	920	209	876	162	623
1972	1,269	72	1,025	61	1,072	234	1,017	180	706
		Requirements to Replace $100 Million of Non-Competitive Imports							
1966	180.4	10.0	154.3	8.3	158.8	33.4	153.1	26.8	(538)
1967	170.6	10.4	147.8	8.4	151.1	33.1	144.2	25.7	(701)
1968	169.6	10.1	145.6	8.3	149.2	31.9	141.5	24.3	(962)
1969	169.6	10.2	145.5	8.4	147.8	32.3	139.8	24.5	(1,117)
1970	174.2	10.0	146.2	8.4	146.2	33.0	138.7	25.5	(1,110)
1971	177.1	10.2	146.5	8.5	147.7	33.6	140.6	26.0	(1,223)
1972	179.7	10.3	145.2	8.7	151.9	33.1	144.0	25.4	(1,163)

Note: Figures in the parentheses are total competitive imports which are presented here to enable an easy comparison with the magnitude of total non-competitive imports. (Competitive or non-competitive as of 1968.)

Table 9.3. Estimates of Capital and Labor Requirements to Replace Non-Competitive Imports: 1970 Basis

In Million 1970 Dollars or 1,000 Persons

	1947 U.S. Coefficients (Leontief's Data) Capital	Labor	1958 U.S. Coefficients (Baldwin's Data) Capital	Labor	1965 Japanese Coefficients (Manufacturing Census & I-O Data) Capital	Labor	1970 Japanese Coefficients (Manufacturing Census & I-O Data) Capital	Labor	Total Non-competitive Imports
				Total Requirements					
1966	149	7	129	6	108	29	106	25	79
1967	223	13	197	11	172	46	166	37	129
1968	334	19	295	16	282	62	266	48	198
1969	487	28	418	23	400	96	381	76	284
1970	559	30	464	25	447	109	430	87	313
1971	731	40	594	33	585	142	563	113	400
1972	861	46	679	39	708	161	678	128	460
			Requirements to Replace $100 Million of Non-Competitive Imports						
1966	189.1	8.9	162.8	7.8	136.7	36.9	133.6	31.3	(617)
1967	173.0	9.7	152.5	8.2	133.3	35.5	128.7	28.9	(823)
1968	168.4	9.7	148.9	8.0	142.2	31.1	134.2	24.0	(1,174)
1969	171.3	9.9	147.0	8.1	140.5	33.8	134.1	26.6	(1,323)
1970	178.6	9.7	148.3	8.1	143.0	34.9	137.5	28.0	(1,314)
1971	182.8	9.9	148.5	8.3	146.3	35.4	140.8	28.4	(1,447)
1972	187.3	10.0	147.7	8.6	154.0	34.9	147.4	27.8	(1,409)

Note: Figures in the parentheses are total competitive imports which are presented here to enable an easy comparison with the magnitude of total non-competitive imports. (Competitive or non-competitive as of 1970.)

Table 9.4. *Factor Requirements per $100 Million Exports or Import Replacements: U.S. (1947), Japan (1951) and Korea (1970)*

	Capital(K) (million 1970 $)	Labor(N) (1,000 persons)	Factor Intensity (K)/(N)
Korea (1970)			
Exports	98.2	65.7	1,495
Competitive-Imports	116.5	69.5	1,676
Non-Competitive Imports			
1947 U.S. Coefficients	178.6	9.7	18,466
1958 U.S. Coefficients	148.3	8.1	18,393
1965 Japanese Coefficients	143.0	34.9	4,102
1970 Japanese Coefficients	137.5	28.0	4,918
Japan (1951)			
Exports	138.6	125.8	1,102
Competitive Imports	133.1	187.6	710
U.S. (1947)			
Exports	255.1	10.1	25,258
Competitive Imports	309.1	9.4	32,883

Source: Tables 7.10., 9.1. and 9.2., Leontief, *op. cit.* (1953 & 1956) and S. Ichimura and M. Tatemoto, *op. cit.*
Note: The GNP deflator of the U.S. was applied to both Leontief's and Ichimura's data in order to get 1970 dollar figures. If we apply the GNP deflator of Japan (1970 = 100) and its official exchange rate of 360 yen per dollar in 1970 to Ichimura's data, we get about $1,400/worker for the capital intensity of Japan's exports and $900/worker for that of Japan's competitive imports in 1951.

more capital than Korea in 1970 but about 50 percent less labor per unit of output, which was reflected in the capital intensity of Korea's non-competitive imports estimated by using the 1965 Japanese coefficients, which was nearly three times higher that of Korea's exports or competitive imports. By 1970, Japan's capital requirements per unit of output have decreased slightly, while labor requirements have declined by more than 20 percent. This change was reflected in the capital intensity of Korea's non-competitive imports estimated by using the 1970 Japanese coefficients, which yielded results which were more than 3.4 times that of Korea's exports or competitive imports in 1970.

The U.S. in 1958 seems to have required a slightly more capital per unit of output than Japan in 1970 but required almost two-third less labor. The impression is that the enormous differences between the (sectoral) labor-output ratios of the U.S. and Japan might be explained partly by capital-labor substitutions but mostly by technological differences, or in terms of human capital inputs. However, the differences between the (sectoral) labor-output ratios of Japan and Korea might be more readily explained by capital-labor substitution in production processes, although the effect of technological differences and human capital element may also be significant.

In any case, if Korea attempts to replace its non-competitive imports in the immediate future, as it has sought to do in the past, the required capital intensity may be expected to be between that of the U.S. and Japan, although it is likely to be lower than that of Japan because of expected further capital-labor substitution arising from a lower wage/rental ratio in Korea than in Japan.[4]

We can see in Table 9.2. that there was no significant change in the factor intensity of Korea's non-competitive imports during 1966–72. Therefore, we can still conclude that the capital intensity of exports has been steadily increasing but the capital intensity of improts, whether competitive or non-competitive, has not changed in any consistent way to a specific direction.

In this chapter, we could conclude that Korea's trade of exports vs. non-competitive imports has clearly been conducted along the classical comparative advantage doctrine of Heckscher-Ohlin. We can draw the same conclusion with respect to the natural-resource intensive imports.

One might interpret the similarity of the factor intensity of exports and that of competitive imports as the limited usefulness of the Heckscher-Ohlin theorem. However, once we put our empirical findings into a dynamic disequilibrium framework, the changing pattern of these factor intensities may rather indicate a common sense sequence of evolution in growth process, i.e., the progress in import substitutions of capital-intensive goods. The competitive imports of Korea were about twice as capital intensive as its exports in 1966. However, with the rapid accumulation of per capita capital stock after 1966, Korea achieved significant import substitutions in capital intensive (import-competing) production which resulted in a significant fall in the capital intensity of competitive imports estimat-

---

[4] We may speculate that, in order for Korea to reach the level of industrialization Japan achieved in 1970, Korea may need approximately 30–40 percent more over-all capital deepening than in 1970. But the real constraints which will control the speed of Korea's industrialization are the rate of increase in the over-all ability to exploit advanced technology in production and management and the ability to allocate resources efficiently. Furthermore, because of the large expected annual net increase in the labor supply, capital deepening with labor-saving technical progress may not proceed rapidly in Korea unless the annual investment rate can be maintained at a high level.

Table 9.5. *Factor Requirements and Factor Intensity of Competitive and Non-Competitive Imports: 1968–70*

In Million 1970 Dollars or Thousand Persons

	Competitive Imports As of 1968			Competitive Imports As of 1970		
	Capital	Labor	K/L	Capital	Labor	K/L

(Applying 1968 A matrix and 1968 set of sectoral factor coefficients.)

1968	1,135	748	1.52	1,380	892	1.55
1969	1,213	942	1.29	1,464	1,085	1.35
1970	1,170	940	1.24	1,418	1,081	1.31

(Applying 1970 A matrix and 1970 set of sectoral factor coefficients.)

1968	1,188	624	1.90	1,443	753	1.92
1969	1,298	790	1.64	1,559	914	1.71
1970	1,274	791	1.61	1,534	913	1.68

	Non-Competitive Imports As of 1968			Non-Competitive Imports As of 1970		
	Capital	Labor	K/L	Capital	Labor	K/L

(Applying 1947 U.S. sectoral direct plus indirect factor coefficients.)

1968	695	41	16.95	334	19	17.58
1969	832	50	16.64	487	28	17.39
1970	901	52	17.33	559	30	18.63

(Applying 1958 U.S. sectoral direct plus indirect factor coefficients).

1968	597	34	17.56	295	16	18.44
1969	714	41	17.41	418	23	18.17
1970	756	43	17.58	464	25	18.56

(Applying 1965 Japanese sectoral direct plus indirect factor coefficients.)

1968	612	131	4.67	282	62	4.55
1969	725	158	4.59	400	96	4.17
1970	756	171	4.42	447	109	4.10

(Applying 1970 Japanese sectoral direct plus indirect factor coefficients.)

1968	580	100	5.80	266	48	5.54
1969	686	120	5.72	381	76	5.01
1970	717	132	5.43	430	88	4.89

ed by using any constant set of sectoral coefficients and in no change in the capital intensity of competitive imports estimated by using different sets of sectoral coefficients, reflecting capital intensive sectoral factor substitutions. At the same time, the capital intensity of exports also increased due to shifts in the composition of exports and factor substitutions in export production. All such changing patterns can be explained in a comparative static framework based on the Heckscher-Ohlin theorem or the variation employing a dynamic disequilibrium sequence which was presented in Chapter 2.[5]

With per capita capital accumulation, domestic production of some non-competitive capital intensive goods can begin. Since the import substitution of non-competing goods can be expected to begin with the relatively less capital intensive group of non-competitive imports, we may expect an increase in the factor intensity of non-competitive imports because the imports would then be limited to those which are extremely capital intensive.[6]

On the other hand, the domestic production of formerly non-competitive capital intensive imports will likely cause an increase in the capital intensity of competitive imports because these goods will now be classified as import competing goods and the competitive imports will now include items which were formerly classified as non-competitive (capital intensive) imports.

In order to verify this proposition, we computed the factor intensity of Korea's competitive and non-competitive imports during 1968-70 classifying imports as competitive or non-competitive based first on the 1968 classification and then based on the 1970 classification. As can be seen in Table 9.5., the estimates of the capital intensity of competitive imports were higher when we applied the 1970 classification. On the other hand, the estimates of the capital intensity of non-competitive imports became higher when we applied the 1970 classification than when we applied the 1968 basis of calssification when the U.S. sectoral factor coefficients were used. However, the opposite results were obtained when we used the Japanese coefficients. Hence the empirical results do not seem to support our proposition without reservation.

---

[5] There are those who argue that once a developing country becomes successful in exporting a large amount of labor-intensive goods to developed countries, the developed countries tend to erect such high barriers to these imports that the developing country has no other choice than to expand capital-intensive exports.

[6] Of course, we also have to consider possible shifts in demand pattern for non-competitive imports.

CHAPTER 10

SKILL INTENSITY OF TRADE

Altering the two-factor Heckscher-Ohlin model to incorporate natural resources and labor skills, Keesing assumes differences in the mobility of factors of production, i.e., natural resources are immobile, capital moves internationally at a low cost, and labor of whatever kind moves at high cost. Economic activities can then be divided into primary activities, those that must be located around the natural resources which they require as direct inputs, and secondary activities, which are free to locate away from natural resources. Since the indirect natural resource requirements of secondary activities can be imported in processed form, these industries will be located according to the availability of skilled and unskilled labor and capital. Because the movement of capital to labor is cheaper than the reverse, Keesing hypothesizes that the chief influence on location will be the skill endowment.[1]

Training can reshape the specific skills of a labor force in a short period of time, but only within narrow limits dictated by the cultural and educational background of the population involved, the availability of skilled people to supply training, and opportunities for on-the job training. Some occupational skills can be acquired only through a long process of professional training. The general training and experience of a population, as well as attitudes and working habits, resist rapid change. Therefore,

---
[1] D. B. Keesing, "Labor Skills and Comparative Advantage," *American Economic Review*, May 1966 and "Labor Skills and the Structure of Trade in Manufactures," in P. B. Kenen, ed., *The Open Economy: Essays on International Trade and Finance*, New York: Columbia University Press, 1968.

104   Factor Intensity of Trade

broad classes of skills in any population can only be altered slowly. The postulation that the endowment of labor skills is one of the major determinants of comparative advantage implies that there can be a skill bottleneck present in the expansion of industrial production. A country will not be able to expand its production of more skill intensive proucts until it acquires a larger skill endownment through training and other investments in human capital.

Using the sectoral skill coefficients of the United States derived from Leontief's skill calculations, Keesing measured the direct skill content of exports and imports for the United States, Japan and seven European countries, and showed that those whose exports are more skill intensive have higher per capita income and less skill intensive imports. From this study Keesing concluded that skill availability is a major factor in the determination of trade patterns, and that the United States has abundant skilled labor and hence tends to export skill intensive goods and import unskilled labor intensive goods.

In this chapter, we will also classify labor into various skill groups and analyze the skill intensity of Korea's trade and its implications.[2]

In order to assume a causal connection flowing from skill endownents to the trade pattern, and also considering the limited availability of data on labor skills, we decided to divide the labor force of each industry into seven occupational skill groups:

      I. Engineers & Scientists
     II. Technicians
    III. Clerical Workers
    IV. Skilled Workers
     V. Semi-Skilled Workers
    VI. Apprentices
   VII. Other Workers

We first disaggregated the 1970 (total) sectoral labor coefficients into the above seven categories and then, using the 1970 input-output table of 117 sector classification, computed the direct and indirect requirements for each skill group.

On the other hand, we can argue that differences in average monthly wages paid to various occupations reflect differences in the amount of skill-training and education required by those occupations. On the as-

---

[2] The original version of this chapter was published as "Skill Intensity of Trade: The Case of Korea (1762-71)," *The Developing Economies*, September 1974.

sumption that differences in monthly labor earnings are due mainly to differences in skill (or, more broadly, in human capital embedded in workers), we can disaggregate the sectoral labor requirements according to wage classes in order to get what might be a more reliable index of skill content, and then examine the skill intensity of trade. Here we decided to group the wage classes in the following fashion:

   I. 70,000 won & over per month: Professional
  II. 50,000 won-69,999 won per month: Highly Skilled (1)
 III. 40,000 won-49,999 won per month: Highly Skilled (2)
  IV. 20,000 won-39,999 won per month: Skilled
   V. 10,000 won-19,999 won per month: Semi-Skilled
  VI. Less than 10,000 won per month: Unskilled

For the former classification of occupational skill groups, we used the 1970 OLA (Office of Labor Affairs) survey results on actual labor conditions at all establishments employing 10 or more workers. For the latter classification of wage groups, we used the 1971 OLA sample observation of 2,014 establishments employing 10 or more workers. Since both data exclude establishments with less than 10 workers, both have a kind of built-in bias in their estimation of skill composition. For instance, the agricultural and service sectors tend to show an unduly high rate of skilled labor employment.

The total number of workers included in the former comprehensive survey was 1,084.1 thousand, but only 4.1 thousand were agricultural and forestry workers while 692.6 thousand were mining and manufacturing workers. It is clear, therefore, that the mining and manufacturing sectors were best represented, while the service sectors were reasonably well represented, but that the agricultural and forestry sectors were very badly represented in the survey. As a result, 52.3 percent of workers in agriculture and 90.9 percent of workers in forestry were classified as clerical workers, while 4.7 percent of agricultural workers were technicians and 2.5 percent were engineers. It is obvious that the survey data on the establishments employing 10 or more workers can not be used to compute the skill composition of the entire agricultural and forestry sectors.

According to these survey data, the total number of workers at agricultural and forestry establishments employing 10 or more workers was 4,139 in 1970. The total number of engineers, technicians, and clerical workers in these two sectors were 96, 184, and 2,248 respectively. If we divide these figures by the total number of workers in the agricultural and forestry sectors in 1970 (4,745 thousand), we get 0.002 percent, 0.004 percent and

Table 10.1. Skill Composition of Labor Directly and Indirectly Employed for Export Production (Based on 1970 Occupational Skill Group): 1963–72

In Thousand Persons & Percent (%)

1970 A^d Matrix

	Engineers & Scientists	Technicians	Clerical Workers	Skilled Workers	Semi-Skilled Workers	Apprentices	Other Workers	Total Labor Employed
				Direct Employment				
1963	1.1%	3.6%	8.1%	27.7%	25.6%	9.7%	24.2%	38.6
1964	1.1%	3.2%	7.6%	30.5%	27.8%	9.7%	20.1%	57.8
1965	1.0%	3.2%	7.2%	30.9%	28.1%	10.9%	18.7%	81.8
1966	0.9%	3.0%	6.6%	33.1%	30.5%	10.7%	15.3%	121.1
1967	0.9%	3.3%	7.1%	31.6%	28.4%	12.3%	16.5%	147.8
1968	0.9%	3.3%	7.0%	32.0%	28.5%	12.9%	15.5%	198.1
1969	0.9%	3.2%	6.8%	32.8%	29.5%	13.0%	13.9%	261.5
1970	0.8%	3.2%	6.9%	32.4%	29.2%	13.9%	13.6%	324.1
1971	0.9%	3.2%	6.9%	33.4%	29.5%	13.8%	12.5%	375.0
1972	1.0%	3.5%	7.8%	32.2%	28.3%	14.5%	12.8%	522.9
				Direct plus Indirect Employment				
1963	0.9%	3.1%	10.0%	28.2%	25.7%	8.0%	24.0%	71.8
1964	0.9%	3.0%	9.9%	28.6%	25.6%	8.3%	23.6%	103.3
1965	0.9%	3.0%	9.9%	29.3%	26.0%	9.1%	21.8%	140.7
1966	0.8%	2.8%	9.3%	30.8%	27.7%	9.1%	19.4%	201.6
1967	0.8%	3.0%	9.6%	30.2%	26.8%	9.9%	19.6%	251.2
1968	0.9%	3.0%	9.7%	30.5%	26.7%	10.5%	18.8%	333.6
1969	0.9%	2.9%	9.5%	31.2%	27.5%	10.6%	17.4%	434.7
1970	0.8%	2.9%	9.6%	30.9%	27.3%	11.0%	17.5%	548.7
1971	0.9%	2.9%	9.8%	31.4%	27.3%	11.0%	16.7%	642.3
1972	0.9%	3.1%	10.5%	30.5%	26.4%	11.4%	17.1%	915.7

Table 10.2. *Skill Composition of Direct and Indirect Labor Requirements for Competitive Import Replacements (Based on 1970 Occupational Skill Group): 1963-72*

In Thousand Persons & Percent (%)

1970 A Matrix

	Engineers & Scientists	Technicians	Clerical Workers	Skilled Workers	Semi-Shilled Workers	Apprentices	Other Workers	Total Labor Employed
				Direct Requirements				
1963	0.7%	1.5%	4.1%	43.0%	42.6%	4.3%	3.8%	196.3
1964	0.9%	1.9%	5.5%	40.7%	40.2%	5.6%	5.2%	110.2
1965	1.1%	2.6%	7.2%	37.8%	37.1%	7.4%	6.9%	99.5
1966	1.6%	3.6%	9.4%	34.1%	33.3%	10.2%	8.0%	148.4
1967	1.5%	3.4%	8.7%	35.2%	34.4%	9.5%	7.4%	225.1
1968	1.4%	3.3%	8.2%	35.8%	35.0%	9.7%	6.7%	340.9
1969	1.0%	2.5%	6.3%	39.0%	38.4%	7.5%	5.4%	469.2
1970	1.0%	2.3%	5.8%	39.6%	39.0%	7.0%	5.5%	478.3
1971	0.9%	2.1%	5.4%	40.2%	39.5%	6.6%	5.4%	564.6
1972	1.0%	2.2%	5.7%	39.7%	38.9%	6.8%	5.8%	537.9
				Direct plus Indirect Requirements				
1963	0.8%	1.9%	7.8%	37.5%	36.0%	5.3%	10.6%	305.0
1964	1.0%	2.2%	9.2%	35.3%	33.7%	6.1%	12.3%	186.8
1965	1.1%	2.7%	10.6%	33.2%	31.2%	7.2%	13.9%	186.1
1966	1.4%	3.3%	12.5%	30.1%	28.0%	9.0%	15.6%	295.5
1967	1.4%	3.4%	12.1%	30.5%	28.4%	9.1%	15.1%	418.0
1968	1.3%	3.2%	11.4%	31.4%	29.5%	9.0%	14.1%	623.9
1969	1.1%	2.6%	9.7%	34.2%	32.6%	7.6%	12.2%	789.6
1970	1.0%	2.5%	9.3%	34.6%	33.0%	7.3%	12.2%	790.5
1971	1.0%	2.4%	8.8%	35.4%	33.9%	6.9%	11.6%	920.0
1972	1.0%	2.5%	9.2%	34.8%	33.1%	7.2%	12.1%	865.9

Table 10.3. Skill Composition of Labor Directly and Indirectly Employed for Export Production
(Based on 1971 Monthly Wage Group): 1963-72

1970 A^a Matrix

In Thousand Persons & Percent (%)

	Professional 70,000 won & over	Highly Skilled 50,000 - 69,999 won	Highly Skilled 40,000 - 49,999 won	Skilled 20,000 - 39,999 won	Semi-Skilled 10,000 - 19,999 won	Unskilled 0 - 9,999 won	Total Labor Employed
				Direct Employment			
1963	0.8%	2.0%	3.5%	20.9%	41.6%	31.2%	38.6
1964	0.7%	1.7%	2.9%	18.3%	42.3%	34.2%	57.8
1965	0.7%	1.6%	2.8%	17.6%	42.4%	34.9%	81.8
1966	0.6%	1.4%	2.4%	15.5%	43.0%	37.2%	121.1
1967	0.6%	1.4%	2.5%	16.5%	42.2%	36.7%	147.8
1968	0.6%	1.3%	2.4%	16.3%	42.1%	37.3%	198.1
1969	0.6%	1.3%	2.3%	15.6%	42.1%	38.2%	261.5
1970	0.6%	1.3%	2.3%	15.8%	41.9%	38.2%	324.1
1971	0.6%	1.2%	2.2%	15.7%	41.7%	38.6%	375.0
1972	0.7%	1.4%	2.5%	17.2%	41.0%	37.3%	522.9
				Direct plus Indirect Employment			
1963	1.7%	3.0%	4.8%	21.0%	39.9%	29.4%	71.8
1964	1.7%	2.8%	4.5%	19.8%	40.2%	30.9%	103.3
1965	1.7%	2.8%	4.5%	19.8%	39.8%	31.3%	140.7
1966	1.6%	2.6%	4.1%	18.2%	40.4%	33.0%	201.6
1967	1.6%	2.6%	4.2%	18.6%	39.8%	32.9%	251.2
1968	1.7%	2.6%	4.2%	18.6%	39.5%	33.3%	333.6
1969	1.6%	2.5%	4.1%	18.3%	39.5%	33.9%	434.7
1970	1.7%	2.6%	4.1%	18.4%	39.3%	33.8%	548.7
1971	1.7%	2.6%	4.1%	18.6%	39.0%	33.8%	642.3
1972	1.8%	2.8%	4.5%	19.9%	38.3%	32.6%	915.7

Table 10.4. Skill Composition of Direct and Indirect Labor Requirements for Competitive Import Replacements (Based on 1971 Monthly Wage Group): 1963–72

1970 A Matrix

In Thousand Persons & Percent (%)

	Professional 70,000 won & over	Highly Skilled 50,000 - 69,999 won	Highly Skilled 40,000 - 49,999 won	Skilled 20,000 - 39,999 won	Semi-Skilled 10,000 - 19,999 won	Unskilled 0 - 9,999 won	Total Labor Employed
Direct Requirements							
1963	0.4%	1.0%	1.4%	8.8%	45.6%	42.8%	196.3
1964	0.6%	1.3%	1.9%	11.5%	44.2%	40.4%	110.2
1965	0.8%	1.7%	2.4%	14.8%	42.5%	37.9%	99.5
1966	0.9%	2.0%	3.1%	20.3%	39.9%	33.7%	148.4
1967	0.8%	1.7%	2.8%	18.8%	40.6%	35.3%	225.1
1968	0.7%	1.5%	2.6%	18.1%	41.3%	35.7%	340.9
1969	0.6%	1.2%	2.0%	13.8%	43.4%	39.0%	469.2
1970	0.5%	1.2%	1.9%	12.9%	44.1%	39.4%	478.3
1971	0.5%	1.1%	1.8%	12.0%	44.8%	39.9%	564.6
1972	0.5%	1.2%	1.9%	12.7%	44.1%	39.7%	537.9
Direct plus Indirect Requirements							
1963	1.4%	2.4%	3.5%	15.3%	41.5%	35.8%	305.0
1964	1.6%	2.8%	4.1%	17.6%	40.1%	33.6%	186.8
1965	1.9%	3.1%	4.7%	20.3%	38.7%	31.2%	186.1
1966	2.1%	3.6%	5.5%	24.7%	36.5%	27.3%	295.5
1967	2.0%	3.4%	5.2%	24.1%	36.9%	28.2%	418.0
1968	1.9%	3.1%	4.9%	23.1%	37.7%	29.1%	623.9
1969	1.6%	2.7%	4.1%	19.4%	39.7%	32.4%	789.6
1970	1.5%	2.6%	4.0%	18.7%	40.2%	32.8%	790.5
1971	1.4%	2.5%	3.8%	17.6%	40.9%	33.7%	920.0
1972	1.5%	2.6%	3.9%	18.4%	40.2%	33.2%	865.9

0.05 percent respectively. Since we do not expect to find any significant number of engineers, technicians and clerical workers in agricultural and forestry establishments employing less than 10 persons, we decided simply to classify half of all agricultural and forestry workers as skilled and the other half as semi-skilled. Similarly, since the average farm household income per worker in 1971 was about 10,000 won, we put half of the agricultural and forestry workers in the lowest wage group (0–9,999 won) and the other half to the second lowest wage group (10,000–19,999).

We first examined the "direct" skill requirements for export production and competitive import replacement in 1970 on the basis of the occupational skill classification. About 32 percent of all labor directly employed for export production were skilled workers and about 57 percent were semi-skilled and unskilled workers. On the other hand, about 40 percent of the total labor directly required for competitive import replacements would have been skilled labor and about 52 percent would have been semi-skilled and unskilled workers. Hence export production seems to use a little bit more unskilled labor than would competitive imports. Less than ten percent of the total labor directly required for both export production and competitive import reqlacements were engineers, technicians or clerical workers. However, when we examine the direct skill requiremets based on the monthly wage-based classification, no significant differences between the skill requirements for export production or competitive import replacment are apparent.

Next, let us consider the total (direct plus indirect) skill requirements for export production and competitive import substitution in 1970. The skill requirements estimated on the basis of occupational skill classification indicate that export production was a slightly more unskilled labor intensive than competitive imports. However, the skill requirements estimated on the basis of the monthly wage group classification do not reveal any significant differences between the skill requirements for export production and those for competitive import replacements.

Since all non-competitive imports are excluded from our estimations of skill requirements, and since the excluded items are likely to be highly skill intensive, we may argue that the statistiacl results are not inconsistent with the implicit hypothesis that Korea is a relatively skill-scarce country and hence enjoys a comparative advantage in the production of relatively unskilled-labor intensive goods.

However, when we computed the direct and indirect skill requirements for the entire 1963–72 period, we found virtually no change in the skill composition of labor required for either export production or import replacement. One immediate implication is that there seems to have been no close correlation between sectoral capital intensity and sectoral skill intensity. Another implication is that either there was no significant accumulation of skill during the period 1960–72 or that there has been significant skill accumulation but, as far as production costs are concerned, it was not significant enough to change the comparative advantage of Korea toward more skill intensive sectors. The latter implication may also be interpreted as meaning that the skill factor itself was not very important in production processes at least with respect to the kind of commodities exported from and competitively imported to Korea during the 1963–72 period.

In Chapter 4, we observed that although there was a significant increase in the supply of educated labor during 1960–70, there was no disproportionate increase in number of workers in occupations which use large numbers of relatively highly educated persons. Instead, the overriding impression is that the general level of education improved in every occupational group. Therefore, it would appear that if there was any significant increase in the level of general education and informal training, this must have been spread evenly over every skill group, and hence did not work to shift Korea's comparative advantage specifically toward relatively more skill intensive sectors.

Since we have limited confidence in the basic data on labor skills, we will not speculate further on possible implications of these fidnings. However, since it is generally believed that the skill supply will play a decisive role in Korea's export expansion in the future, more rigorous investigation in this area is warranted.

CHAPTER 11

A STATIC ESTIMATE OF GAINS FROM TRADE

The primary application of input-output analysis by Leontief and his followers has been in the testing of the Heckscher-Ohlin theory. In this chapter, the techniques of input-output analysis are used to demonstrate that the promotion of exports can result in static inefficiency for the economy.[1] This result should be of interest to those who consider that export promotion is sometimes as chaotic as import substitution and that the chief causes of the difference in the economic performance of export-promoting and import-substituting economies may well lie in other asymmetries between the two developmental strategies, as suggested by Bhagwati and Krueger.[2] This result should also be of interest to anyone who believes in the unavoidability of some temporary losses in obtaining long-term gains of welfare, since our method identifies those static losses which should be justified in terms of dynamic gains.

The term 'static inefficiency' in this chapter may be understood as the net loss of production factors arising from satisfying the domestic demand indirectly via export production instead of satisfying it directly via import-substitution at any specific point in time. Consequently, "dynamic inefficiency" might be understood as the net loss of production factors in trade even when (dynamic) external economies *a la* the infant industry argu-

---

[1] This chapter is a revised and extended version of my paper "Distortions and Static Negative Marginal Gains from Trade," *Journal of International Economics* (May, 1976).

[2] J. N. Bhagwati and A. O. Krueger, "Exchange Control, Liberalization, and Economic Development," *American Economic Review,* May 1973,

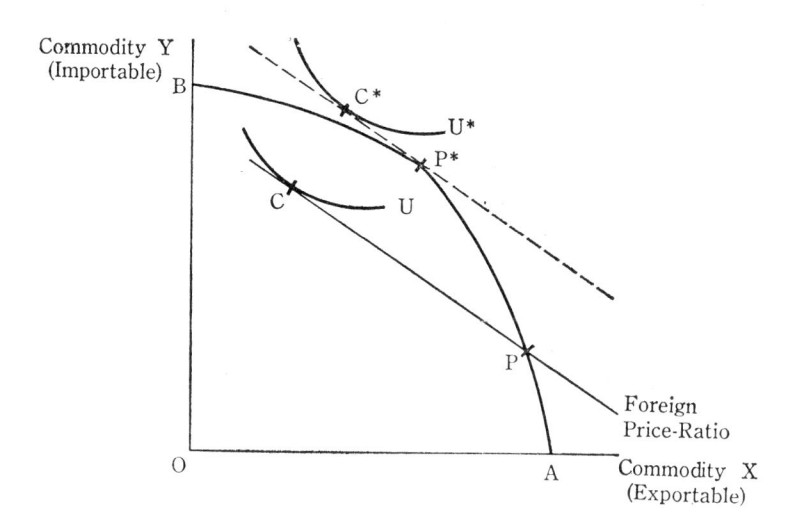

Figure 1

ment are taken into account over the long-run.

Note first that it is well-known from the theory of unified exchange rates that the possibility of wasteful export promotion or import-substitution in any activity, i.e., the presence of static inefficiency in economic activities, is ruled out for a small country with no internal distortions. Hence, we must necessarily deal with the case of Korea on the realistic and valid presumption that there are a fair number of distortions in the Korean economy. It should be useful then to spell out, in the context of the traditional 2-sector model of trade theory, the precise manner in which some wasteful export promotion may arise under distortions, before we proceed to compute corresponding estimates for the Korean economy.

Thus, in Figure 1, AB is the production possibility frontier in the 2-good economy and PC is the given foreign price-ratio between commodities X and Y for this small country. If there were no distortions, the economy would produce optimally at P* and consume optimally at C* with the trade thus arising being optimal (in the static sense). Assume, however, that the economy has a production distortion such that X-production increases and the equilibrium production vector shifts to P, the resulting consumption vector being C, and with social welfare declining from U* to U.

Now, if we were to compare the observed production-cum-trade equilibrium with a *marginal* decrease in X-production and the trade equilibrium associated therewith, it is clear that welfare would be greater in the latter case. This would be equally true, in this model, if we had unchanging consumption distortion in both equilibria, ruling out pathologies arising from inferior goods and associated multiple equilibria, as discussed by Vanek, Bhagwati, and Kemp.[3]

Moreover, in this instance it is clear that a marginal reduction in X-production, say *via* a production subsidy to Y, would be associated with a reduction in trade volume (ruling out strong inferiority in X-consumption). Thus, we could conclude that the economy was exporting too much *at the margin*. Hence we have shown that, given a (domestic) distortion, a country could be exporting too much: a conclusion which is, of course, paralleled by the well-known Mill argument for an optimal tariff where the (foreign) distortion represented by the existence of monopoly power in trade under laissez faire implies over-exportation by the country calling for the imposition of a suitable optimal tariff.

Having briefly underlined the possibility of wasteful export expansion and the corresponding static inefficiency under distortions, we now proceed to show how, in the Korean case, export expansion in certain sectors of the economy resulted in a static loss in efficiency to the economy. This is done simply by showing that the direct-plus-indirect capital and labour requirements for exports of some selected "capital-intensive group of commodities" exceed *both* the capital and the labor requirements for the replacement of "competitive imports of the same value" through direct domestic production.[4]

If we further assume that (i) the average capital and labour coefficients in different activities will not change as the economy shifts out of these exports and into import-competing commodities in the above comparison, and that (ii) the international prices will remain invariant to the required changes in trade volumes as the production shift is carried out, then we can also take the net saving in capital and labour, as computed above, as a measure of the resources/GNP saved by eliminating the wasteful exports.

---

[3] J. Vanek, *General Equilibrium of International Discrimination: The Case of Customs Unions*, Cambridge: Harvard University Press, 1965, J. N. Bhagwati, "The Gains from Trade Once Again," *Oxford Economic Papers,* July 1968 and M. C. Kemp, "Some Issues in the Analysis of Trade Gains," *Oxford Economic Papers,* July 1968.

[4] Since we are analyzing in terms of two-factor model, our analysis may be vulnerable to Vanek type criticism. However, we excluded most of the natural resource intensive goods from our computation as non-competitive natural resource intensive imports. See Vanek, *op. cit.* (1957).

Note, however, that no such conclusion can be drawn when the capital and labor requirements of an exported good do not dominate both the capital and labor requirements of the competitively imported goods. This happens, for example, to be the case for most of the Korean exports in the "non-capital-intensive group of commodities" where the capital requirements fall below and the labor requirements exceed the corresponding capital and labor requirements for competitive-import production. Admittedly, some of these exports may also be wasteful; but only detailed cost-benefit analysis would seem to be capable of determining this.

We turn now therefore to discussing Korean exports in the context of the above theory and attempt to estimate the resource-loss from export expansion in certain sectors as discussed above. We will focus on the period 1966–73. We will apply the 1970 set of sectoral factor coefficients, the 1970 A^d and A matrices, and employ the 1970 classification of competitive and non-competitive imports in our computation of (direct-plus-indirect) factor requirements.

As we can see in Table 11.1., in order to produce $100 million (in 1970 dollar prices) worth of commodity exports in 1966, Korea used $100 million worth of fixed capital stock and 69 thousand man-years of labor plus other non-primary inputs such as competitive and non-competitive imports.

With $100 million exports, Korea could finance the same amount of competitive imports, though part of these imports were required for export production and hence were not available for domestic consumption. Let us assume that trade (exports vs. competitive imports) was balanced at $100 million in 1966. Table 11.1. shows that the amount of primary factors which would be required to replace the $100 million worth of competitive imports that could be financed by this volume of exports in 1966 are $137 million worth of fixed capital (in 1970 dollar prices) and 56 thousand man-years of labor. However, part of the competitive imports were used as inputs for export production. Since we excluded them from our computation of factor requirements for exports, they should also be excluded from our computation of factor requirements for import replacements. That is, the absence of export production will eliminate the requirements for those competitive and non-competitive imports which were previously absorbed in export production. Now, if we subtract the factor requirements for competitive imports which were used as inputs in export production, we can argue that Korea saved $119 million worth of fixed capital (in 1970 dollar prices) and 49 thousand labor through imports of competitive goods in 1966.

Table 11.1. *Factor Savings Per $100 Million of Trade (1970 Basis): 1966–73*

In Million 1970 Dollars or Thousand Persons

	Factor Requirements Per $100 Million Exports				Factor Requirements Per $100 Million of Import Replacements Applying A Matrix				Factor Savings via Trade in Exports vs.			
	Capital		Labor		Capital	Labor	Capital	Labor	Competitive Imports		Non-Competitive Imports	
	A^d Matrix (A)	A^m Matrix (B)	A^d Matrix (C)	A^m Matrix (D)	(E)	(F)	(G=E-B)	(H=F-D)	Capital (G-A)/(A)	Labor (H-C)/(C)	Capital (K-A)/(A)	Labor (L-C)/(C)
1966	99.8	17.7	68.7	6.5	137.0	55.6	119.3	49.1	19.5%	-28.5%	19.2%	-55.9%
1967	102.2	19.3	68.3	6.8	130.5	60.0	111.2	53.2	8.8%	-22.1%	11.6%	-58.0%
1968	100.4	20.8	66.3	7.2	122.6	64.1	101.8	56.9	1.4%	-14.2%	20.9%	-63.8%
1969	99.5	21.7	66.2	7.5	117.6	69.1	95.9	61.6	-3.6%	-7.0%	19.4%	-60.3%
1970	98.2	22.3	65.7	7.7	116.5	69.5	94.2	61.8	-4.1%	-5.9%	22.9%	-58.6%
1971	100.0	22.8	63.1	8.0	116.5	72.9	93.7	64.9	-6.3%	2.9%	23.5%	-56.6%
1972	100.9	23.3	60.6	8.4	119.6	72.2	96.3	63.8	-4.6%	5.3%	29.5%	-56.3%
1973	99.7	24.1	59.8	9.0	119.9	71.4	95.8	62.4	-3.9%	4.4%	29.0%	-56.9%

	Factor Requirements Per $100 Million of Non-Competitive Import Replacements Applying 1965 Japanese Coefficients			
	Capital (I)	Labor (J)	Capital (K=I-B)	Labor (L=J-D)
1966	136.7	36.8	119.0	30.3
1967	133.3	35.5	114.0	28.7
1968	142.2	31.2	121.4	24.0
1969	140.5	33.8	118.8	26.3
1970	143.0	34.9	120.7	27.2
1971	146.3	35.4	123.5	27.4
1972	154.0	34.9	130.7	26.5
1973	152.7	34.8	128.6	25.8

Due to data limitations, we could not compute the factor requirements for non-competitive imports which are required as inputs both in export production and import replacement activities. Assuming that such factor requirements roughly offset one another, we computed the factor savings from trade in competitive goods. Korea's gain in fixed capital per $100 million worth of trade (exports vs. competitive imports) was equivalent to about 20 percent of the capital used in the export production and its loss in labor was equivalent to about 29 percent of the labor used in the export production in 1966. That is, by selling labor which is the abundant factor in Korea, it could get in return a significant amount of capital, which is the relatively scarce factor in Korea.

However, when we computed such factor gains through trade in competitive goods for the entire 1966–73 period, the results suggested that the amount of gains in capital per labor lost in trade was rapidly falling and became negative after 1969. That is, Korea lost some significant amount of both capital and labor via trade in competitive goods in 1969 and 1970 and, quite perversely, gained significant amount of labor at the expense of capital in the period of 1971–73.

We may interpret the above observations in the following fashion. Korea used to produce and export mainly labor intensive competitive goods while importing primarily capital intensive competitive goods. However, with the accumulation of capital, Korea started to produce and export an increasing amount of capital intensive goods. Furthermore, the over-expansion of some inefficient sectors seems to have even resulted in a net loss of both capital and labor in 1969 and 1970. Since 1971, Korea started to export capital through its trade in exports vs. competitive imports, which seems to be a reproduction of the Leontief paradox.

We also examined Korea's gains from trade in exports vs. non-competitive imports. We applied the 1965 Japanese factor coefficients to approximate the factor content of Korea's non-competitive imports. We found that Korea has been saving a fairly large amount of capital (equivalent to about 20–30 percent of capital stock employed in export production at the expense of labor during 1966–73. Hence specialization and trade in Korea *a la* Heckscher-Ohlin seem to have been limited mostly to trade in competitive exports vs. non-competitive imports. This is consistent with our conclusion in Chapter 9.

In order to identify the most capital intensive exports, we listed 92 commodity sectors (in 117 I-O sector classification) in the order of the magnitude of direct plus indirect factor requirements per $1,000 of outputs in 1970.(See Table A.31.). Among the top 15 industries which required

Table 11.2. Exports of Eight Capital Intensive Commodities: 1966–73

In Thousand 1970 Dollars

	Cement	Chemical Fertilizer	Chemical Fibre Yarn	Fishery Products	Woolen Yarn	Other Chemical Products	Chemical Fibre Fabrics	Silk Fabrics
1966	621	—	1,600	14,649	582	474	9,600	338
1967	204	1,886	1,211	22,273	1,167	267	16,281	259
1968	211	2,100	812	24,827	738	1,302	24,566	1,475
1969	3,456	6,572	977	24,707	1,606	2,029	17,903	855
1970	4,442	6,333	3,026	28,815	2,269	6,044	14,876	940
1971	10,129	7,205	10,407	28,755	1,587	14,662	18,954	1,243
1972	11,772	10,701	7,911	42,192	8,955	16,312	44,319	3,115
1973	15,510	4,003	23,327	63,783	19,402	20,186	102,452	52,698
	Direct plus Indirect Capital-Output Ratios (1970 Basis)							
Total (A)	2.98	2.02	2.40	1.97	1.86	1.93	1.99	1.57
Domestic (A^d)	2.92	1.99	1.91	1.89	1.75	1.71	1.51	1.37
	Direct plus Indirect Labor-Output Ratios (1970 Basis)							
Total (A)	0.32	0.23	0.45	1.08	0.67	0.33	0.69	0.83
Domestic (A^d)	0.29	0.21	0.35	1.04	0.64	0.28	0.59	0.75

Source: Tables A.12., A.31. and A.32.

the largest amount of capital per $1,000 of outputs, eight sectors exported fairly large amount of their products. The exports of cement, chemical fertilizer,chemical fibre yarn, fishery products, woolen yarn, other chemical products, chemical fibre fabrics, and silk fabrics amounted to about 9 percent of total commodity exports during 1966–73.

Since those eight commodities belong to the most capital intensive group (measured by the direct plus indirect capital requirements per $1,000 of outputs) among the 92 commodity sectors, they directly and indirectly took about 16 percent of total capital employed for export production in 1969 and about 15 percent of the total in 1970 while their share in total exports was 9 percent in 1969 and 8 percent in 1970. Quite clearly, as a result of exporting such capital intensive goods Korea realized a smaller saving of capital through its trade in competitive goods than it might otherwise have.

However, the more important fact is that this "capital-intensive eight-commodity group" directly and indirectly absorbed about 10 percent of the total labor employed in export production in 1969 and about 8 percent of it in 1970. Since these commodities used more than a proportionate amount of capital in production, we might naturally expect a less than proportionate use of labor. However, these commodities used "as much" (in 1970) or "a little bit more" (in 1969) labor than the average for all export commodities. This seems to reflect either an extraordinarily high rate of domestic value added content or the presence of inefficiencies in in these sectors, or both.

In order to check whether this capital-intensive eight-commodity group used an extraordinarily small amount of imported goods, we computed the factor requirements needed to replace competitive imports used in $100 million worth of export production of these commodities, i.e., we computed the differences between the results obtained with the A matrix and A^d matrix, respectively, in the factor requirement computations for $100 million worth of these eight commodities. In 1969, for example, the capital requirements needed to replace competitive imports used in the production of $100 million worth of this "eight-commodity" group amounted to $21.3 million while the labor requirements amounted to 5.5 thousand man-years. On the other hand, the capital requirements needed to replace competitive imports used in $100 million worth of all commodity exports amounted to $21.7 million and the labor requirements amounted to 7.5 thousand man-years in 1970. (See Tables 11.1. and 11.3.) The results were similar for other years as well. Therefore, although we could not compute the non-competitive import content of the export

Table 11.3. *Factor Savings Per $100 Million of Trade Excluding Capital Intensive Export Group: 1966-73*
In Million 1970 Dollars or Thousand Persons

	Factor Requirements Per $100 Million Exports				Per $100 Million Imports Applying 1970 A Matrix		Factor Savings via Trade in Competitive Imports	
	Capital		Labor		Capital	Labor	Capital	Labor
	A^d Matrix (A)	A^m Matrix (B)	A^d Matrix (C)	A^m Matrix (D)	(G = E-B)	(H = F-D)	(G-A)/A	(H-C)/C

Trade of Capital Intensive Export Group vs. Competitive Imports

1966	177.2	24.6	80.3	6.2	112.4	49.4	−36.6	−38.5
1967	175.0	24.3	79.5	6.1	106.2	53.9	−39.3	−32.2
1968	171.2	26.8	76.8	6.5	95.8	57.6	−44.1	−25.0
1969	182.8	21.3	70.9	5.5	96.3	63.6	−47.3	−10.3
1970	185.7	19.7	69.2	5.3	96.8	64.2	−47.9	−7.2
1971	189.8	22.5	59.4	5.5	94.0	67.4	−50.5	13.5
1972	182.6	24.0	62.7	5.8	95.6	66.4	−47.7	5.9
1973	170.5	27.9	65.7	6.9	92.0	64.5	−46.1	−1.8

Trade of Competitive Goods Excluding Capital Intensive Export Group

1966	91.7	16.9	67.4	6.6	120.1	49.0	31.0%	−27.3%
1967	92.4	18.7	66.8	6.9	111.8	53.1	21.0%	−20.5%
1968	91.5	20.1	65.0	7.3	102.5	56.8	12.0%	−12.6%
1969	91.4	21.7	65.8	7.7	95.9	61.4	4.9%	−6.7%
1970	90.7	22.4	65.4	7.9	94.1	61.6	3.8%	−5.8%
1971	91.0	22.8	63.4	8.3	93.7	64.6	3.0%	1.9%
1972	92.2	23.2	60.4	8.7	96.4	63.5	4.6%	5.1%
1973	90.2	23.6	59.1	9.2	96.3	62.2	6.8%	5.3%

production of this group, we can argue that the more than proportionate requirement of not only capital but also labor in their export production reflects inefficiency rather than an extraordinarily high rate of domestic value added.

As can be seen in Table 11.3, Korea lost both capital and labor in its trade in capital intensive exports vs. competitive imports during 1966–70. We then computed the factor earnings ratio of trade in competitive goods during 1966–73 excluding these eight capital-intensive commodities, which reduced the magnitude of total commodity exports by about 9 percent. We found that the net earnings of capital per $100 million worth of trade in competitive goods were equivalent to about 5 percent of the total capital required for $100 million worth of export production and the loss of labor was equivalent to about 7 percent of the total labor required for $100 million worth of export production in 1969. In 1970, the gains of capital amounted to about 4 percent, and the loss of labor amounted to about 6 percent. That is, the exclusion of this "eight-commodity" group of capital intensive exports changed the "loss of both capital and labor" into "gains of capital at the expense of labor" in 1969 and 1970, and the loss of labor itself was reduced. Furthermore, with these commodities excluded, Korea gained significant amounts of *both* capital and labor via trade in exports vs. competitive imports from 1971, and the gain of labor itself was increased.

We can conclude, therefore, that were it not for these eight capital-intensive export commodities, Korea would not have registered negative earnings of "both" capital and labor during 1969–70. Furthermore, the perverse phenomenon whereby Korea was in effect exporting capital and importing labor in the period 1971–73 would have been transformed into gains of "both capital and labor" during these years.

Although the selection of only these eight commodities for this analytical exercise is a bit arbitrary, we can still deduce some useful implications from our observations.

The first implication is that in a static analytic framework and assuming fixed input coefficients, Korea's gains from trade in this eight capital-intensive commodity group was negative and, more broadly speaking (since the selection of those eight items was more or less arbitrary), we can argue that the marginal gains from trade were negative in the sense that a cut in export production and an expansion in import substitution, while resulting in decreased trade in competitive goods, may have saved factors of production in Korea during 1966–73.[5]

---

[5] However, the wasteful (in a static sense) exportation of these eight commodities

Second implication is that if we want to justify the vigorous export expansion policy of the Korean government which resulted in such perverse results, we have to justify it in a dynamic framework, such as encompassed by the infant (export) industry argument.[6] Otherwise, "negative earnings" of both capital and labor from trade in competitive goods must be taken as a signal that the export promotion policy needs some adjustment in its extent and direction and that import substitution should receive more attention even though export promotion might be a superior strategy overall than an import-substitution oriented strategy.[7]

Note finally that the estimates of resource losses from apparently wasteful export promotion in Korea is an *underestimate* because we have not been able to separate out the wasteful exports from those exports whose requirements of capital are below, but whose requirements for labor exceed, those of import-substitutes. At the same time, it is an *overestimate* because we have not taken into account possible externalities from export promotion, possibly less-than-infinitely-elastic supply elasticities at home, or possible monopoly power in trade.

---

does not necessarily imply inefficiencies in only these eight sectors. Since we included the indirect requirements when computing total factor requirements, what we observed may be the result of either inefficiency in these eight sectors themselves or of inefficiencies in other sectors which supplied intermediate inputs to these sectors or combinations of both. That is, what is implied is the simple fact that, under the given industrial structure, exports of these eight commodities were, in a static sense, wasteful.

[6] See H. G. Johnson, "Optimal Trade Intervention in the Presence of Domestic Distortions," in Baldwin and Others, *Trade, Growth, and the Balance of Payments*, Chicago: Rand McNally, 1965, J.N. Bhagwati, *The Theory and Practice of Commercial Policy: Departures from Unified Exchange Rates*, International Finance Section, Princeton University Press, 1968, and D. B. Keesing, *op. cit.* (1967).

Even a casual observation can show that export promotion in Korea sometimes carries reckless aspects. Exports of cement in spite of a slowdown in the domestic construction sector due to shortages of cement, exports of fertilizer in spite of insufficient supplies of fertilizers through legal channels, and exports of chemical fiber yarn in spite of the contraction of domestic production activities using chemical fiber yarn as raw material, etc. indicate the undesirable side effects of government drives to achieve annually set export targets. On the other hand, one may justify the exports of cement on the basis of an almost infinite domestic supply of its raw materials (limestone) and the necessity of developing international markets at an early stage prior to beginning export on a mass scale, and exports of chemical fertilizers and chemical fiber yarn to realize dynamic external economies through learning by doing which may enormously enhance the development potential of Korea in more sophisticated industrial sectors whose long run rate of return more than offsets the initial losses. One may also justify such exports in terms of so-called vent-for-surplus exports arising from a temporary domestic over-supply.

[7] See J. N. Bhagwati and A. O. Krueger, *op. cit.* (1973).

We would like to conclude this chapter, therefore, by emphasizing that although the simple existence of static loss at any specific point in time does not necessarily imply welfare losses to the economy on a long-term basis, the fact that such static losses can be observed implies that we should question whether their existence is justified in terms of dynamic gains and if not, seek to eliminate such inefficiencies.

CHAPTER 12

SUMMARY AND CONCLUSION

(1) The annual commodity exports of Korea, which amounted to less than $0.1 billion before 1962, increased at the average annual rate of 40 percent during the period of 1962–73, amounting to around $3.2 billion in 1973 and $4.5 billion in 1974. The share of manufactured goods in total commodity exports, which never exceeded the 20 percent level during 1953–61, steadily increased thereafter reaching about 80 percent in 1966 and rising to over 90 percent after 1970.

(2) The total net fixed capital stock in Korea increased by an average annual rate of 3.5 percent during 1953–61, 6.7 percent during 1962–66, and a remarkable 13.4 percent during 1967–73. The net fixed capital stock of all industries amounted to about $14.3 billion in 1973.

(3) Per capita capital stock in Korea increased by about 30 percent during the fourteen year period of 1953–66, and it was only after 1966 that per capita capital stock started to increase rapidly. Per capita capital stock more than doubled during 1966–73, but due to rapidly increasing employment (about a 30 percent increase), the fixed capital stock per employed person increased by around 80 percent. However, this still implies that significant overall capital deepening occurred in Korea during 1966–73.

(4) The per worker farm income started to rise significantly after 1967, as did the wage rate for employees in the manufacturing sector. On the other hand, the weighted average real interest rates on all types of loans supplied by both monetary and non-monetary financial institutions as well as by

the curb markets reached their peak in 1967 and declined gradually thereafter. Hence, we conclude there was rapid and significant capital accumulation and capital deepening in Korea since 1966 which was accompanied by increases in the wage/rental ratio.

(5) The factor intensity of Korea's export commodity bundle grew significantly in capital intensity during 1960-73. However, the factor intensity of competitive import replacements did not shift much in any specific direction. Consequently, although competitive imports were much more capital intensive than exports before 1968, the difference became smaller and there seems to have been only slight differences in their factor intensities after 1970.

(6) The increase in the factor intensity (i.e., capital/labor ratio) of Korea's exports was partly due to changes in the export pattern but more significantly due to capital-labor substitutions in the production process. On the other hand, the factor intensity of Korea's competitive import replacements became less capital intensive due to changes in the import pattern, but due to the offsetting increases in sectoral capital-labor substitutions we could not observe any consistent decreases in the estimates of the capital intensity of competitive import replacements.

(7) The capital intensity of Korea's non-competitive imports estimated by using the U.S. and Japanese sectoral factor coefficients was much higher than that of either exports or competitive imports. Therefore, Korea's trade was consistent with the comparative advantage doctrine of Heckscher-Ohlin principally with regard to exports vs. non-competitive imports and exports vs. natural resource intensive imports.

(8) Korea's exports seem to be slightly more skill intensive than its competitive imports. However, when we computed the skill intensity of trade for the entire 1963-72 period, we found out that there was virtually no change in the skill composition of labor required for either export production or import replacement. Therefore, there seems to have been no close correlation between sectoral capital intensity and sectoral skill intensity, and the effects of increases in general education and informal training seem to have been spread evenly over all skill groups and thus did not exert an influence working to shift Korea's comparative advantage specifically towards relatively more skill intensive sectors. Furthermore, one might argue that the skill factor itself was not extremely important in production processes insofar as regards the kinds of commodities exported from and competitively imported to Korea during 1963-72.

(9) According to estimates of static gains from trade based on the fixed coefficients assumption, the gain of capital per labor lost through trade in exports vs. competitive imports fell rapidly during the period 1966–73 and became negative from 1969. That is, Korea lost a significant amount of both capital and labor via trade in competitive goods in 1969 and 1970 and, quite perversely, gained a significant amount of labor at the expense of capital in the period 1971–73. We computed the gains from trade excluding some selected capital intensive export group and found that were it not for this capital intensive export group Korea would not have registered negative earnings in both capital and labor during 1969–70, and the perverse phenomenon of Korea's exporting capital and importing labor during 1971–73 would have turned into gains of "both capital and labor". Although the simple existence of static losses at any specific point in time does not necessarily imply welfare losses to the economy over the long-term, the fact that we can observe such losses implies that we should at least try to justify their existence in terms of dynamic gains.

BIBLIOGRAPHY

1. Baldwin, R.E., "Determinants of the Commodity Structure of U.S. Trade," *American Economic Review* (March 1971)
2. Bhagwati, J.N., "The Gains from Trade Once Again," *Oxford Economic Papers* (July 1968)
3. _____, "The Heckscher-Ohlin Theorem in the Multi-Commodity Case," *Journal of Political Economy* (September/October 1972)
4. _____, "The Pure Theory of International Trade: A Survey," *Economic Journal* (March 1964)
5. _____, *The Theory and Practice of Commercial Policy: Departures from Unified Exchange Rates*, International Finance Section, Princeton University Press, 1968
6. _____ and Krueger, A.O., "Exchange Control, Liberalization, and Economic Development", *American Economic Review*, (May 1973)
7. Bharadwaj, R., "Factor Proportions and the Structure of Indo-U.S. Trade," *The Indian Economic Journal* (October 1962)
8. Cho, Y.S., *Disguised Unemployment in Underdeveloped Areas, With Special Reference to South Korean Agriculture*, Berkeley, 1963
9. Cole, D.C., "The Contribution of Exports to Employment in Korea," in *Trade and Development in Korea*, ed. by Wontack Hong and A. O. Krueger, Seoul: KDI Press, 1975
10. Denison, E.F., *Why Growth Rates Differ*, Washington D.C.: The Brookings Institution, 1967
11. Hong, Wontack, "A Global Equilibrium Pattern of Specialization: A Model to Approximate Linder's World of Production and Trade," *The Swedish Journal of Economics* (December 1969)
12. _____, "Capital Accumulation, Factor Substitution, and the Changing Factor Intensity of Trade: The Case of Korea (1966–72)," in *Trade and Development in Korea*, ed. by Wontack Hong and A. O. Krueger, Seoul: KDI Press, 1975

13. _____, "Distortions and Static Negative Marginal Gains from Trade," *Journal of International Economics* (May 1976)
14. _____, "Skill Intensity of Trade: The Case of Korea (1962–71)," *The Developing Economies* (September 1974)
15. _____, "The Heckscher-Ohlin Theory of Factor Price Equalization and the Indeterminacy in International Specialization," *International Economic Review* (June 1970)
16. _____ and Krueger, A.O., editors, *Trade and Development in Korea*, Seoul: KDI Press, 1975
17. Ichimura, S. and Tatemoto, M., "Factor Proportions and Foreign Trade: The Case of Japan," *Review of Economics and Statistics* (November 1959)
18. Johnson, H.G., "Optimal Trade Intervention in the Presence of Domestic Distortions", in Baldwin and others, *Trade, Growth, and the Balance of Payments*, Chicago: Rand McNally, 1965
19. Keesing, D.B., "Labor Skills and Comparative Advantage," *American Economic Review* (May 1966)
20. _____, "Labor Skills and the Structure of Trade in Manufactures," in P. Kenen ed., *The Open Economy: Essays on International Trade and Finance*, New York: Columbia University Press, 1968
21. _____, "Outward-Looking Policies and Economic Development", *Economic Journal* (June 1967)
22. Kemp, M.C., "Some Issues in the Analysis of Trade Gains," *Oxford Economic Papers* (July 1968)
23. _____, *The Pure Theory of International Trade and Investment*, New Jersey: Prentice Hall, 1969
24. Kim, K.S., "Outward-Looking Industrialization Policy: The Case of Korea," in *Trade and Development in Korea*, ed. by Wontack Hong and A. O. Krueger, Seoul: KDI Press, 1975
25. Kim, Y.C., "Sectoral Output-Capital Ratios and Levels of Economic Development: A Cross-Sectional Comparison of Manufacturing Industry," *The Review of Economics and Statistics* (November 1969)
26. Leontief, W., "Domestic Production and Foreign Trade: The American Capital Position Re-Examined," *Proceedings of the American Philosophical Society* (September 1953)
27. _____, "Factor Proportions and the Structure of American Trade: Further Theoretical and Empirical Analysis," *Review of Economics and Statistics* (November 1956)
28. Lewis, A., "Economic Development with Unlimited Supplies of

Labour," *The Manchester School* (May 1954)
29. Meade, J.E., *A Neo-Classical Theory of Economic Growth*, London: Allen & Unwin, 1962
30. Ranis, G.R. and Fei, J.H., "A Theory of Economics Development," *American Economic Review* (September 1961)
31. Rybczynski, T.N., "Factor Endowments and Relative Commodity Prices," *Economica* (November 1955)
32. Stolper, W.F. and Samuelson, P.A., "Protection and Real Wages," *Review of Economic Studies* (November 1941)
33. Vanek, J., *General Equilibrium of International Discrimination: The Case of Customs Unions*, Cambridge: Harvard University Press, 1965
34. _____, "The Natural Resource Content of Foreign Trade, 1870–1955, and the Relative Abundance of Natural Resources in the United States," *Review of Economics and Statistics* (May 1959)
35. Watanabe, Susumu, "Exports and Employment: The Case of the Republic of Korea," *International Labor Review* (December 1972)
36. Weiser, L.A., "Changing Factor Requirements of United States Foreign Trade," *Review of Economics and Statistics* (August 1968)

STATISTICAL REFERENCES

1. Bank of Korea, *Employment Requirement Coefficient for 1970* (mimeographed)
2. _____, *External Trade Statistics* (1960 through 1963)
3. _____, *Korean Input-Output Tables for 1960, 1963, 1966, 1968* (mimeographed)
4. _____, *Monthly Economic Statistics* (various issues)
5. _____, *Monthly Foreign Exchange Statistics* (various issues)
6. _____, *National Income Statistics Yearbook* (various issues)
7. _____, *1970 Input-Output Table*
8. _____, *Economic Statistics Yearbook* (various issues)
9. Economic Planning Board, *Annual Report on the Economically Active Population* (various issues)
10. _____, *1960 Population and Housing Census of Korea, 1966 Census Report of Korea, and 1970 Population and Housing Census Report*
11. _____, *Korea Statistical Yearbook* (various issues)
12. _____, *Report on National Wealth Survey* (as of December 31, 1968), 1972
13. _____ & The Korea Development Bank, *Report on Mining and Manufacturing Survey:* 1963, 1967, 1969–1972, and *Report on Mining and Manufacturing Census:* 1960, 1963, 1966, 1967 & 1968
14. Government of Korea, *First Five-Year Economic Development Plan (1962–66)*, Seoul, January 1961
15. Han, K. C., *Estimates of Korean Capital and Inventory Coefficients in 1968*, Seoul: Yonsei University, 1970 (mimeographed)
16. Hong, Wontack, *Statistical Data on Korea's Trade and Growth*, Seoul: Korea Development Institute, 1975 (mimeographed)
17. Medium Industry Bank, *Mining and Manufacturing Census: 1962*
18. Ministry of Agriculture & Forestry, *The Results of Farm Household Economy Survey and Production Cost Survey of Agricultural Products* (various issues since 1962)

19. _____, *Yearbook of Agriculture and Forestry Statistics* (various issues)
20. Ministry of Finance, *Foreign Trade of Korea* (1964–68)
21. Office of Customs Administration, *Statistical Yearbook of Foreign Trade* (1969–74)
22. Office of Fisheries, *Fisheries Census Report of Korea: 1970,* 1972
23. Office of Labor Affairs, *Survey Report on Actual Labor Conditions at Establishment,* 1970
24. _____, *Survey Report on Occupational Wages,* 1971
25. Shim, B.K., et. al., *A Study of Preferential Interest Rate Structure: The Korean Experience (1963–71),* Seoul: Seoul National University, 1972 (mimeographed)

STATISTICAL APPENDIX

STATISTICAL APPENDIX

A. 1. Summary of Exports and Imports *137*
A. 2. Invisible Trade by Type: Receipts (1953–74) *138*
A. 3. Invisible Trade by Type: Payments (1953–74) *139*
A. 4. Official Exchange Rates and Parity Rates *140*

A. 5. Index Numbers of Foreign Trade and Terms of Trade *141*
A. 6. Major Commodities Exported: 1955–74 .... *142*
A. 7. Major Commodities Imported: 1955–74 .... *145*
A. 8. Commodity Trade (At Current Dollar Prices): 1960–74 ...... *148*

A. 9. Commodity Trade (At 1970 Constant Dollar Prices): 1960–74 .... *149*
A.10. Natural Resource Intensive Imports *150*
A.11. Commodity Exports: 1952–59 .... *151*
A.12. Commodity Exports: 1960–74 .... *152*

A.13. Commodity Imports: 1952–59 .... *163*
A.14. Competitive Imports (1968 Basis): 1960–74 .... *164*
A.15. Non-Competitive Imports (1968 Basis): 1960–74 .... *176*
A.16. Competitive Imports (1970 Basis): 1960–74 .... *184*

A.17. Non-Competitive Imports (1970 Basis): 1960–74 .... *194*
A.18. Amount of Commodities Transferred from 1963 Non-Competitive Imports to 1966 Competitive Imports *201*
A.19. Amount of Commodities Transferred from 1966 Non-Competitive Imports to 1968 Competitive Imports *203*
A.20. Raw Material Imports for Export Production (Competitive Imports as of 1968): 1966–74 .... *204*

A.21. Raw Material Imports for Export Production (Non-Competitive as of 1968): 1966–74 206
A.22. Industrial Origin of Gross National Product (At 1970 Constant Market Prices): 1953–74 208
A.23. Sectoral Gross and Net Fixed Capital Stock: 1968 209
A.24. Sectoral Gross Fixed Capital Formation (1953–74) 210

A.25. Sectoral Provisions for the Consumtion of Fixed Capital (1953–74).................................... 211
A.26. Sectoral Net Fixed Capital Formation (1953–74) 212
A.27. Sectoral Net Fixed Capital Stock (1953–74) 213
A.28. Age Structure of Fixed Capital Stock: 1953–74..................... 214

A.29. Age Structure of Fixed Capital Stock (Excluding the Ownership of Dwellings): 1953–74 216
A.30. Direct Factor Requirements Per $1,000 (1970 Dollar Prices) of Outputs: 1960, 1963, 1966, 1968 & 1970 218
A.31. Direct Plus Indirect Factor Coefficients (Applying the A^d Matrix): 1966, 1968 & 1970 225
A.32. Direct Plus Indirect Factor Coefficients (Applying the A Matrix): 1960, 1963, 1966, 1968 & 1970 231

Table A.1. Summary of Exports and Imports

In Million U.S. Dollars

	Exports			Imports				
	Total	Commercial	Bonded Process	Total	Commercial	Official Aid	Foreign Loans	Relief & Others	P.A.C.*
1953	39.6	39.6	—	345.4	153.6	191.8	—	—	—
1954	24.2	24.2	—	243.3	93.9	149.4	—	—	—
1955	18.0	18.0	—	341.4	108.6	232.8	—	—	—
1956	24.6	24.6	—	386.1	66.2	319.9	—	—	—
1957	22.2	22.2	—	442.2	46.9	374.0	—	21.2	—
1958	16.5	16.5	—	378.2	48.7	311.0	—	18.5	—
1959	19.8	19.2	—	303.8	81.0	210.7	—	12.1	—
1960	32.8	31.8	—	343.5	97.2	231.9	—	14.4	—
1961	40.9	38.6	—	316.1	103.1	196.8	—	16.2	—
1962	54.8	52.8	1.0	421.8	179.0	218.5	4.5	19.7	—
1963	86.8	76.7	4.9	560.3	232.7	232.6	52.1	42.8	—
1964	119.1	111.0	5.4	404.4	184.5	142.6	34.6	42.6	—
1965	175.1	153.4	16.3	463.4	248.4	135.5	31.5	48.1	—
1966	250.3	215.8	28.8	716.4	397.8	143.6	108.4	62.5	4.1
1967	320.2	259.6	49.8	996.2	640.7	119.2	167.3	36.2	32.8
1968	455.4	356.3	87.0	1,462.9	921.8	125.7	299.6	73.1	42.6
1969	622.5	478.9	130.7	1,823.6	1,052.3	120.5	475.7	140.4	34.7
1970	835.2	659.8	152.3	1,984.0	1,229.9	161.2	400.2	166.4	26.3
1971	1,067.6	839.2	208.8	2,394.3	1,595.4	105.6	541.4	131.8	20.2
1972	1,624.1	1,308.9	285.3	2,522.0	1,657.5	21.7	628.6	169.4	44.7
1973	3,225.0	2,459.1	703.1	4,240.3	3,295.6	—	628.4	292.9	23.3
1974	4,460.4	3,334.0	1,064.8	6,851.8	5,524.6	—	638.8	658.5	29.9

Source: The Bank of Korea, *Economic Statistics Yearbook: 1975*.
*Imports financed with Properties and Claims funds from Japan.

Table A.2. Invisible Trade by Type: Receipts (1953–74)

In Thousand U.S. Dollars

	Total	Trans-portation	Insurance	Misc. Services	Foreign Travel	Investment Income	Gov't* Transactions	Donations
1953	133,713	370	5	1,093	60	543	122,026	9,616
1954	52,595	588	30	2,153	65	1,366	40,507	7,886
1955	66,420	755	13	1,282	352	1,646	54,803	7,569
1956	37,027	985	14	876	59	1,811	20,164	13,118
1957	55,319	1,166	53	597	153	2,515	41,204	9,631
1958	80,695	550	6	1,274	323	2,905	65,499	10,138
1959	78,254	1,693	23	2,044	358	3,743	64,145	6,248
1960	79,410	1,091	802	3,386	436	4,501	63,006	6,188
1961	123,597	1,167	81	4,758	1,353	4,563	80,581	31,094
1962	122,318	1,451	25	5,971	3,092	5,160	86,825	19,794
1963	91,817	2,606	24	4,920	2,726	3,355	59,744	18,442
1964	97,102	4,315	169	3,053	2,789	3,755	65,485	17,536
1965	125,763	4,336	141	6,477	7,724	3,726	75,251	28,108
1966	238,434	5,639	937	20,129	16,186	5,571	135,478	54,494
1967	375,199	10,076	6,793	46,776	16,316	10,104	214,946	70,188
1968	424,500	15,658	5,346	71,786	16,883	12,360	247,791	54,676
1969	497,070	23,139	3,715	89,389	16,233	37,850	276,342	50,402
1970	490,743	36,654	5,560	89,091	18,719	38,011	261,631	41,077
1971	486,592	46,472	6,030	87,994	31,193	28,768	237,985	48,150
1972	579,157	79,775	3,656	91,334	74,729	20,892	241,595	67,176
1973	936,324	147,075	10,554	163,535	264,062	40,468	185,322	125,305
1974	987,325	227,217	7,497	206,163	153,326	82,900	161,390	148,832

Source: The Bank of Korea, *Economic Statistics Yearbook*: 1961 & 1975.
*Government transactions include sales of goods and services to the U.S. army stationed in Korea. Repayments for the liabilities in open A/C by P.A.C. fund were also included.

Table A.3. Invisible Trade by Type: Payments (1953–74)

In Thousand U.S. Dollars

	Total	Trans-portation	Insurance	Misc. Services	Foreign Travel	Investment Income	Gov't Transaction	Donations
1953	13,998	1,996	446	1,335	736	1	—	9,484
1954	7,374	530	328	1,004	1,244	—	403	3,865
1955	10,091	12	0	1,455	1,683	415	2,162	4,364
1956	14,734	396	—	1,736	943	743	2,714	8,202
1957	11,836	1,146	65	1,411	631	581	3,987	4,015
1958	13,468	2,110	12	2,231	2,937	77	3,741	2,360
1959	16,525	3,742	293	5,031	3,948	146	3,141	224
1960	17,379	5,932	338	3,557	4,596	185	2,611	160
1961	15,541	5,919	187	3,624	2,374	47	3,116	274
1962	29,964	11,717	263	8,251	2,166	35	7,507	25
1963	39,403	20,694	715	7,202	2,276	170	8,298	48
1964	38,606	22,144	929	5,663	2,381	1,785	5,559	145
1965	38,499	23,312	652	5,567	1,662	2,011	5,274	21
1966	44,726	20,125	1,399	9,173	3,193	3,251	7,538	47
1967	89,358	33,202	3,232	25,054	8,396	10,807	8,403	264
1968	127,808	47,075	4,670	37,390	10,487	17,469	10,501	216
1969	159,454	46,071	4,591	39,221	10,964	41,518	16,822	269
1970	220,745	42,376	4,707	56,192	12,424	81,226	23,395	425
1971	294,460	66,346	8,176	57,871	14,808	118,648	25,408	3,203
1972	348,586	82,499	9,711	52,803	12,570	160,824	28,200	1,979
1973	483,165	140,102	15,971	69,064	17,074	205,640	33,045	2,268
1974	774,968	245,185	21,809	121,517	27,618	320,649	32,568	5,622

Source: The Bank of Korea, *Economic Statistics Yearbook: 1961 & 1975.*

140

Table A. 4. Official Exchange Rates and Parity Rates

	Official Exchange Rate		Wholesale Price Index			Parity Rate 310.6 ×		GNP Deflator of			Parity Rate 310.6 ×	
	(End of the Month)	12-Month Average	Korea (A)	U.S. (B)	Japan (C)	(A/B)	(A/C)	Korea (A')	U.S. (B')	Japan (C')	(A'/B')	(A'/C')
1953	18.00(12)	12.00	8.2	79.2	87.9	32.1	34.2	5.7	65.3	51.1	27.1	34.6
1954	18.00(12)	18.00	10.5	79.3	87.3	41.1	37.4	7.5	66.3	52.0	35.2	44.8
1955	50.00 (8)	31.33	19.1	79.5	85.7	74.6	69.2	12.4	67.2	52.8	57.3	72.9
1956	50.00 (8)	50.00	25.1	82.2	89.5	94.9	87.1	16.2	69.5	55.5	72.4	90.7
1957	50.00 (8)	50.00	29.2	84.5	92.2	107.3	98.4	19.5	72.1	58.0	84.0	104.4
1958	50.00 (8)	50.00	27.3	85.7	86.2	99.0	98.4	19.4	73.9	57.5	81.5	104.8
1959	50.00 (8)	50.00	28.0	85.9	87.0	101.3	100.0	19.9	75.2	59.4	82.2	104.1
1960	65.00 (2)	63.75	31.0	86.0	88.0	112.0	109.4	21.8	76.4	62.5	88.7	108.3
1961	130.00 (2)	127.50	35.1	85.6	88.9	127.3	122.6	25.1	77.4	66.9	100.8	116.5
1962	130.00 (2)	130.00	38.4	85.9	87.4	138.8	136.5	28.6	78.2	68.2	113.6	130.3
1963	130.00 (2)	130.00	46.3	85.6	89.0	168.0	161.6	36.8	79.2	71.2	144.3	160.5
1964	256.53 (5)	214.35	62.3	85.8	89.2	225.5	216.9	48.6	80.5	74.4	187.5	202.9
1965	264.00 (3)	266.48	68.5	87.5	89.8	243.2	236.9	52.6	82.0	78.2	199.3	208.9
1966	272.20 (4)	272.19	74.6	90.4	92.0	256.3	251.9	60.1	84.3	82.0	211.6	227.6
1967	274.60(12)	272.50	79.4	90.6	93.7	272.2	263.2	68.5	87.0	85.9	244.7	247.7
1968	281.50(12)	276.37	85.8	92.8	94.5	287.2	282.0	76.6	90.4	89.8	263.1	264.9
1969	304.45(12)	286.80	91.6	96.5	96.5	294.8	294.8	86.7	94.8	93.8	284.1	287.1
1970	316.65(12)	310.12	100.0	100.0	100.0	310.6	310.6	100.0	100.0	100.0	310.6	310.6
1971	373.30(12)	346.08	108.6	103.2	99.2	326.8	340.0	111.5	104.5	104.5	330.8	331.4
1972	387.10 (3)	391.83	123.8	107.9	100.0	356.4	384.5	127.7	108.0	109.6	367.2	361.9
1973	397.50(12)	398.43	132.4	122.0	115.9	335.2	354.8	139.9	114.1	122.2	382.0	355.6
1974	484.00(12)	405.97	188.2	145.0	152.2	403.1	384.1	177.2	125.8	147.6	437.3	372.9
1975	484.00(12)	484.00	238.0	158.4	156.8	466.7	471.5	220.4p	135.9p	..	503.6p	..

Source: The Bank of Korea, *Economic Statistics Yearbook*, U.S. Government, *Economic Report of the President*, and the Bank of Japan, *Economic Statistics Annual* and *Foreign Economic Statistics Quarterly*.

Table A.5. *Index Numbers of Foreign Trade and Terms of Trade*

	Quantum Index		Unit Value Index		Net Barter Terms of Trade	Income Terms of Trade
	Exports	Imports	Exports	Imports		
1968	54.1	75.6	100.8	97.9	102.9	55.7
1969	77.8	95.3	95.8	96.4	99.4	77.3
1970	100.0	100.0	100.0	100.0	100.0	100.0
1971	129.4	121.2	98.8	99.6	99.2	128.4
1972	194.6	125.5	99.9	101.3	98.6	191.9
1973	305.2	158.1	126.5	135.2	93.6	285.5
1974	333.4	164.2	160.2	210.3	76.2	254.1

Source: The Bank of Korea, *Monthly Economic Statistics*.

Table A.6. Major Commodities Exported: 1955–74

In Thousand U.S. Dollars

SITC	1955	Value	SITC	1961	Value
2839	Base Metal Ores & Concentrates	5,206	2839	Base Metal Ores & Concentrates	4,616
2762	Clay & Other Refractory Minerals	1,322	2813	Iron Ore & Concentrates	4,252
2929	Materials of Vegetable Origin	1,303	2613	Raw Silk	2,849
2613	Raw Silk	1,275	0312	Fish (salted, in brine, dried)	2,674
2919	Materials of Animal Origin	667	0013	Swine	2,464
3214	Coal	488	3214	Coal	2,209
2924	Plants for Medicines & Perfumes	466	2929	Materials of Vegetables Origin	1,523
6895	Base Metals	416	0311	Fish (fresh, chilled, frozen)	1,274
2840	Non-Ferrous Metal Scrap	387	6312	Plywood	1,217
2120	Fur Skins, undressed	366	2919	Materials of Animal Origin	1,070
2612	Silk Waste	354	2762	Clay & Other Refractory Minerals	1,055
8999	Other Manufactured Articles	338	2924	Plants for Medicines & Perfumes	1,021
2813	Iron Ore & Concentrates	326	0548	Vegetable Products	893
2831	Ores & Concentrates of Copper	307	6521	Cotton Fabrics	771
2820	Iron & Steel Scrap	295	2765	Fluorspar, Felspar, etc.	688
0548	Vegetable Products	294	8999	Other Manufactured Articles	596
0542	Dried Leguminous Vegetables	291	2769	Minerals, crude	524
6821	Copper & Alloys, unworked	285	0422	Rice	507
0312	Fish (salted, in brine, dried)	283	6821	Copper & Alloys, unworked	459
2765	Fluorspar, Felspar, etc.	272	2214	Soya Beans	436
2769	Minerals, crude	269	2840	Non-ferrous Metal Scraps	407
2440	Cork	215	6712	Pig Iron	390
2670	Waste from Textile Fabrics	206	0542	Dried Leguminous Vegetables	305
0311	Fish (fresh, chilled, frozen)	175	0320	Fish & Fish Preparations	299
2837	Manganese Ores & Concentrates	134	2612	Silk Waste	297
	Subtotal (S)	15,940		Subtotal (S)	32,796
	(S)/Total Exports	91%		(S)/Total Exports	80%

SITC	1966	Value	SITC	1971	Value
6312	Plywood	30,150	8414	Clothes & Accessories thereof	132,921
8414	Clothes & Accessories thereof	15,937	8411	Clothing of Textile Fabrics	129,135
8999	Other Manufactured Articles	15,925	6312	Plywood	126,823
8411	Clothing of Textile Fabrics	13,593	8999	Other Manufactured Articles	70,586
2613	Raw Silk	11,632	7293	Thermionic, Valves & Tubes	48,472
2839	Base Metal Ores & Concentrates	11,402	2613	Raw Silk	39,273
0311	Fish (fresh, chilled, frozen)	8,663	8510	Footwear	37,436
0548	Vegetable Products	8,415	8412	Clothing Accessories of Fabrics	36,205
6521	Cotton Fabrics (unbleached)	7,479	6521	Cotton Fabrics (unbleached)	20,716
6748	Plates & Sheets of Iron or Steel	7,046	0311	Fish (fresh, chilled, frozen)	20,020
1210	Tobacco, unmanufactured	6,469	6516	Yarn & Thread of Synthetic Fibres	19,197
2813	Iron Ore & Concentrates	6,091	6743	Plates & Sheets of Iron or Steel	19,156
8510	Footwear	5,467	6556	Twines, Cordage, Ropes, etc.	17,159
0320	Fish & Fish Preparations	4,852	6535	Fabrics of Synthetic Fibres	14,402
0421	Rice, unpolished	4,634	0313	Crustacea & Mollusca	14,077
0313	Crustacea & Mollusca	4,481	1210	Tobacco, unmanufactured	14,076
6535	Woven Fabrics of Synthetic Fibres	4,402	2924	Plants for Medicines & Perfumes	12,654
0312	Fish (salted, dried)	3,677	2839	Base Metal Ores & Concentrates	11,834
6536	Fabric of Regenerated Fibre	3,549	6537	Knitted or Crocheted Fabrics	11,433
2929	Materials of Vegetables Origin	3,546	6612	Cement	10,587
8412	Clothing Accessories of Fabrics	3,472	6514	Cotton Yarn & Thread	10,306
7242	Radio Receivers & Parts	3,186	6522	Cotton Fabrics (bleached, dyed)	10,288
6539	Fabrics, woven	3,068	0548	Vegetable Products	9,329
6556	Twines, Cordage, Ropes, etc.	3,015	6513	Cotton Yarn & Thread, grey	5,923
6989	Articles of Base Metal	3,015	7242	Radio Receivers & Parts	5,785
	Subtotal (S)	193,166		Subtotal (S)	847,793
	(S)/Total Exports	78%		(S)/Total Exports	79%

Table A.6. (Continued)

In Thousand U.S. Dollars

SITC	1973	Value	SITC	1974	Value
8414	Clothes & Accessories thereof	346,389	8411	Clothing of Taxtile Fabrics	415,234
8411	Clothing of Textile Fabrics	314,635	8414	Clothes & Accessories thereof	410,918
6312	Plywood	273,989	7293	Thermionic, Valves & Tubes	242,679
7293	Thermionic, Valves & Tubes	179,697	8510	Footwear	179,547
8510	Footwear	106,371	6312	Plywood	163,409
6743	Plates & Sheets of Iron or Steel	104,468	6743	Plates & Sheets of Iron or Steel	150,770
6535	Woven Fabrics of Synthetic Fibers	103,593	6535	Woven Fabrics of Synthetic Fibers	107,015
8999	Other Manufactured Articles	83,732	8999	Other Manufactured Articles	75,905
2613	Raw Silk (not thrown)	72,844	7353	Tankers	73,956
6531	Silk Fabrics	67,276	6531	Silk Fabrics	71,277
0311	Fish (fresh, chilled or frozen)	56,756	8413	Clothing & Accessories of Leather	69,199
8412	Clothing Accessories of Fabrics	49,313	0311	Fish (fresh, chilled or frozen)	63,829
0313	Crustacea & Mollusca	45,438	6513	Cotton Yarn & Thread, grey	60,027
6521	Cotton Fabrics, woven	43,819	2613	Raw Silk (not thrown)	59,828
8911	Gramophones, Tape Recorders, etc.	42,344	6291	Rubber Tyres & Tubes for Vehicles	59,796
7242	Radio Receivers & Parts	32,753	6741	Heavy Plates & Sheets	56,862
8310	Trunks, Suitcases, etc.	32,093	6783	Tubes and Pipes of Iron or Steel	56,219
6516	Yarn & Thread of Synthetic Fibers	30,984	7249	Telecommunications Equipments	56,089
8942	Children's Toys, Indoor Games, etc.	29,981	8911	Gramophones, Tape Recorders, etc.	54,113
0320	Fish, in Airtight Containers	29,322	8310	Trunks, Suitcases, etc.	50,119
8413	Clothing & Accessories of Leather	26,741	7242	Radio Receivers & Parts	49,597
6513	Cotton Yarn & Thread, grey	24,609	6612	Cement	48,946
7241	Television Receivers & Parts	23,894	1210	Tobacco, unmanufactured	46,711
7249	Telecommunications Equipments	23,074	0313	Crustacea & Mollusca	45,732
1210	Tobacco, unmanufactured	22,106	8942	Children's Toys, Indoor Games, etc.	45,460
	Subtotal (S)	2,166,221		Subtotal (S)	2,713,237
	(S)/Total Exports	67%		(S)/Total Exports	61%

Source: The Bank of Korea, *Economic Statistics Yearbook*; Ministry of Finance, *Foreign Trade of Korea*; and Office of Customs Administration, *Statistical Yearbook of Foreign Trade*.

Table A.7.   Major Commodities Imported: 1955–74

In Thousand U.S. Dollars

SITC	1955	Value	SITC	1961	Value
5611	Nitrogenous Fertilizer	46,892	2631	Raw Cotton	29,423
3214	Coal	28,581	0410	Wheat & Meslin	24,019
2631	Raw Cotton	20,145	5611	Nitrogenous Fertilizer	21,298
7314	Railway & Tramway Cars	14,870	5619	Fertilizer, n.e.s.	15,872
6512	Yarn of Wool & Animal Hair	10,831	7221	Electrical Power Machinery	7,155
6516	Yarn & Thread of Synthetic Fibres	7,616	2627	Wool or Other Animal Hair	7,063
6517	Yarn of Regenerated Fibres	7,306	3324	Residual Fuel Oils	6,999
7171	Textile Machines	6,445	6517	Yarn of Regenerated Fibres	6,627
3321	Motor Spirit	6,042	0611	Raw Sugar	5,577
112	Alcoholic Beverage	5,798	0430	Barley, unmilled	5,237
0410	Wheat & Meslin	4,188	2423	Sawlogs & Veneer Logs	5,192
6411	News Print Paper	3,514	2311	Natural Rubber	5,184
8411	Clothing of Textile Fabrics	3,430	3323	Distrillate Fuels	4,529
2423	Sawlogs & Veneer Logs	2,890	7171	Textile Machines	4,422
6412	Printing & Writing Paper	2,718	3321	Motor Spirit	4,345
3323	Distillate Fuels	2,495	3214	Coal	4,331
6522	Cotton Fabrics, woven	2,419	6516	Yarn & Thread of Synthetic Fibres	4,290
7221	Electrical Power Machinery	2,383	7115	Internal Combustion Engines	3,819
3324	Residual Fuel Oils	2,014	5310	Synthetic Organic Dyestuffs	3,121
5417	Medicaments	2,011	5612	Phosphatic Fertilizer	3,118
6612	Cement	1,975	2663	Regenerated Fibres	2,797
0611	Raw Sugar	1,949	5417	Medicaments	2,769
3325	Lubricating Oils & Greases	1,860	5812	Synthetic Plastic Materials	2,754
6743	Plates & Sheets of Iron or Steel	1,789	0615	Molasses	2,551
2311	Natural Rubber	1,630	4113	Animal Oils & Greases	2,335
	Subtotal (S)	191,791		Subtotal (S)	184,827
	(S)/Total Imports	56%		(S)/Total Imports	59%

145

146

Table A.7. (Continued)

In Thousand U.S. Dollars

SITC	1966	Value	SITC	1971	Value
2631	Raw Cotton	42,774	3310	Crude Oil	173,989
0410	Wheat & Meslin	40,481	0421	Rice, unhulled & unpolished	146,053
5611	Nitrogenous Fertilizer	39,139	2423	Sawlogs & Veneer Logs	135,819
2423	Sawlogs & Veneer Logs	35,662	0410	Wheat & Meslin	115,101
5612	Phosphatic Fertilizer	34,773	2631	Raw Cotton	84,188
7171	Textile Machines	30,839	7171	Textile Machines	78,879
3310	Crude Oil	30,289	6535	Woven Fabrics of Synthetic Fibres	56,683
7353	Ships & Boats	25,884	7353	Ships & Boats	55,671
6516	Yarn & Thread of Synthetic Fibres	17,513	2820	Iron & Steel Scrap	53,535
6517	Yarn of Regenerated Fibres	14,094	6727	Iron or Steel Coils for Re-rolling	49,306
5613	Potassic Fertilizer	13,647	7293	Thermionic Valves, Tubes, Transistors	41,357
2820	Iron & Steel Scrap	12,373	6516	Yarn & Thread of Synthetic Fibres	38,430
0460	Flour of Wheat & Meslin	11,751	7191	Heating & Cooling Equipments	38,297
7198	Machinery, n.e.s.	11,401	0611	Raw Sugar	31,069
7192	Pumps & Centrifuges	10,559	2662	Synthetic Fibres	30,541
2662	Synthetic Fibres	9,939	2517	Sulphate Wood Pulp	29,401
7191	Heating & Cooling Equipments	9,652	5812	Synthetic Plastic Materials	28,500
6743	Plates & Sheets of Iron or Steel	9,589	0819	Food Waste & Animal Feed	28,048
2311	Natural Rubber	7,590	7221	Electrical Power Machinery	27,933
2517	Sulphate Wood Pulp	7,129	..7192	Pumps & Centrifuges	25,953
5812	Synthetic Plastic Materials	6,709	7341	Aircraft	25,108
2422	Sawlogs & Veneer Logs	6,389	7198	Machinery, n.e.s.	24,894
6911	Structures of Iron & Steel	6,300	7222	Electrical Apparatus (switch gear)	23,471
0611	Raw Sugar	5,434	0440	Maize, unmilled	22,614
7221	Electrical Power Machinery	5,332	7323	Trucks, Vans or Lorries	22,513
	Subtotal (S)	445,242		Subtotal (S)	1,387,353
	(S)/Total Imports	62%		(S)/Total Imports	58%

SITC	1973	Value	SITC	1974	Value
3310	Crude Oil	277,388	3310	Crude Oil	965,845
2423	Sawlogs & Veneer Logs	273,858	7353	Ships & Boats	373,657
0410	Wheat & Meslin	256,621	0410	Wheat & Meslin	297,562
7293	Thermionic, Valves & Tubes	162,005	2423	Sawlogs & Veneer Logs	288,295
6727	Iron or Steel Coils for Re-rolling	148,178	7293	Thermionic, Valves & Tubes	218,489
7171	Textile Machines	147,308	6727	Iron or Steel Coils for Re-rolling	211,745
2631	Raw Cotton	112,426	2631	Raw Cotton	189,450
6535	Woven Fabrics of Synthetic Fibres	104,089	7171	Textile Machines	186,542
7341	Aircraft	101,943	2820	Waste & Scrap Metal of Iron or Steel	171,811
6516	Yarn & Thread of Synethtic Fibres	78,774	0611	Beet Sugar & Cane Sugar, solid	131,490
2820	Waste & Scrap Metal of Iron or Steel	74,323	6535	Woven Fabrics of Synethetic Fibres	97,113
2662	Synthetic Fibres, discontinuous	73,340	2517	Chemical Wood Pulp	85,736
7193	Mechanical Handling Equipments	71,046	0430	Barley & Naked Barley, unmilled	84,499
0421	Rice, in the husk or husked	66,108	0421	Rice, in the husk or husked	80,373
0611	Beet Sugar & Cane Sugar, solid	63,015	7191	Heating & Cooling Equipments	70,026
7249	Telecommunications Equipments	55,069	0440	Maize, unmilled	66,544
0430	Barley & Naked Barley, unmilled	54,160	7341	Aircraft	65,930
7198	Machinery & Mechanical Appliances	51,664	7151	Metal-Working Machinery	62,988
6725	Blooms, Billets of Iron or Steel	48,270	5812	Synthetic Plastic Materials	62,703
2517	Chemical Wood Pulp	47,590	2662	Synthetic Fibres, discontinuous	62,380
7353	Ships & Boats	46,832	5128	Organic-Inorganic Compounds	61,531
7191	Heating & Cooling Equipments	44,639	7249	Telecommunications Equipments	60,881
0440	Maize, unmilled	41,272	7198	Machinery & Mechanical Appliances	58,878
5128	Organic-Inorganic Compounds	38,034	2311	Natural Rubber & Natural Gums	56,718
5812	Synthetic Plastic Materials	37,779	6516	Yarn & Thread of Synthetic Fibres	55,320
	Subtotal (S)	2,475,731		Subtotal (S)	4,066,506
	(S)/Total Imports	58%		(S)/Total Imports	59%

Source: The Bank of Korea, *Economic Statistics Yearbook*; Ministry of Finance, *Foreign Trade of Korea*; and Office of Customs Administration, *Statistical Yearbook of Foreign Trade*.

Table A.8. Commodity Trade (At Current Dollar Prices): 1960–74

In Million U.S. Dollars

	Commodity Exports		Commodity Imports		(1968 Basis)		(1970 Basis)		Natural Resource Intensive Imports
	BOK	OCA Tape	BOK	OCA Tape	Competitive Imports	Non-Competitive Imports	Competitive Imports	Non-Competitive Imports	
1960	32.8	31.8	343.5	329.1	223.8	45.2	233.0	36.0	60.1
1961	40.9	38.6	316.1	300.0	193.9	50.7	202.9	41.7	55.3
1962	54.8	54.8	421.8	421.8	256.0	100.9	275.7	81.3	64.8
1963	86.8	86.8	560.3	560.3	367.4	121.6	387.7	101.3	71.3
1964	119.1	118.9	404.4	404.3	246.9	79.8	272.9	53.8	77.6
1965	175.1	175.0	463.4	463.1	263.3	103.8	296.6	70.5	96.0
1966	250.3	247.6	716.4	717.4	453.5	132.5	519.4	66.6	131.3
1967	320.2	320.3	996.2	996.2	609.6	218.2	715.8	112.0	168.4
1968	455.4	455.3	1,462.9	1,464.1	870.2	370.9	1,061.7	179.4	223.0
1969	622.5	622.6	1,823.6	1,825.9	1,058.4	465.1	1,254.0	269.6	302.4
1970	835.2	835.2	1,984.0	1,985.0	1,109.9	517.2	1,314.3	312.9	357.8
1971	1,067.6	1,067.6	2,394.3	2,395.0	1,280.9	652.2	1,514.5	418.5	461.9
1972	1,624.1	1,632.6	2,522.0	2,522.0	1,256.7	762.5	1,522.5	496.7	502.8
1973	3,225.0	3,225.3	4,240.3	4,241.5	2,072.0	1,329.5	2,506.3	895.3	840.0
1974	4,460.4	4,456.3	6,851.8	6,844.7	3,250.7	1,883.8	3,784.6	1,349.8	1,710.2

Source: The Bank of Korea, *Economic Statistics Yearbook*, *External Trade Statistcs* (1960–63), Ministry of Finance, *Foreign Trade of Korea*, taped, (1964–69), and Office of Customs Administration, *Statistical Yearbook of Foreign Trade*, taped, (1970–74).

Table A.9. Commodity Trade (At 1970 Constant Dollar Prices): 1960-74

In Million 1970 Dollars

	Commodity Exports		Commodity Imports		(1968 Basis)		(1970 Basis)		Natural Resource Intensive Imports
	BOK	OCA Tape	BOK	OCA Tape	Competitive Imports	Non-Competitive Imports	Competitive Imports	Non-Competitive Imports	
1960	42.9	41.6	449.7	430.8	293.0	59.2	350.1	47.1	78.7
1961	42.9	49.9	408.6	387.8	250.6	65.5	262.3	53.9	71.5
1962	70.1	70.1	539.2	539.2	327.3	129.0	352.5	103.9	82.8
1963	109.5	109.5	707.0	707.0	463.7	153.5	489.3	127.8	90.0
1964	148.0	147.7	502.4	502.3	306.7	99.1	339.0	66.8	96.4
1965	213.6	213.5	565.3	564.9	321.2	126.6	361.8	86.0	117.1
1966	297.1	293.9	850.3	851.5	538.3	157.3	616.5	79.0	155.8
1967	368.3	368.4	1,145.7	1,145.7	701.1	251.0	823.2	128.8	193.7
1968	503.6	503.4	1,617.7	1,619.0	962.3	410.1	1,174.0	198.4	246.6
1969	656.7	656.8	1,923.7	1,926.1	1,116.5	490.6	1,322.8	284.4	319.0
1970	835.2	835.2	1,984.0	1,985.0	1,109.9	517.2	1,314.3	312.9	357.8
1971	1,021.4	1,021.4	2,290.8	2,291.4	1,225.5	624.0	1,449.0	400.4	441.9
1972	1,503.2	1,511.1	2,334.3	2,334.3	1,163.2	705.8	1,409.2	459.7	465.4
1973	2,549.4	2,549.6	3,136.3	3,137.2	1,532.5	983.4	1,853.8	662.2	621.3
1974	2,784.3	2,781.7	3,258.1	3,254.7	1,545.7	895.8	1,799.6	641.8	813.2

Source: The same as Table A.8.

Table A.10. Natural Resource Intensive Imports

In Thousand U.S. Dollars

	Crude Oil (11)	Timber (7)	Timber (39)	Raw Cotton (5)	Raw Sugar (18)	Crude Rubber (7)	Wool (6)	Wool (26)	Total
1960	—	7,848	—	28,631	6,118	6,359	11,185	—	60,141
1961	—	6,832	594	29,423	5,577	5,846	7,063	—	55,335
1962	17	14,470	—	34,179	3,802	5,477	1,784	5,083	64,812
1963	27	16,088	—	38,153	3,978	6,931	1,459	4,686	71,322
1964	12,331	16,316	—	37,294	3,577	4,675	223	3,155	77,571
1965	21,791	19,954	—	40,837	3,458	6,352	538	3,048	95,978
1966	29,269	40,918	117	42,570	5,433	7,516	345	5,050	131,308
1967	37,973	55,257	115	49,328	8,963	7,925	2,040	6,844	168,445
1968	56,108	85,780	10	49,051	10,169	9,339	3,239	9,313	223,009
1969	99,316	103,768	11	52,038	17,454	13,888	3,508	12,423	302,406
1970	123,229	122,275	7	62,669	23,478	13,244	3,192	9,755	357,849
1971	172,003	151,241	13	84,188	31,069	14,179	2,268	6,910	461,871
1972	206,273	139,013	13	85,478	36,448	14,764	3,557	17,221	502,767
1973	275,101	305,968	83	112,427	63,015	33,034	9,938	40,471	840,037
1974	961,626	337,641	65	189,449	131,489	56,720	5,961	27,250	1,710,201

Source: The same as Table A.8.
Note: Figures in the parentheses represent I-0 117 sectoral classification.

Table A.11. Commodity Exports: 1952–59

In Thousand U.S. Dollars

I-O 43 Sector Classification	1952	1953	1954	1955	1956	1957	1958	1959
1. Rice, Barley & Wheat	—	—	16	247	—	—	—	775
2. Other Agriculture	2,971	3,465	2,997	3,462	5,034	2,945	2,868	3,598
3. Forestry	—	—	—	—	—	—	—	329
4. Fishery	898	1,198	632	416	718	2,294	707	602
5. Coal	—	—	—	—	—	—	—	657
6. Other Minerals	21,153	29,252	15,009	9,061	14,938	11,506	7,275	7,807
7. Processed Foods	—	—	259	405	214	183	1,936	2,277
8. Beverages	88	80	—	—	—	—	—	106
10. Fibre Spinning	—	—	—	8	5	—	31	745
11. Textile Fabrics	880	2,589	2,693	2,230	2,767	3,260	899	1,420
12. Textile Products	—	—	—	—	—	—	136	8
13. Lumber & Plywood	—	—	1	—	—	41	212	—
18. Rubber Products	—	—	—	—	—	—	—	—
19. Basic Chemicals	—	—	—	—	—	6	10	115
20. Other Chemicals	—	—	1,685	247	18	—	—	—
22. Petroleum Products	—	—	668	387	—	—	297	—
23. Coal Products	—	1,133	17	91	135	—	—	121
24. Nonmetallic Mineral Products	1,254	1,021	2	—	13	—	124	—
26. Steel Products	—	—	126	590	1,285	1,195	1,249	431
27. Nonferrous Metals	—	—	—	—	—	—	—	—
28. Finished Metal Products	—	—	4	371	—	—	4	48
31. Transport Equipments	489	848	120	70	27	91	148	86
32. Misc. Manufacturing	—	—	14	—	—	—	172	37
41. Other Services	—	—	—	19	—	—	383	3
43. Unclassifiable	—	—	—	—	—	—	—	—
Total Commodity Exports	27,733	39,586	24,243	17,604	25,154	21,521	16,451	19,165

Source: The Bank of Korea, *Monthly Foreign Exchange Statistics*, *External Trade Statistics*, and *Economic Statistics Yearbook*.

Table A.12. Commodity Exports: 1960-74

In Thousand U.S. Dollars

I-O 117 Sector Classification	1960	1961	1962	1963	1964	1965	1966	1967
(1) Rice, Barley & Wheat								
1. Rice, Barley & Wheat	3,762	508	8,960	809	2,352	3,242	6,850	12
(2) Other Agriculture								
2. Other Cereals	34	741	247	97	43	1,447	993	704
3. Vegetables	—	379	40	3	27	48	105	82
4. Fruit	75	81	886	279	310	263	359	457
5. Industrial Crops	1,064	1,376	342	723	3,330	3,840	9,485	10,868
6. Livestock & Sericulture	1,907	2,494	1,483	3,676	1,361	421	427	554
(3) Forestry								
7. Forestry	816	156	117	90	120	170	141	150
(4) Fishery								
8. Fishery	1,820	1,496	4,642	5,722	8,388	10,589	12,342	19,366
(5) Coal								
9. Coal	1,147	2,209	2,760	2,578	2,405	1,899	1,500	1,752
(6) Other Minerals								
10. Metallic Ores	7,713	9,577	7,887	10,471	13,249	17,680	20,763	21,523
11. Nonmetallic Minerals	2,393	2,338	1,605	2,128	4,362	4,185	4,369	5,510
12. Salt	119	688	—	—	—	—	0	1
(7) Processed Foods								
13. Meat & Dairy Products	154	326	569	1,531	621	1,265	279	135
14. Vegetable & Fruit Processing	—	4	405	270	638	352	442	732
15. Processing of Sea Foods	3,983	5,405	6,971	8,527	15,029	13,359	18,606	17,488
16. Grain Milling	—	—	—	527	—	4	2	21
17. Bakery & Confectionery	—	—	—	—	3	—	8	—

18. Sugar Refining	—	3	685	1,262	857	1,131	3,233	2,973
19. Seasonings	9	25	17	158	227	173	172	173
20. Other Processed Foods	—	26	13	23	23	65	746	1,066
(8) Beverages								
21. Alcoholic Beverages	—	173	74	46	30	27	391	351
22. Soft Drinks	—	—	—	—	—	—	4	—
(9) Tobacco								
23. Tobacco	—	—	—	—	13	15	29	28
(10) Fibre Spinning								
24. Cotton Yarn	—	—	—	—	181	34	8	—
25. Silk Yarn	1,337	3,146	4,248	5,109	6,882	8,081	12,816	17,488
26. Woolen Yarn	—	47	37	58	391	818	490	1,015
27. Hemp & Flax Yarn	—	—	—	—	26	7	7	5
28. Chemical Fibre Yarn	—	21	67	1,322	425	741	1,348	1,053
(11) Textile Fabrics								
29. Cotton Fabrics	2,443	857	1,834	4,289	11,118	10,522	10,121	12,626
30. Silk Fabrics	—	—	—	—	250	392	285	225
31. Woolen Fabrics	—	4	1	5	758	2,842	3,143	4,397
32. Hemp Fabrics	—	—	—	—	867	1,589	1,397	94
33. Chemical Fibre Fabrics	—	66	304	1,823	3,136	4,771	8,088	14,156
34. Dyeing & Finishing	—	—	—	—	—	—	0	—
(12) Textile Products								
35. Knit Products	—	—	—	—	641	5,580	15,994	24,974
36. Rope & Fishing Nets	—	42	—	77	308	1,634	2,836	3,938
37. Apparels & Accessories	—	2	1,119	4,643	6,566	15,524	16,924	27,723
38. Misc. Textile Products	20	4	13	287	1,195	2,018	6,178	16,835

Table A. 12. (Continued)

In Thousand U.S. Dollars

I–O 117 Sector Classification	1960	1961	1962	1963	1964	1965	1966	1967
(13) Lumber & Plywood								
39. Lumber & Plywood	—	1,217	2,289	6,309	11,421	18,177	29,993	39,128
(14) Wood & Furniture								
40. Wood Products	3	17	38	38	176	273	454	376
41. Furniture	—	10	47	15	108	60	131	236
(15) Paper & Products								
42. Pulp	—	—	—	—	—	—	2	—
43. Paper	—	85	5	63	40	76	154	222
44. Paper Products	—	2	22	1	48	108	920	1,606
(16) Printing & Publishing								
45. Printing & Publishing	—	23	24	156	93	103	369	513
(17) Leather Products								
46. Leather & Fur	—	1	—	1	12	26	12	5
47. Leather Products	—	—	2	—	62	520	1,485	2,037
(18) Rubber Products								
48. Rubber Products	—	30	314	1,249	1,726	4,794	5,543	8,326
(19) Basic Chemicals								
49. Inorganic Chemicals	—	—	701	291	75	103	276	142
50. Organic Chemicals	190	397	276	590	392	271	349	186
(20) Other Chemical Products								
51. Explosives	—	—	—	—	—	—	0	0
52. Paint	—	—	—	—	—	—	1	103
53. Drugs	—	266	49	52	87	56	58	149
54. Soap	—	—	—	1	—	—	—	12

55. Cosmetics	—	—	—	1	1	17	4	18
56. Pesticides	—	—	—	—	—	—	—	0
57. Other Chemical Products	401	1	1	17	73	86	399	232
(21) Chemical Fertilizer								
58. Chemical Fertilizer	—	—	—	—	—	—	—	1,640
(22) Petroleum Products								
59. Petroleum Products	—	—	—	2	83	—	5	20
(23) Coal Products								
60. Coal Products	—	—	—	—	—	—	—	—
(24) Nonmetallic Mineral Products								
61. Cement	—	19	6	16	305	848	523	177
62. Ceramic Products	—	2	6	27	116	13	59	102
63. Glass Products	—	—	76	583	937	1,531	868	458
64. Pottery	—	—	—	98	213	190	110	74
65. Other Stone & Clay	—	3	2	5	360	170	73	218
(25) Iron & Steel								
66. Pig Iron	—	390	—	—	—	—	0	3
67. Steel Ingots	—	62	6	13	44	469	—	243
(26) Steel Products								
68. Rolled Steel	—	—	475	9,598	1,710	2,026	483	250
69. Pipes & Plated Steel	—	—	9	340	2,328	9,848	7,292	1,158
70. Cast & Forged Steel	—	—	60	652	9	5	15	141
(27) Nonferrous Metals								
71. Nonferrous Smelting	334	316	—	—	1,147	470	1,047	1,117
72. Primary Nonferrous	218	641	165	123	1,302	2,101	1,481	842
(28) Finished Metal Products								
73. Structural Metallic	—	—	140	1,167	523	778	446	664

Table A.12. (Continued)

In Thousand U.S. Dollars

I-O 117 Sector Classification	1960	1961	1962	1963	1964	1965	1966	1967
74. Other Metallic Products	864	230	579	621	902	2,170	4,467	6,220
(29) Machinery								
75. Prime Movers & Boilers	—	5	94	445	98	730	1,300	899
76. Working Machinery	—	—	—	2	64	77	90	196
77. Industrial Machinery	88	724	59	83	73	538	805	1,101
78. Other Machinery	—	—	101	512	73	115	152	642
79. Office Machines	—	3	—	3	2	1	6	24
80. Household Machines	—	—	44	46	23	464	662	825
81. Machine Spare Parts	—	—	—	—	—	91	132	98
(30) Electrical Machinery								
82. Electrical Machinery	—	—	96	517	33	161	65	1,874
83. Electronic & Comm. Eq.	—	3	10	143	610	1,431	3,409	3,763
84. Household Elec. Appliances	—	50	2	23	3	120	1,012	1,411
85. Other Electric Equipments	—	—	—	68	362	159	625	313
(31) Transport Equipments								
86. Shipbuilding	—	—	1	15	78	50	174	1,460
87. Railroad Transport Eq.	—	16	—	—	1	1	14	1
88. Motor Vehicles	—	114	289	2,081	741	1,316	794	1,147
89. Other Transport Equipments	—	20	752	146	33	179	180	557
(32) Misc. Manufacturing								
90. Measuring & Optical	—	—	7	24	399	397	388	774
91. Synthetic Resin Products	—	—	90	17	51	136	474	944
92. Other Manufactures	897	1,718	1,305	2,746	4,571	8,258	18,505	28,247
(41) Other Services								
107. Education	—	—	—	—	—	—	1	14
111. Business Service	—	—	—	—	—	—	—	—
112. Recreation	—	18	81	59	384	197	161	171

157

(42) Scrap							
115. Iron Scrap	—	37	1,144	1,059	127	214	243	307
116. Other Scrap	42	34	51	99	612	225	364	382
(43) Unclassifiable								
117. Unclassifiable	—	—	57	146	97	121	120	93
Whole Industry	31,833	38,648	54,804	86,796	118,860	174,998	247,576	320,325
	31,991	38,559	53,491	85,433	119,646	174,241	246,689	

Table A.12. (Continued)

In Thousand U.S. Dollars

I-O 117 Sector Classification	1968	1969	1970	1971	1972	1973	1974
(1) Rice, Barley & Wheat							
1. Rice, Barley & Wheat	224	233	25	14	20	8,342	220
(2) Other Agriculture							
2. Other Cereals	285	817	794	3,649	509	769	455
3. Vegetables	205	215	204	203	1,972	4,917	4,714
4. Fruit	537	795	662	517	1,994	3,671	4,795
5. Industrial Crops	13,574	22,169	25,343	27,174	25,732	42,787	63,348
6. Livestock & Sericulture	878	1,048	933	804	1,766	4,858	5,942
(3) Forestry							
7. Forestry	433	262	409	425	1,274	2,291	4,142
(4) Fishery							
8. Fishery	22,451	23,420	28,815	30,055	45,584	80,685	99,297
(5) Coal							
9. Coal	2,248	2,681	3,900	4,347	1,999	2,732	424
(6) Other Minerals							
10. Metallic Ores	25,633	25,924	31,250	23,567	23,446	23,561	31,427
11. Nonmetallic Minerals	5,833	6,931	8,290	8,751	8,275	16,506	29,156
12. Salt	48	—	—	—	21	5	—
(7) Processed Foods							
13. Meat & Dairy Products	157	904	246	690	8,943	14,051	24,980
14. Vegetable & Fruit Processing	656	1,493	3,328	6,249	10,542	34,819	38,170
15. Processing of Sea Foods	20,287	21,858	30,058	25,129	34,407	85,566	86,129
16. Grain Milling	1	20	51	2	7	7	58
17. Bakery & Confectionery	21	798	860	686	1,516	3,248	3,534
18. Sugar Refining	807	503	1,171	724	1,671	10,695	39,735
19. Seasonings	443	382	729	758	1,653	3,953	21,605

20. Other Processed Foods	832	1,394	2,042	4,094	3,478	5,008	6,255
(8) Beverages							
21. Alcoholic Beverages	850	1,286	769	1,156	1,332	758	652
22. Soft Drinks	—	—	5	—	34	24	—
(9) Tobacco							
23. Tobacco	128	188	28	52	27	77	151
(10) Fibre Spinning							
24. Cotton Yarn	121	1,603	4,973	16,229	16,794	25,263	61,104
25. Silk Yarn	20,958	27,206	40,426	43,900	58,731	84,314	68,031
26. Woolen Yarn	667	1,522	2,269	1,659	9,675	24,544	8,127
27. Hemp & Flax Yarn	1	39	210	241	157	1,261	1,425
28. Chemical Fibre Yarn	734	926	3,026	10,877	8,547	29,509	35,532
(11) Textile Fabrics							
29. Cotton Fabrics	13,668	19,409	27,173	32,732	40,931	62,534	58,796
30. Silk Fabrics	1,334	810	940	1,299	3,365	66,663	71,325
31. Woolen Fabrics	4,672	3,849	3,753	3,283	7,938	14,102	12,001
32. Hemp Fabrics	158	93	30	23	173	616	721
33. Chemical Fibre Fabrics	22,215	16,970	14,876	19,811	47,882	129,602	134,052
34. Dyeing & Finishing	—	—	—	—	—	—	—
(12) Textile Products							
35. Knit Products	51,891	79,645	93,993	136,371	238,936	365,937	420,663
36. Rope & Fishing Nets	3,920	5,712	6,835	16,975	9,970	19,913	38,393
37. Apparels & Accessories	45,954	60,875	92,787	143,578	164,805	341,072	453,390
38. Misc. Textile Products	23,983	30,620	38,915	40,541	52,277	71,457	64,476
(13) Lumber & Plywood							
39. Lumber & Plywood	65,695	79,721	92,458	127,979	169,285	308,872	194,979
(14) Wood & Furniture							
40. Wood Products	540	1,059	2,031	1,915	3,405	19,798	27,651
41. Furniture	893	1,257	2,107	2,080	6,968	20,711	18,049

Table A.12. (Continued)

In Thousand U.S. Dollars

I-O 117 Sector Classification	1968	1969	1970	1971	1972	1973	1974
(15) Paper & Products							
42. Pulp	—	1	1	2	1	69	73
43. Paper	73	4	46	142	1,972	16,381	18,712
44. Paper Products	2,228	2,143	3,552	2,984	5,710	9,724	19,704
(16) Printing & Publishing							
45. Printing & Publishing	243	258	605	1,695	11,515	28,310	12,771
(17) Leather Products							
46. Leather & Fur	23	42	146	272	2,106	1,281	1,033
47. Leather Products	1,559	1,405	2,496	5,396	10,931	27,475	69,546
(18) Rubber Products							
48. Rubber Products	12,112	11,797	18,016	36,470	54,201	90,167	192,241
(19) Basic Chemicals							
49. Inorganic Chemicals	119	193	1,077	477	632	4,907	10,398
50. Organic Chemicals	330	373	500	1,126	13,733	18,098	37,651
(20) Other Chemical Products							
51. Explosives	1	—	23	12	35	254	268
52. Paint	16	9	4	—	101	413	474
53. Drugs	163	1,042	1,369	2,074	2,381	4,599	6,119
54. Soap	1	15	21	232	483	945	1,367
55. Cosmetics	9	4	116	13	10	8	153
56. Pesticides	—	2	1	301	207	434	1,589
57. Other Chemical Products	1,177	1,923	6,044	15,325	17,623	25,535	36,267
(21) Chemical Fertilizer							
58. Chemical Fertilizer	1,899	6,230	6,333	7,531	11,561	5,064	—
(22) Petroleum Products							
59. Petroleum Products	74	2,155	4,742	6,941	16,196	32,640	107,633

(23) Coal Products							
60. Coal Products	21	4	6	—	3	185	317
(24) Nonmetallic Mineral Products							
61. Cement	191	3,276	4,442	10,587	12,718	19,620	48,946
62. Ceramic Products	158	1,091	856	749	3,066	11,334	14,328
63. Glass Products	455	481	762	1,703	6,148	8,535	10,475
64. Pottery	30	257	187	136	1,046	3,245	2,954
65. Other Stone & Clay	55	88	404	278	957	4,134	8,005
(25) Iron & Steel							
66. Pig Iron	20	—	24	83	276	990	1,858
67. Steel Ingots	26	306	3,158	450	1,189	2,192	9,970
(26) Steel Products							
68. Rolled Steel	844	3,818	9,251	22,285	80,027	143,971	268,993
69. Pipes & Plated Steel	122	445	464	1,182	9,534	25,701	135,750
70. Cast & Forged Steel	92	200	186	202	866	9,253	19,923
(27) Nonferrous Metals							
71. Nonferrous Smelting	1,366	4,718	5,592	3,098	4,668	2,284	3,466
72. Primary Nonferrous	52	19	35	73	1,160	4,925	4,938
(28) Finished Metal Products							
73. Structural Metallic	552	865	2,325	3,004	5,401	22,176	60,830
74. Other Metallic Products	9,310	9,086	10,456	11,363	18,442	51,851	86,901
(29) Machinery							
75. Prime Movers & Boilers	240	1,061	1,772	2,164	4,220	1,428	399
76. Working Machinery	57	201	212	186	3,012	1,621	1,923
77. Industrial Machinery	652	641	1,062	1,841	4,039	9,185	9,203
78. Other Machinery	180	495	1,102	901	2,414	3,390	3,083
79. Office Machines	2,386	4,979	3,339	5,289	13,786	32,753	40,667
80. Household Machines	309	1,014	431	844	2,625	5,817	9,038
81. Machine Spare Parts	25	49	111	123	639	1,808	2,255

Table A.12. (Continued)

In Thousand U.S. Dollars

I-0 117 Sector Classification	1968	1969	1970	1971	1972	1973	1974
(30) Electrical Machinery							
82. Electrical Machinery	4,412	8,659	6,316	3,886	8,684	24,803	47,248
83. Electronic & Comm. Eq.	13,569	26,836	35,873	65,025	117,990	311,817	446,151
84. Household Elec. Appliances	676	995	1,739	2,422	5,926	12,176	15,082
85. Other Electric Equipments	234	149	709	1,433	2,127	5,976	18,980
(31) Transport Equipments							
86. Shipbuilding	40	6,417	2,526	3,042	667	5,995	78,284
87. Railroad Transport Equipments	—	23	—	196	256	3,689	11,709
88. Motor Vehicles	1,358	1,124	1,733	2,256	4,081	4,762	4,596
89. Other Transport Equipments	271	473	5,280	1,916	10,755	13,199	34,840
(32) Misc. Manufacturing							
90. Measuring & Optical	900	1,767	2,695	3,521	7,988	22,041	54,119
91. Synthetic Resin Products	1,317	1,719	3,132	5,568	13,922	55,112	95,649
92. Other Manufactures	39,991	67,246	113,672	88,993	115,779	194,217	250,849
(41) Other Services							
107. Education	13	2	1	3	2	8	11
111. Business Service	—	—	—	3	—	1	259
112. Recreation	230	412	690	1,102	702	522	443
(42) Scrap							
115. Iron Scrap	553	994	1,302	979	688	724	1,131
116. Other Scrap	580	411	1,534	1,188	1,356	2,228	2,770
(43) Unclassifiable							
117. Unclassifiable	0	3	—	—	—	—	—
Whole Industry	455,249	622,556	835,185	1,067,606	1,632,599	3,225,292	4,456,246

Source: The same as Table A.8.

Table A.13. Commodity Imports: 1952-59

In Thousand U.S. Dollars

I-0 43 Sector Classification	1952	1953	1954	1955	1956	1957	1958	1959
1. Rice, Barley & Wheat	57,776	118,080	19,827	4,460	30,205	80,813	45,353	14,495
2. Other Agriculture	11,474	9,198	17,710	24,718	26,921	42,311	37,948	35,118
3. Forestry	4,815	3,806	4,103	1,630	4,932	3,871	4,463	6,653
4. Coal	1,773	1,779	—	—	—	—	—	—
5. Other Minerals	—	—	793	382	457	1,741	709	284
7. Processed Foods	13,731	41,669	19,195	9,635	12,421	12,110	15,360	8,750
8. Beverages	—	—	—	5,798	5,285	5,393	4,104	14
9. Tobacco	—	—	—	12	4,850	2,125	—	—
10. Fibre Spinning	16,535	17,893	29,449	27,763	27,504	21,202	20,270	19,578
11. Textile Fabrics	14,061	1,969	3,367	3,062	5,216	8,229	9,186	8,946
12. Textile Products	11,662	17,115	3,231	8,727	2,208	4,138	3,672	2,103
13. Lumber & Plywood	5,024	11,045	1,668	4,134	8,775	7,445	11,053	6,385
14. Furniture	—	—	3,851	1,007	513	788	770	336
15. Paper & Products	4,032	9,042	14,209	9,236	11,994	12,302	17,620	9,965
17. Leather Products	—	—	360	451	947	694	641	444
18. Rubber Products	476	6,369	2,089	1,171	1,979	1,012	296	144
19. Basic Chemicals	3,785	9,317	13,477	5,547	7,224	6,480	8,088	7,257
20. Other Chemicals	6,426	3,705	6,531	8,778	11,554	13,907	17,215	15,936
21. Chemical Fertilizer	25,964	29,069	28,775	48,233	58,261	58,935	45,969	48,049
22. Petroleum Products	7,432	11,474	14,034	14,634	19,942	23,333	21,731	29,196
23. Coal Products	—	415	1,213	28,581	24,661	20,220	15,362	8,994
24. Nonmetallic Mineral Products	744	2,213	1,531	3,424	8,429	9,074	7,621	1,800
26. Steel Products	108	890	3,775	3,754	8,647	8,975	8,706	6,851
27. Nonferrous Metal	—	—	483	1,195	1,644	3,334	3,845	3,485
28. Finished Metal Products	—	—	—	1,827	9,576	6,578	8,406	2,971
29. Machinery	729	3,610	11,191	17,566	17,067	18,989	16,541	24,233
30. Electrical Machinery	—	6,537	3,569	21,516	13,446	11,404	10,702	9,493
31. Transport Equipments	7,429	9,441	10,477	18,142	12,410	12,045	8,985	8,129
32. Misc. Manufacturing	534	1,056	3,056	3,226	7,632	5,377	7,459	5,552
43. Unclassifiable	19,655	29,744	25,363	62,800	41,358	39,349	26,089	18,635
Total Commodity Imports	214,165	345,436	243,327	341,409	386,058	442,174	378,165	303,796

Table A. 14. Competitive Imports (1968 Basis): 1960-74

In Thousand U.S. Dollars

I-O 117 Sector Classification	1960	1961	1962	1963	1964	1965	1966	1967
(1) Rice, Barley & Wheat								
1. Rice, Barley & Wheat	19,394	29,297	32,634	98,193	51,324	41,651	44,348	71,515
(2) Other Agriculture								
2. Other Cereals	759	1,155	1,593	1,128	1,684	144	288	4,112
3. Vegetables	61	101	20	0	206	211	176	179
4. Fruit	0	0	0	0	0	7	138	7
5. Industrial Crops	1,604	2,117	1,282	1,316	445	528	341	597
6. Livestock & Sericulture	1,981	913	787	238	440	468	793	680
(3) Forestry								
7. Forestry	457	436	4,192	6,296	2,077	682	1,621	2,065
(4) Fishery								
8. Fishery	2	56	15	9	69	374	173	2,113
(5) Coal								
9. Coal	584	4,852	0	0	24	98	17	2
(6) Other Minerals								
10. Metallic Ores	67	55	575	1,494	1,656	806	910	1,383
11. Nonmetallic Minerals	211	141	1,242	2,185	1,145	1,598	2,174	4,180
12. Salt	0	0	0	0	97	273	1	3
(7) Processed Foods								
13. Meat & Dairy Products	1,868	1,493	3,079	3,581	2,104	3,359	3,030	2,368
14. Vegetable & Fruit Processing	167	4	185	313	336	436	365	465
15. Processing of Sea Foods	0	1	49	7	18	16	46	38
16. Grain Milling	4	6	5,785	7,829	8,755	12,480	16,603	3,900
17. Bakery & Confectionery	53	40	19	21	83	62	168	182

18. Sugar Refining	2,618	2,653	687	657	246	536	816	681
19. Seasonings	67	305	313	561	56	93	239	229
20. Other Processed Foods	360	42	247	4,396	505	644	772	4,030
(8) Beverages								
21. Alcoholic Beverages	368	196	72	82	108	159	211	507
22. Soft Drinks	0	32	10	113	4	17	32	35
(9) Tobacco								
23. Tobacco	0	0	6	12	7	7	23	101
(10) Fibre Spinning								
24. Cotton Yarn	15	35	57	58	210	177	738	531
25. Silk Yarn	0	23	60	23	2	5	69	323
26. Woolen Yarn	58	12	107	26	4	19	327	147
27. Hemp & Flax Yarn	0	0	0	0	1	10	—	1
28. Chemical Fibre Yarn	6,307	10,300	14,299	9,649	5,160	5,869	5,327	10,988
(11) Textile Fabrics								
29. Cotton Fabrics	19	0	1	1,740	1,579	2,428	2,332	2,882
30. Silk Fabrics	0	0	0	0	104	430	1,197	5,465
31. Woolen Fabrics	137	142	44	40	292	305	526	750
32. Hemp Fabrics	0	0	0	0	754	925	729	105
33. Chemical Fibre Fabrics	0	19	267	3,496	1,235	2,664	6,167	9,814
34. Dyeing & Finishing	0	0	0	0	0	0	0	—
(12) Textile Products								
35. Knit Products	0	0	0	0	184	438	236	77
36. Rope & Fishing Nets	268	457	602	347	418	358	532	611
37. Apparels & Accessories	57	67	213	323	184	241	170	82
38. Misc. Textile Products	660	1,158	825	537	661	651	713	856

Table A.14. (Continued)

In Thousand U.S. Dollars

I-O 117 Sector Classification	1960	1961	1962	1963	1964	1965	1966	1967
(13) Lumber & Plywood								
39. Lumber & Plywood	252	0	926	1,095	336	373	1,614	2,030
(14) Wood & Furniture								
40. Wood Products	104	143	123	109	105	56	105	151
41. Furniture	6	9	130	136	66	35	67	103
(15) Paper & Products								
42. Pulp	1,691	1,538	1,019	737	1,860	1,604	3,103	4,311
43. Paper	7,237	4,106	3,256	1,922	1,400	889	2,421	3,117
44. Paper Products	495	369	384	328	356	552	999	1,290
(16) Printing & Publishing								
45. Printing & Publishing	629	684	1,083	1,079	1,029	890	1,017	1,597
(17) Leather Products								
46. Leather & Fur	0	0	6	2	27	5	68	87
47. Leather Products	12	8	48	56	58	157	247	377
(18) Rubber Products								
48. Rubber Products	69	132	344	939	700	878	1,436	4,399
(19) Basic Chemicals								
49. Inorganic Chemicals	3,379	3,039	2,405	3,825	2,446	2,638	3,685	6,035
50. Organic Chemicals	7,154	7,062	9,714	9,361	2,828	3,322	4,906	9,662
(20) Other Chemical Products								
51. Explosives	0	74	46	50	45	53	67	91
52. Paint	373	335	680	515	190	227	591	549
53. Drugs	2,524	4,127	3,257	2,050	1,807	1,690	2,004	3,366
54. Soap	58	0	216	470	462	1,017	981	1,590

55. Cosmetics	0	15	2	5	13	30	91	58
56. Pesticides	717	456	1,247	1,800	1,309	2,147	679	1,158
57. Other Chemical Products	18,522	14,249	21,281	25,854	16,009	22,163	42,063	58,237
(21) Chemical Fertilizer								
58. Chemical Fertilizer	30,532	19,138	33,084	23,293	45,538	49,702	81,314	44,148
(22) Petroleum Products								
59. Petroleum Products	21,851	20,778	24,452	28,520	11,533	4,026	8,350	19,552
(23) Coal Products								
60. Coal Products	561	1,870	3,629	2,860	1,275	2,255	2,650	1,426
(24) Nonmetallic Mineral Products								
61. Cement	1,146	1,489	3,595	5,246	729	257	3,186	8,497
62. Ceramic Products	926	372	1,476	908	772	583	1,383	1,659
63. Glass Products	1,130	693	494	350	306	295	923	1,034
64. Pottery	0	6	121	255	592	488	730	1,717
65. Other Stone & Clay	118	510	270	387	284	499	676	1,497
(25) Iron & Steel								
66. Pig Iron	0	0	547	496	1,006	500	2,568	2,023
67. Steel Ingots	1,213	2,319	1,137	4,580	3,055	1,270	4,999	2,271
(26) Steel Products								
68. Rolled Steel	7,287	3,633	11,435	16,896	5,461	14,935	20,610	30,547
69. Pipes & Plated Steel	1,118	468	2,179	6,219	1,091	1,407	3,019	4,703
70. Cast & Forged Steel	248	216	215	29	205	146	444	1,632
(27) Nonferrous Metals								
71. Nonferrous Smelting	772	1,125	1,719	2,783	1,549	4,052	3,478	3,649
72. Primary Nonferrous	139	166	660	1,444	307	271	869	1,172
(28) Finished Metal Products								
73. Structural Metallic	1,217	653	3,947	5,522	967	2,060	8,477	10,107

Table A.14. (Continued)

In Thousand U.S. Dollars

I-O 117 Sector Classification	1960	1961	1962	1963	1964	1965	1966	1967
74. Other Metallic Products	3,269	1,767	4,284	2,860	2,426	4,729	9,704	17,100
(29) Machinery								
75. Prime Movers & Boilers	865	1,274	1,546	8,292	5,376	1,574	3,807	12,484
76. Working Machinery	84	1,975	300	668	1,356	1,984	3,602	6,720
77. Industrial Machinery	7,326	7,228	8,718	14,595	12,562	11,524	35,993	34,253
78. Other Machinery	752	1,224	992	2,109	3,851	5,034	13,295	17,489
79. Office Machines	0	0	0	0	22	15	30	133
80. Household Machines	322	245	1,531	917	359	1,373	2,240	2,668
81. Machine Spare Parts	135	160	0	0	672	439	567	1,342
(30) Electrical Machinery								
82. Electrical Machinery	2,337	2,777	6,665	4,594	5,250	2,599	6,038	15,053
83. Electronic & Comm. Eq.	4,530	4,811	12,325	3,440	5,303	1,963	5,159	4,096
84. Household Elec. Appliances	156	123	961	683	278	293	1,641	1,060
85. Other Electric Equipments	1,757	2,703	1,000	2,389	1,515	521	1,250	4,006
(31) Transport Equipments								
86. Shipbuilding	15,350	5,557	749	4,316	2,018	10,475	38,984	56,155
87. Railroad Transport Eq.	283	169	1,795	8,960	1,835	3,295	997	21,060
88. Motor Vehicles	60	349	2,887	7,219	5,110	7,090	8,832	22,456
89. Other Transport Equipments	49	222	90	29	61	32	53	44
(32) Misc. Manufacturing								
90. Measuring & Optical	1,937	858	654	415	699	712	1,614	2,865
91. Synthetic Resin Products	0	0	0	0	2	6	11	24
92. Other Manufactures	1,013	945	1,303	1,125	403	428	758	1,712

(41) Other Services								
107. Education	0	0	0	0	3	0	16	15
111. Business Service	0	0	0	0	4	0	4	24
112. Recreation	141	603	865	921	414	418	892	1,208
(42) Scrap								
115. Iron Scrap	0	6	981	3,437	2,549	4,545	12,377	18,869
116. Other Scrap	1,507	84	2,620	4,522	5,543	3,609	3,459	4,304
(43) Unclassifiable								
117. Unclassifiable	32,267	14,961	1,385	1,130	1,261	2	4	—
Whole Indstury	223,766	193,931	256,045	367,412	246,891	263,331	453,535	609,555

Table A.14. (Continued)

In Thousand U.S. Dollars

I-O 117 Sector Classification	1968	1969	1970	1971	1972	1973	1974
(1) Rice, Barley & Wheat							
1. Rice, Barley & Wheat	118,002	218,344	225,851	269,418	253,224	395,167	535,375
(2) Other Agriculture							
2. Other Cereals	3,414	11,426	18,571	31,572	28,058	60,987	87,046
3. Vegetables	281	625	2,491	1,434	301	432	8,430
4. Fruit	1	8	5	6	177	526	836
5. Industrial Crops	1,861	2,284	2,582	5,863	9,688	12,856	17,194
6. Livestock & Sericulture	1,690	3,200	3,962	5,518	5,110	12,184	10,057
(3) Forestry							
7. Forestry	4,042	3,122	3,442	2,523	2,383	5,646	7,429
(4) Fishery							
8. Fishery	70	103	293	295	1,605	5,908	8,552
(5) Coal							
9. Coal	6	0	1	24	218	10	4
(6) Other Minerals							
10. Metallic Ores	4,794	7,893	8,283	10,133	17,395	49,775	88,955
11. Nonmetallic Minerals	4,069	5,596	7,117	8,242	11,862	18,709	19,664
12. Salt	1	298	2,600	5,212	2,981	550	31
(7) Processed Foods							
13. Meat & Dairy Products	9,927	8,219	11,656	15,273	17,264	33,667	52,670
14. Vegetable & Fruit Processing	730	1,330	2,217	2,992	3,659	6,121	4,592
15. Processing of Sea Foods	132	450	223	124	477	6,560	1,042
16. Grain Milling	8,159	24,309	3,355	10,888	5,770	3,858	3,535
17. Bakery & Confectionery	464	585	391	525	789	684	989

18. Sugar Refining	2,077	3,713	5,243	7,097	6,237	13,209	15,752
19. Seasonings	961	2,263	2,786	3,091	3,004	2,561	2,161
20. Other Processed Foods	13,233	15,295	18,769	30,061	4,213	3,348	4,212
(8) Beverages							
21. Alcoholic Beverages	351	446	717	339	496	932	664
22. Soft Drinks	130	275	124	33	18	6	1
(9) Tobacco							
23. Tobacco	196	315	424	424	263	130	93
(10) Fibre Spinning							
24. Cotton Yarn	2,663	853	1,033	647	668	12,960	2,776
25. Silk Yarn	88	50	377	1,588	303	1,904	2,793
26. Woolen Yarn	600	912	554	774	972	3,440	5,136
27. Hemp & Flax Yarn	27	10	51	71	92	179	241
28. Chemical Fibre Yarn	23,970	23,959	19,075	12,366	12,799	21,961	31,558
(11) Textile Fabrics							
29. Cotton Fabrics	6,211	5,485	4,969	6,295	10,549	20,479	34,013
30. Silk Fabrics	1,942	2,711	3,922	4,340	3,783	9,308	328
31. Woolen Fabrics	1,010	3,539	6,522	6,576	5,375	12,463	13,103
32. Hemp Fabrics	242	654	878	326	730	469	639
33. Chemical Fibre Fabrics	20,670	28,855	46,294	63,341	48,013	115,606	107,231
34. Dyeing & Finishing	—	—	—	—	—	—	—
(12) Textile Products							
35. Knit Products	80	55	270	8,467	22,759	24,662	15,841
36. Rope & Fishing Nets	742	636	406	283	315	295	613
37. Apparels & Accessories	283	341	292	1,453	3,435	2,256	2,152
38. Misc. Textile Products	2,029	3,153	4,303	4,965	7,454	15,891	19,764

Table A.14. (Continued)

In Thousand U.S. Dollars

I-O 117 Sector Classification	1968	1969	1970	1971	1972	1973	1974
(13) Lumber & Plywood							
39. Lumber & Plywood	2,657	3,544	1,898	1,399	843	2,903	1,889
(14) Wood & Furniture							
40. Wood Products	400	450	551	895	671	822	1,778
41. Furniture	605	1,125	1,169	1,051	920	2,594	2,389
(15) Paper & Products							
42. Pulp	5,719	6,600	9,224	9,535	4,253	6,067	41,438
43. Paper	5,309	4,327	5,745	7,636	6,474	7,050	8,023
44. Paper Products	2,063	2,199	2,826	3,170	3,349	6,314	10,888
(16) Printing & Publishing							
45. Printing & Publishing	4,424	10,844	5,801	6,223	4,566	4,900	6,232
(17) Leather Products							
46. Leather & Fur	176	440	1,472	2,510	3,741	13,183	23,668
47. Leather Products	369	343	334	553	721	1,571	1,059
(18) Rubber Products							
48. Rubber Products	6,312	7,915	8,832	11,078	12,891	12,484	23,779
(19) Basic Chemicals							
49. Inorganic Chemicals	6,298	3,971	3,493	6,206	6,056	11,514	14,764
50. Organic Chemicals	11,681	14,772	18,746	16,341	29,878	28,039	38,067
(20) Other Chemical Products							
51. Explosives	107	119	109	253	243	178	285
52. Paint	963	1,489	2,276	2,342	3,082	7,279	14,970
53. Drugs	1,953	1,294	1,434	1,170	2,181	1,414	2,266
54. Soap	2,027	2,136	2,514	2,514	3,251	5,219	8,304

55. Cosmetics	193	361	880	472	256	448	417
56. Pesticides	1,302	1,641	848	946	969	953	678
57. Other Chemical Products	67,767	67,056	83,451	77,408	83,290	154,154	143,709
(21) Chemical Fertilizer							
58. Chemical Fertilizer	20,289	8,013	2,774	6,340	9,061	15,010	50,057
(22) Petroleum Products							
59. Petroleum Products	13,819	5,561	5,462	10,392	7,806	14,803	47,740
(23) Coal Products							
60. Coal Products	2,566	..	3,118	3,526	3,004	2,049	3,948	8,420
(24) Nonmetallic Mineral Products							
61. Cement	2,529	366	63	154	95	124	1,687
62. Ceramic Products	2,953	3,042	3,311	3,334	10,551	5,881	11,879
63. Glass Products	2,416	4,200	3,686	3,196	4,315	8,424	10,665
64. Pottery	2,089	1,985	2,416	3,100	2,399	3,182	7,052
65. Other Stone & Clay	1,132	1,845	1,920	2,628	3,553	2,525	5,275
(25) Iron & Steel							
66. Pig Iron	4,335	3,333	919	3,268	4,720	7,787	15,171
67. Steel Ingots	1,698	6,035	2,605	7,902	14,460	47,544	23,033
(26) Steel Products							
68. Rolled Steel	17,328	17,564	17,007	23,526	20,010	60,561	121,167
69. Pipes & Plated Steel	10,216	12,037	9,375	17,050	11,475	8,887	18,419
70. Cast & Forged Steel	1,586	1,567	3,941	2,046	2,402	4,737	6,845
(27) Nonferrous Metals							
71. Nonferrous Smelting	4,208	4,590	10,005	8,880	7,312	19,345	40,733
72. Primary Nonferrous	1,479	3,585	4,142	5,337	5,883	11,873	23,047
(28) Finished Metal Products							
73. Structural Metallic	17,173	26,590	24,373	26,942	22,272	16,093	18,125

Table A.14. (Continued)

In Thousand U.S. Dollars

I-O 117 Sector Classification	1968	1969	1970	1971	1972	1973	1974
74. Other Metallic Products	19,377	22,047	21,554	24,413	18,622	29,444	45,987
(29) Machinery							
75. Prime Movers & Boilers	25,299	20,828	25,214	22,839	23,837	18,062	28,403
76. Working Machinery	9,421	8,624	11,452	23,553	35,427	36,239	38,431
77. Industrial Machinery	80,228	82,013	89,197	95,259	52,366	168,717	220,551
78. Other Machinery	31,125	38,272	34,967	39,185	55,285	34,980	65,352
79. Office Machines	1,246	768	777	616	676	2,581	3,424
80. Household Machines	3,826	4,260	5,631	6,542	5,703	15,479	15,130
81. Machine Spare Parts	1,609	2,881	4,083	5,761	6,382	8,475	11,083
(30) Electrical Machinery							
82. Electrical Machinery	27,533	31,622	37,382	39,102	50,734	52,153	79,684
83. Electronic & Comm. Eq.	5,204	6,342	5,798	12,664	34,118	76,390	109,182
84. Household Elec. Appliances	2,061	2,804	3,339	3,250	2,314	2,338	3,727
85. Other Electric Equipments	3,862	3,265	3,555	7,819	8,546	10,832	17,042
(31) Transport Equipments							
86. Shipbuilding	59,887	61,366	45,794	57,656	73,387	51,620	388,453
87. Railroad Transport Eq.	28,211	27,428	11,942	8,638	6,107	4,422	9,338
88. Motor Vehicles	62,682	62,124	64,497	51,724	38,135	59,825	91,250
89. Other Transport Equipments	63	52	83	233	1,230	5,618	4,477
(32) Misc. Manufacturing							
90. Measuring & Optical	4,747	7,529	9,332	11,117	11,107	13,512	36,092
91. Synthetic Resin Products	69	121	214	91	129	18	62
92. Other Manufactures	12,846	14,157	7,335	7,757	8,765	16,701	22,917

(41) Other Services							
107. Education	28	62	56	67	38	55	82
111. Business Service	6	10	34	49	44	55	49
112. Recreation	1,395	2,584	2,392	3,110	2,674	2,446	2,153
(42) Scrap							
115. Iron Scrap	22,915	40,326	61,885	53,569	27,740	74,413	172,040
116. Other Scrap	5,277	3,543	6,246	4,514	4,944	14,125	26,381
(43) Unclassifiable							
117. Unclassifiable	—	—	—	—	—	—	—
Whole Industry	870,206	1,058,397	1,109,936	1,280,908	1,256,747	2,072,009	3,250,680

Source: The same as Table A.8.

Table A.15. Non-Competitive Imports (1968 Basis): 1960-74

In Thousand U.S. Dollars

I-O 117 Sector Classification	1960	1961	1962	1963	1964	1965	1966	1967
(2) Other Agriculture								
3. Vegetables	—	—	—	—	2	1	8	15
4. Fruit	154	142	22	95	27	12	17	283
5. Industrial Crops	357	253	714	611	1,378	2,183	4,044	3,378
6. Livestock & Sericulture	—	—	121	73	46	41	131	416
(3) Forestry								
7. Forestry	0	5	4	46	58	116	90	135
(4) Fishery								
8. Fishery	171	0	265	131	27	164	385	605
(5) Coal								
9. Coal	0	0	2,213	2,173	2,362	1,732	845	990
(6) Other Minerals								
10. Metallic Ores	—	—	0	0	21	5	58	350
11. Nonmetallic Minerals	—	—	834	1,241	366	476	690	1,234
(7) Processed Foods								
13. Meat & Diary Products	—	—	—	—	—	1	—	1
14. Vegetable & Fruit Processing	—	—	25	5	—	—	9	8
16. Grain Milling	—	23	—	—	18	—	2	1
18. Sugar Refining	14	24	5	2	—	—	1	1
19. Seasonings	24	24	119	427	44	45	55	100
20. Other Processed Foods	350	271	291	44	20	28	12	82
(10) Fibre Spining								
26. Woolen Yarn	0	18	0	0	0	0	0	5
28. Chemical Fibre Yarn	—	—	—	—	—	—	—	—

(12) Textile Products							
38. Misc. Textile Products	—	—	—	—	—	309	360
(13) Lumber & Plywood							
39. Lumber & Plywood	0	0	182	158	43	34	0	0
(14) Wood & Furniture							
40. Wood Products	—	—	—	—	—	—	2	13
(15) Paper & Products							
42. Pulp	1,687	3,444	7,136	7,976	6,398	7,207	9,199	11,318
43. Paper	—	—	—	—	82	40	42	79
44. Paper Products	—	—	—	—	59	33	56	68
(17) Leather Products							
46. Leather & Fur	—	—	—	—	17	4	29	43
(18) Rubber Products							
48. Rubber Products	—	—	—	—	56	24	38	73
(19) Basic Chemicals							
49. Inorganic Chemicals	680	1,163	2,263	2,292	2,517	3,001	3,712	6,765
50. Organic Chemicals	2,599	3,269	6,283	5,999	10,816	12,451	16,158	24,981
(20) Other Chemical Products							
51. Explosives	—	—	—	—	44	68	146	125
52. Paint	—	—	—	—	6	11	33	25
53. Drugs	840	1,088	2,444	2,413	1,968	3,247	4,109	4,445
57. Other Chemical Products	2,156	783	3,358	2,592	8,269	13,511	14,077	19,132
(21) Chemical Fertilizer							
58. Chemical Fertilizer	24,843	21,150	29,233	25,629	13,179	18,309	8,251	3,876
(22) Petroleum Products							
59. Petroleum Products	37	34	43	50	1,043	1,452	1,057	192

Table A.15. (Continued)

In Thousand U.S. Dollars

1-O 117 Sector Classification	1960	1961	1962	1963	1964	1965	1966	1967
(23) Coal Products								
60. Coal Products	—	—	—	—	—	—	35	18
(24) Nonmetallic Mineral Products								
63. Glass Products	—	—	—	—	34	45	5	—
65. Other Stone & Clay	—	—	—	—	10	22	38	22
(25) Iron & Steel								
66. Pig Iron	—	0	—	—	7	8	—	149
67. Steel Ingots	—	0	—	—	109	253	312	870
(26) Steel Products								
68. Rolled Steel	815	747	3,007	3,544	3,242	5,626	6,973	12,249
69. Pipes & Plated Steel	—	—	—	—	11	3	108	38
(27) Nonferrous Metals								
71. Nonferrous Smelting	—	2,110	5,104	4,084	1,920	3,715	5,887	6,445
72. Primary Nonferrous	2,169	60	95	123	156	187	826	1,250
(28) Finished Metal Products								
73. Structural Metallic	—	—	0	0	146	381	456	659
74. Other Metallic Products	146	196	37	44	230	680	40	69
(29) Machinery								
75. Prime Movers & Boilers	1,501	3,414	7,805	7,225	2,415	894	2,136	11,562
76. Working Machinery	856	0	1,234	1,841	799	1,339	2,029	4,596
77. Industrial Machinery	2,282	1,582	796	2,077	3,980	6,627	12,567	19,974
78. Other Machinery	0	0	—	—	4,595	2,939	14,052	17,198
79. Office Machines	—	328	1,045	570	84	329	510	1,956
80. Household Machines	—	0	—	—	—	—	—	—

81. Machine Spare Parts	—	—	—	—	583	430	2,593	2,497
(30) Electrical Machinery								
82. Electrical Machinery	1,151	7,155	3,241	7,217	4,291	3,733	6,171	11,884
83. Electronic & Comm. Eq.	276	840	1,868	1,539	2,048	2,156	2,732	7,740
84. Household Elec. Appliances	0	0	—	—	46	23	102	424
85. Other Electric Equipments	—	0	2,332	2,071	472	889	2,141	2,263
(31) Transport Equipments								
86. Shipbuilding	—	—	10,894	23,219	23	1	678	1,114
87. Railroad Transport Eq.	42	174	1,159	10,360	305	232	286	11,619
88. Motor Vehicles	—	—	164	476	320	824	1,355	4,395
89. Other Transport Equipments	21	0	224	681	2,386	4,178	921	9,705
(32) Misc. Manufacturing								
90. Measuring & Optical	2,039	2,423	5,153	3,818	2,274	3,234	4,260	7,572
91. Synthetic Resin Products	—	—	183	107	263	364	1,022	1,829
92. Other Manufactures	—	—	—	—	—	—	8	11
(42) Scrap								
116. Other Scrap	—	—	1,013	595	1	1	727	1,034
(43) Unclassifiable								
117. Unclassifiable	—	—	—	—	209	482	—	—
Whole Industry	45,210	50,696	100,909	121,548	79,825	103,791	132,535	218,242

179

Table A.15. (Continued)

In Thousand U.S. Dollars

I-O 117 Sector Classification	1968	1969	1970	1971	1972	1973	1974
(2) Other Agriculture							
3. Vegetables	82	55	145	146	127	242	486
4. Fruit	263	429	523	654	3,420	1,172	1,549
5. Industrial Crops	2,359	2,743	3,509	4,841	5,143	6,878	7,672
6. Livestock & Sericulture	138	211	266	359	466	574	207
(3) Forestry							
7. Forestry	882	656	936	814	693	640	1,127
(4) Fishery							
8. Fishery	508	732	893	875	943	2,021	2,099
(5) Coal							
9. Coal	860	481	308	306	—	14,276	28,657
(6) Other Minerals							
10. Metallic Ores	39	70	222	412	410	757	1,507
11. Nonmetallic Minerals	7,026	8,125	8,413	8,375	7,810	10,495	25,471
12. Salt	—	284	193	—	152	3,327	7,442
(7) Processed Foods							
13. Meat & Dairy Products	5	5	11	13	9	19	29
14. Vegetable & Fruit Processing	15	9	8	12	11	20	112
16. Grain Milling	2	4	—	—	1	0	503
17. Bakery & Confectionery	—	—	—	—	—	0	0
18. Sugar Refining	0	0	0	0	0	0	1
19. Seasonings	87	246	125	740	74	260	516
20. Other Processed Foods	20	19	76	78	73	106	331

(10) Fibre Spinning								
26. Woolen Yarn	0	0	0	0	0	0	1	0
(11) Textile Fabrics								
29. Cotton Fabrics	—	—	—	—	3	1	1	585
(12) Textile Products								
37. Apparels & Accessories	—	6	1	11	9	0	0	0
38. Misc. Textile Products	528	705	729	815	893	1,591	2,343
(13) Lumber & Plywood								
39. Lumber & Plywood	0	0	0	0	0	0	0	1
(14) Wood & Furniture								
40. Wood Products	49	60	114	112	91	90	78
(15) Paper & Products								
42. Pulp	19,045	17,910	21,965	25,700	30,786	58,940	69,791
43. Paper	116	113	256	377	493	666	897
44. Paper Products	673	941	1,233	2,054	1,969	3,418	3,896
(17) Leather Products								
46. Leather & Fur	78	110	129	287	809	2,483	9,590
(18) Rubber Products								
48. Rubber Products	72	78	174	59	40	207	237
(19) Basic Chemicals								
49. Inorganic Chemicals	6,699	10,378	11,895	14,451	12,532	23,311	37,123
50. Organic Chemicals	39,482	53,010	72,373	97,944	97,893	173,042	336,779
(20) Other Chemical Products								
51. Explosives	223	262	304	328	373	507	603
52. Paint	228	299	398	172	201	406	1,108
53. Drugs	9,833	11,513	13,694	12,404	10,816	16,351	22,278

Table A.15. (Continued)

In Thousand U.S. Dollars

I-O 117 Sector Classification	1968	1969	1970	1971	1972	1973	1974
54. Soap	285	370	460	475	523	1,045	1,007
57. Other Chemical Products	26,162	41,804	54,059	65,588	69,585	108,599	150,715
(21) Chemical Fertilizer							
58. Chemical Fertilizer	10,333	3,888	1,309	778	2,084	2,556	2,843
(22) Petroleum Products							
59. Petroleum Products	2,442	2,570	2,640	3,190	2,390	3,880	7,975
(23) Coal Products							
60. Coal Products	—	28	96	45	1	14	12
(24) Nonmetallic Mineral Products							
61. Cement	9	22	37	44	19	44	28
63. Glass Products	24	8	19	21	31	87	73
65. Other Stone & Clay	584	1,343	1,605	1,339	1,493	2,830	5,805
(25) Iron & Steel							
66. Pig Iron	11	—	—	—	—	109	125
67. Steel Ingots	382	415	686	971	1,102	1,685	3,053
(26) Steel Products							
68. Rolled Steel	30,875	40,821	51,787	69,827	110,074	180,622	269,724
69. Pipes & Plated Steel	83	453	119	456	839	676	919
(27) Nonferrous Metals							
71. Nonferrous Smelting	8,053	8,127	3,594	3,448	3,126	8,557	24,516
72. Primary Nonferrous	2,237	2,173	2,603	1,940	3,457	5,408	10,084
(28) Finished Metal Products							
73. Structural Metallic	1,689	3,442	4,363	6,505	5,980	15,346	13,369
74. Other Metallic Products	94	125	82	310	180	662	1,417

(29) Machinery						
75. Prime Movers & Boilers	13,326	26,663	20,529	21,982	9,087	14,408	46,173
76. Working Machinery	5,614	4,828	7,592	6,440	11,877	15,562	28,434
77. Industrial Machinery	57,721	65,056	52,786	44,920	50,296	75,488	120,569
78. Other Machinery	33,838	29,530	28,849	39,829	61,795	92,062	55,805
79. Office Machines	3,943	6,770	8,069	12,469	18,866	33,118	32,621
81. Machine Spare Parts	1,454	1,122	1,581	5,817	2,105	2,458	3,183
(30) Electrical Machinery						
82. Electrical Machinery	26,865	30,722	33,412	28,688	28,836	28,045	46,908
83. Electronic & Comm. Eq.	23,342	34,046	43,912	68,747	77,307	211,519	273,499
84. Household Elec. Appliances	335	333	192	210	272	220	264
85. Other Electric Equipments	3,080	1,948	1,896	4,270	3,332	6,714	7,933
(31) Transport Equipments						
86. Shipbuilding	2,372	4,914	1,609	6,598	8,031	2,142	9,402
87. Railroad Transport Eq.	—	4,050	2,056	12,846	14,879	15,558	50,096
88. Motor Vehicles	7,526	7,700	9,770	12,457	13,437	17,221	14,002
89. Other Transport Equipments	1,795	12,522	22,037	29,042	35,240	109,281	75,332
(32) Misc. Manufacturing						
90. Measuring & Optical	11,477	14,192	14,652	23,068	24,612	36,258	45,090
91. Synthetic Resin Products	2,844	3,258	3,685	5,133	3,844	9,452	13,397
92. Other Manufactures	25	20	118	188	322	1,365	943
(42) Scrap						
115. Iron Scrap	1	17	5	93	75	1,506	1,931
116. Other Scrap	2,777	2,391	2,094	2,093	1,155	3,191	3,480
Whole Industry	370,910	465,125	517,196	652,169	762,490	1,329,486	1,883,745

Source: The same as Table A.8.
Note: Excluding the non-competitive natural-resource-intensive imports.

183

Table A.16. Competitive Imports (1970 Basis): 1960–74

In Thousand U.S. Dollars

I-O 117 Sector Classification	1960	1961	1962	1963	1964	1965	1966	1967
(1) Rice, Barley & Wheat								
1. Rice, Barley & Wheat	19,394	29,297	32,634	98,193	51,324	41,651	44,348	71,515
(2) Other Agriculture								
2. Other Cereals	759	1,155	1,593	1,128	1,684	144	288	4,112
3. Vegetables	61	101	20	0	208	212	184	194
4. Fruit	0	0	0	0	15	18	154	44
5. Industrial Crops	1,604	2,117	1,282	1,316	624	747	606	1,008
6. Livestock & Sericulture	1,981	913	787	238	449	493	825	680
(3) Forestry								
7. Forestry	457	441	4,196	6,342	2,077	682	1,630	2,071
(4) Fishery								
8. Fishery	173	56	280	140	96	538	558	2,718
(5) Coal								
9. Coal	584	4,852	0	0	24	98	17	2
(6) Other Minerals								
10. Metallic Ores	67	55	575	1,494	1,656	806	910	1,383
11. Nonmetallic Minerals	211	141	1,554	2,611	1,490	2,050	2,579	4,363
12. Salt	0	0	0	0	97	273	1	3
(7) Processed Foods								
13. Meat & Dairy Products	1,868	1,493	3,079	3,581	2,104	3,359	3,030	2,368
14. Vegetable & Fruit Processing	167	4	185	313	336	436	365	465
15. Processing of Sea Foods	0	1	49	7	18	16	46	38,
16. Grain Milling	4	6	5,785	7,829	8,755	12,480	16,603	3,900
17. Bakery & Confectionery	53	40	19	21	83	62	168	182
18. Sugar Refining	2,632	2,676	690	659	246	536	816	681
19. Seasonings	91	329	432	988	56	93	294	329

20. Other Processed Foods	360	42	247	4,396	505	644	772	4,033
(8) Beverages								
21. Alcoholic Beverages	368	196	72	82	108	159	211	507
22. Soft Drinks	0	32	10	113	4	17	32	35
(9) Tobacco								
23. Tobacco	0	0	6	12	7	7	23	101
(10) Fibre Spinning								
24. Cotton Yarn	15	35	57	58	210	177	738	531
25. Silk Yarn	0	23	60	23	2	5	69	323
26. Woolen Yarn	58	12	107	26	4	19	327	147
27. Hemp & Flax Yarn	0	0	0	0	1	10	0	1
28. Chemical Fibre Yarn	6,307	10,300	14,299	9,469	5,160	5,869	5,327	10,988
(11) Textil Fabrics								
29. Cotton Fabrics	19	0	1	1,740	1,579	2,428	2,332	2,882
30. Silk Fabrics	0	0	0	0	104	430	1,197	5,465
31. Woolen Fabrics	137	142	44	40	292	305	526	750
32. Hemp Fabrics	0	0	0	0	754	925	729	105
33. Chemical Fibre Fabrics	0	19	267	3,496	1,235	2,664	6,167	9,814
34. Dyeing & Finishing	—	—	—	—	—	—	—	—
(12) Textile Products								
35. Knit Products	0	0	0	0	184	438	236	77
36. Rope & Fishing Nets	268	457	602	347	418	358	532	611
37. Apparels & Accessories	57	67	213	323	184	241	170	82
38. Misc. Textile Products	660	1,158	825	537	703	683	1,018	1,216
(13) Lumber & Plywood								
39. Lumber & Plywood	252	0	1,108	1,253	336	373	1,614	2,030
(14) Wood & Furniture								
40. Wood Products	104	143	123	109	105	56	107	164
41. Furniture	6	9	130	136	66	35	67	103

Table A.16. (Continued)

In Thousand U.S. Dollars

I-O 117 Sector Classification	1960	1961	1962	1963	1964	1965	1966	1967
(15) Paper & Products								
42. Pulp	3,378	4,982	5,393	5,294	5,201	5,860	8,373	11,171
43. Paper	7,237	4,106	3,256	1,922	1,432	918	2,458	3,174
44. Paper Products	495	369	384	328	382	559	1,024	1,325
(16) Printing & Publishing								
45. Printing & Publishing	629	684	1,083	1,079	1,029	890	1,017	1,597
(17) Leather Products								
46. Leather & Fur	0	0	6	2	27	5	68	87
47. Leather Products	12	8	48	56	58	157	247	377
(18) Rubber Products								
48. Rubber Products	69	132	344	939	756	902	1,473	4,468
(19) Basic Chemicals								
49. Inorganic Chemicals	3,567	3,176	2,621	3,996	2,756	2,886	4,153	6,015
50. Organic Chemicals	7,677	7,795	10,975	10,711	5,106	5,404	7,978	16,021
(20) Other Chemical Products								
51. Explosives	0	74	46	50	45	53	106	92
52. Paint	373	335	680	515	196	238	624	574
53. Drugs	2,524	4,127	3,257	2,050	1,877	1,758	2,034	3,390
54. Soap	58	0	216	470	462	1,017	981	1,590
55. Cosmetics	0	15	2	5	13	30	91	58
56. Pesticides	717	456	1,247	1,800	1,309	2,147	679	1,158
57. Other Chemical Products	18,522	14,249	21,319	25,876	16,533	22,906	43,830	61,273
(21) Chemical Fertilizer								
58. Chemical Fertilizer	30,532	19,138	33,084	23,293	45,538	49,702	81,314	44,148
(22) Petroleum Products								

59. Petroleum Products	21,851	20,778	24,452	28,520	11,576	4,083	8,371	19,572
(23) Coal Products								
60. Coal Products	561	1,870	3,629	2,860	1,275	2,255	2,650	1,426
(24) Nonmetallic Mineral Products								
61. Cement	1,146	1,489	3,595	5,246	729	257	3,186	8,497
62. Ceramic Products	926	372	1,476	908	772	583	1,383	1,659
63. Glass Products	1,130	693	494	350	340	340	928	1,034
64. Pottery	0	6	121	255	592	488	730	1,717
65. Other Stone & Clay	118	510	270	387	284	499	676	1,497
(25) Iron & Steel								
66. Pig Iron	0	0	547	496	1,006	500	2,568	2,023
67. Steel Ingots	1,213	2,319	1,137	4,580	3,164	1,523	5,311	3,141
(26) Steel Products								
68. Rolled Steel	8,102	4,380	14,442	20,440	8,690	20,557	27,458	41,208
69. Pipes & Plated Steel	1,118	468	2,179	6,219	1,102	1,410	3,127	4,741
70. Cast & Forged Steel	248	216	215	29	205	146	444	1,632
(27) Nonferrous Metals								
71. Nonferrous Smelting	2,941	3,235	6,823	6,867	3,446	7,750	9,342	10,020
72. Primary Nonferrous	139	166	660	1,444	319	272	1,511	2,067
(28) Finished Metal Products								
73. Structural Metallic	1,217	653	3,947	5,522	1,113	2,441	8,933	10,766
74. Other Metallic Products	3,415	1,963	4,321	2,904	2,642	5,349	9,736	17,097
(29) Machinery								
75. Prime Movers & Boilers	865	1,274	1,546	8,292	5,376	1,574	3,807	24,046
76. Working Machinery	940	1,975	1,534	2,509	2,155	3,323	5,631	11,316
77. Industrial Machinery	9,470	8,110	9,258	15,701	15,942	16,291	46,674	50,541
78. Other Machinery	752	1,224	992	2,109	8,446	7,973	27,347	34,687
79. Office Machines	0	0	0	0	78	207	293	674
80. Household Machines	322	245	1,531	917	359	1,373	2,240	2,668

Table A.16. (Continued)

In Thousand U.S. Dollars

I-O 117 Sector Classification	1960	1961	1962	1963	1964	1965	1966	1967
81. Machine Spare Parts	135	160	0	0	1,255	869	3,160	3,839
(30) Electrical Machinery								
82. Electrical Machinery	2,337	2,777	6,665	4,594	6,057	3,025	9,112	19,238
83. Electronic & Comm. Eq.	4,530	4,811	12,325	3,440	6,143	3,089	5,637	6,332
84. Household Elec. Appliances	156	123	961	683	324	316	1,743	1,484
85. Other Electric Equipments	1,757	2,703	1,000	2,389	2,087	1,393	3,441	5,332
(31) Transport Equipments								
86. Shipbuilding	15,350	5,557	749	4,316	2,018	10,475	38,985	56,155
87. Railroad Transport Eq.	283	169	1,795	8,960	1,835	3,295	997	21,060
88. Motor Vehicles	60	349	2,887	7,219	5,118	7,104	9,092	22,470
89. Other Transport Equipments	70	222	112	117	102	46	238	211
(32) Misc. Manufacturing								
90. Measuring & Optical	2,408	1,509	2,532	2,093	1,908	2,450	4,160	7,539
91. Synthetic Resin Products	0	0	183	107	265	370	1,033	1,849
92. Other Manufactures	1,013	945	1,303	1,125	403	428	758	1,722
(41) Other Services								
107. Education	—	—	—	—	3	—	16	15
111. Business Service	—	—	—	—	4	—	4	24
112. Recreation	141	603	865	921	414	418	892	1,208
(42) Scrap								
115. Iron Scrap	0	6	981	3,437	2,549	4,545	12,377	18,869
116. Other Scrap	1,507	84	3,455	4,992	5,543	3,609	3,551	4,304
(43) Unclassifiable								
117. Unclassifiable	32,267	14,961	1,385	1,130	1,261	2	4	0
Whole Industry	232,995	202,883	275,659	387,664	272,923	296,597	519,448	715,829

Table A.16. (Continued)

In Thousand U.S. Dollars

I-O 117 Sector Classification	1968	1969	1970	1971	1972	1973	1974
(1) Rice, Barley & Wheat							
1. Rice, Barley & Wheat	118,002	218,344	225,851	269,418	253,224	395,167	535,375
(2) Other Agriculture							
2. Other Cereals	3,414	11,426	18,571	31,572	28,058	60,987	87,046
3. Vegetables	363	680	2,636	1,580	428	674	8,916
4. Fruit	20	42	38	54	186	545	858
5. Industrial Crops	1,894	2,335	2,649	5,941	9,716	12,882	17,239
6. Livestock & Sericulture	1,799	3,298	4,058	5,640	5,200	12,340	10,221
(3) Forestry							
7. Forestry	4,225	3,356	3,911	2,866	2,694	5,951	7,790
(4) Fishery							
8. Fishery	578	835	1,186	1,170	2,548	7,929	10,651
(5) Coal							
9. Coal	6	0	1	24	218	10	4
(6) Other Minerals							
10. Metallic Ores	4,794	7,893	8,283	10,133	17,395	49,775	88,955
11. Nonmetallic Minerals	4,545	5,732	7,210	8,306	11,928	18,845	19,880
12. Salt	1	298	2,600	5,212	2,981	550	31
(7) Processed Foods							
13. Meat & Diary Products	9,927	8,219	11,656	15,273	17,264	33,667	52,670
14. Vegetable & Fruit Processing	730	1,330	2,217	2,992	3,659	6,121	4,592
15. Processing of Sea Foods	132	450	223	124	477	6,560	1,042
16. Grain Milling	8,159	24,309	3,355	10,888	5,771	3,858	4,038
17. Bakery & Confectionery	464	585	391	525	789	684	989
18. Sugar Refining	2,077	3,713	5,243	7,097	6,237	13,209	15,752

Table A.16. (Continued)

In Thousand U.S. Dollars

I-O 117 Sector Classification	1968	1969	1970	1971	1972	1973	1974
19. Seasonings	1,035	2,497	2,901	3,825	3,004	2,566	2,286
20. Other Processed Foods	13,233	15,296	18,769	30,062	4,213	3,348	4,212
(8) Beverages							
21. Alcoholic Beverages	351	446	717	339	496	932	664
22. Soft Drinks	130	275	124	33	18	6	1
(9) Tobacco							
23. Tobacco	196	315	424	424	263	130	93
(10) Fibre Spinning							
24. Cotton Yarn	2,663	853	1,033	647	668	12,960	2,776
25. Silk Yarn	88	50	377	1,588	303	1,904	2,793
26. Woolen Yarn	600	912	554	774	972	3,440	5,136
27. Hemp & Flax Yarn	27	10	51	71	92	179	241
28. Chemical Fibre Yarn	23,970	23,959	19,075	12,366	12,799	21,961	31,558
(11) Textile Fabrics							
29. Cotton Fabrics	6,211	5,485	4,969	6,295	10,549	20,479	34,013
30. Silk Fabrics	1,942	2,711	3,922	4,340	3,783	9,308	328
31. Woolen Fabrics	1,010	3,539	6,522	6,576	5,375	12,463	13,103
32. Hemp Fabrics	242	654	878	326	730	469	639
33. Chemical Fibre Fabrics	20,670	28,855	46,294	63,341	48,013	115,606	107,231
34. Dyeing & Finishing	—	—	—	—	—	—	—
(12) Textile Products							
35. Knit Products	80	55	270	8,467	22,759	24,662	15,841
36. Rope & Fishing Nets	742	636	406	283	315	295	613
37. Apparels & Accessories	283	341	292	1,453	3,435	2,256	2,152
38. Misc. Textile Products	2,551	3,847	5,004	5,723	8,225	17,462	22,054

(13) Lumber & Plywood							
39. Lumber & Plywood	2,657	3,544	1,898	1,399	843	2,903	1,889
(14) Wood & Furniture							
40. Wood Products	449	510	665	1,007	671	912	1,856
41. Furniture	605	1,125	1,169	1,051	920	2,594	2,389
(15) Paper & Products							
42. Pulp	18,054	20,444	27,353	33,281	34,290	55,600	102,014
43. Paper	5,412	4,411	5,929	7,951	6,925	7,657	8,869
44. Paper Products	2,132	2,256	2,869	3,248	3,436	6,342	10,904
(16) Printing & Publishing							
45. Printing & Publishing	4,424	10,844	5,801	6,223	4,566	4,900	6,232
(17) Leather Products							
46. Leather & Fur	176	440	1,472	2,510	3,741	13,183	23,668
47. Leather Products	369	343	334	553	721	1,571	1,059
(18) Rubber Products							
48. Rubber Products	6,383	7,989	9,000	11,136	12,928	12,689	24,016
(19) Basic Chemicals							
49. Inorganic Chemicals	6,922	4,911	4,275	7,106	7,141	13,921	18,909
50. Organic Chemicals	38,714	22,533	26,082	23,943	35,510	38,028	52,992
(20) Other Chemical Products							
51. Explosives	117	120	112	255	248	179	321
52. Paint	1,167	1,748	2,627	2,453	3,202	7,587	15,856
53. Drugs	3,566	2,954	1,783	1,707	2,514	2,144	3,372
54. Soap	2,027	2,136	2,514	2,514	3,251	5,219	8,304
55. Cosmetics	193	361	880	472	256	448	417
56. Pesticides	1,302	1,641	848	946	969	953	678
57. Other Chemical Products	74,625	82,781	102,629	96,837	98,485	184,591	196,066
(21) Chemical Fertilizer							
58. Chemical Fertilizer	20,289	8,013	2,774	6,340	9,061	15,010	50,057

Table A.16. (Continued)

In Thousand U.S. Dollars

I-O 117 Sector Classification	1968	1969	1970	1971	1972	1973	1974
(22) Petroleum Products							
59. Petroleum Products	13,842	5,589	5,491	10,546	7,810	14,804	47,743
(23) Coal Products							
60. Coal Products	2,566	3,118	3,526	3,004	2,049	3,948	8,420
(24) Nonmetallic Mineral Products							
61. Cement	2,533	375	74	165	103	168	1,715
62. Ceramic Products	2,953	3,042	3,311	3,334	10,551	5,881	11,879
63. Glass Products	2,440	4,208	3,705	3,217	4,346	8,511	10,738
64. Pottery	2,089	1,985	2,416	3,100	2,399	3,182	7,052
65. Other Stone & Clay	1,132	1,846	1,920	2,628	3,553	2,525	5,275
(25) Iron & Steel							
66. Pig Iron	4,335	3,333	919	3,268	4,720	7,787	15,171
67. Steel Ingots	2,080	6,450	3,291	8,869	14,460	47,544	23,033
(26) Steel Products							
68. Rolled Steel	32,684	35,305	37,039	43,989	44,456	92,522	178,665
69. Pipes & Plated Steel	10,299	12,488	9,490	17,487	12,313	9,563	19,338
70. Cast & Forged Steel	1,586	1,567	3,941	2,046	2,402	4,737	6,845
(27) Nonferrous Metals							
71. Nonferrous Smelting	12,221	12,691	13,477	12,153	10,355	26,657	63,884
72. Primary Nonferrous	3,092	5,152	5,941	6,608	8,687	15,624	30,660
(28) Finished Metal Products							
73. Structural Metallic	17,173	30,032	28,736	33,447	28,252	31,439	31,494
74. Other Metallic Products	19,417	22,091	21,573	24,465	18,682	29,755	46,848
(29) Machinery							
75. Prime Movers & Boilers	25,299	20,828	25,214	22,839	23,837	18,062	28,403
76. Working Machinery	14,888	13,423	19,011	29,922	47,113	51,732	66,063

77. Industrial Machinery	121,080	132,583	130,468	133,247	98,490	231,725	318,159
78. Other Machinery	64,856	67,795	63,743	78,607	116,980	124,202	118,678
79. Office Machines	1,503	2,032	2,613	1,701	1,557	3,732	4,386
80. Household Machines	3,826	4,260	5,631	6,542	5,703	15,479	15,130
81. Machine Spare Parts	3,063	4,003	5,664	11,578	8,487	10,933	14,266
(30) Electrical Machinery							
82. Electrical Machinery	38,509	39,761	51,169	48,139	59,033	70,238	96,644
83. Electronic & Comm. Eq.	14,079	16,692	19,899	30,828	52,756	131,351	159,769
84. Household Elec. Appliances	2,345	3,114	3,504	3,436	2,512	2,510	3,896
85. Other Electric Equipments	6,728	4,864	4,275	10,918	10,442	11,413	17,720
(31) Transport Equipments							
86. Shipbuilding	60,056	61,933	45,821	58,818	73,690	53,535	391,313
87. Railroad Transport Eq.	28,211	27,428	11,942	8,638	6,107	4,422	9,338
88. Motor Vehicles	62,828	62,258	64,619	51,968	38,622	60,526	92,239
89. Other Transport Equipments	462	942	2,023	2,313	2,381	8,206	7,006
(32) Misc. Manufacturing							
90. Measuring & Optical	11,437	16,042	18,303	25,793	26,977	30,657	56,419
91. Synthetic Resin Products	2,875	3,354	3,801	4,991	3,699	7,036	10,517
92. Other Manufactures	12,863	14,173	7,438	7,939	9,064	18,066	23,517
(41) Other Services							
107. Education	28	62	56	67	38	55	82
111. Business Service	6	10	34	49	44	55	49
112. Recreation	1,395	2,584	2,392	3,110	2,674	2,446	2,153
(42) Scrap							
115. Iron Scrap	22,915	40,326	61,885	53,569	27,740	74,413	172,040
116. Other Scrap	5,277	3,545	6,246	4,514	4,944	14,126	26,384
(43) Unclassifiable							
117. Unclassifiable	—	—	—	—	—	—	—
Whole Industry	1,061,708	1,253,969	1,314,276	1,514,532	1,522,491	2,506,178	3,784,582

Source: The same as Table A.8.

Table A.17. Non-Competitive Imports (1970 Basis) : 1960–74

In Thousand U.S. Dollars

I-O 117 Sector Classification	1960	1961	1962	1963	1964	1965	1966	1967
(2) Other Agriculture								
4. Fruit	154	142	22	95	12	1	1	246
5. Industrial Crops	357	253	714	611	1,199	1,964	3,779	2,967
6. Livestock & Sericulture	—	—	121	73	37	16	99	416
(3) Forestry								
7. Forestry	0	0	0	0	58	116	81	129
(5) Coal								
9. Coal	0	0	2,213	2,173	2,362	1,732	845	990
(6) Other Minerals								
10. Metallic Ores	—	—	0	0	21	5	58	350
11. Nonmetallic Minerals	—	—	522	815	21	24	285	1,051
(7) Processed Foods								
13. Meat & Dairy Products	—	—	—	—	—	1	—	1
14. Vegetable & Fruit Processing	—	—	25	5	—	—	9	8
16. Grain Milling	—	—	—	—	18	—	2	1
18. Sugar Refining	0	0	2	0	0	0	1	1
19. Seasonings	—	—	—	—	44	45	—	—
20. Other Processed Foods	350	271	291	44	20	28	12	79
(10) Fibre Spinning								
26. Woolen Yarn	0	18	0	0	0	0	0	5
28. Chemical Fibre Yarn	—	—	—	—	—	—	—	—
(12) Textile Products								
38. Misc. Textile Products	—	—	—	—	1	2	4	—

(15) Paper & Products								
42. Pulp	—	—	2,762	3,419	3,057	2,951	3,929	4,458
43. Paper	—	—	—	—	50	11	5	22
44. Paper Products	—	—	—	—	33	26	31	33
(17) Leather Products								
46. Leather & Fur	—	—	—	—	17	4	29	43
(18) Rubber Products								
48. Rubber Products	—	—	—	—	—	—	1	4
(19) Basic Chemicals								
49. Inorganic Chemicals	492	1,026	2,047	2,121	2,207	2,753	3,130	6,189
50. Organic Chemicals	2,076	2,536	5,022	4,649	8,538	10,369	13,086	18,622
(20) Other Chemical Products								
51. Explosives	—	—	—	—	44	68	107	124
53. Drugs	840	1,088	2,444	2,413	1,898	3,179	4,061	4,391
57. Other Chemical Products	2,156	783	3,320	2,570	7,745	12,768	12,310	16,096
(21) Chemical Fertilizer								
58. Chemical Fertilizer	24,843	21,150	29,233	25,629	13,179	18,309	8,251	3,876
(22) Petroleum Products								
59. Petroleum Products	37	34	43	50	1,000	1,395	1,036	172
(23) Coal Products								
60. Coal Products	—	—	—	—	—	—	35	18
(24) Nonmetallic Mineral Products								
65. Other Stone & Clay	—	—	—	—	10	22	38	22
(25) Iron & Steel								
66. Pig Iron	—	—	—	—	7	8	—	149
(26) Steel Products								
68. Rolled Steel	—	—	—	—	13	4	125	1,588

Table A.17. (Continued)

In Thousand U.S. Dollars

I-O 117 Sector Classification	1960	1961	1962	1963	1964	1965	1966	1967
(27) Nonferrous Metals								
71. Nonferrous Smelting	—	—	—	—	23	17	23	74
72. Primary Nonferrous	—	60	95	123	144	186	184	355
(28) Finished Metal Products								
74. Other Metallic Products	—	—	—	—	14	60	8	72
(29) Machinery								
75. Prime Movers & Boilers	1,501	3,414	7,805	7,225	2,415	894	2,136	—
77. Industrial Machinery	138	700	256	971	600	1,860	1,886	3,686
79. Office Machines	—	328	1,045	570	28	137	247	1,415
(30) Electrical Machinery								
82. Electrical Machinery	1,151	7,155	3,241	7,217	3,484	3,307	3,261	8,089
83. Electronic & Comm. Eq.	276	840	1,868	1,539	1,208	1,030	2,254	5,504
85. Other Electric Equipments	—	0	2,332	2,071	26	47	32	132
(31) Transport Equipments								
86. Shipbuilding	—	—	10,894	23,219	23	1	677	1,114
87. Railroad Transport Eq.	42	174	1,159	10,360	305	232	286	11,619
88. Motor Vehicles	—	—	164	476	312	810	1,095	4,381
89. Other Transport Equipments	—	161	202	593	2,345	4,164	736	9,538
(32) Misc. Manufacturing								
90. Measuring & Optical	1,568	1,772	3,275	2,140	1,065	1,496	1,714	2,898
92. Other Manufactures	—	—	—	—	—	—	8	1
(42) Scrap								
116. Other Scrap	—	—	178	125	1	1	725	1,034
(43) Unclassifiable								
117. Unclassifiable	—	—	—	—	209	482	—	—
Whole Industry	35,981	41,744	81,295	101,296	53,793	70,525	197,930	280,413

Table A.17. (Continued)

In Thousand U.S. Dollars

I-O 117 Sector Classification	1968	1969	1970	1971	1972	1973	1974
(2) Other Agriculture							
4. Fruit	244	395	490	606	3,411	1,153	1,527
5. Industrial Crops	2,326	2,692	3,442	4,763	5,115	6,852	7,627
6. Livestock & Sericulture	29	113	170	237	376	418	43
(3) Forestry							
7. Forestry	699	422	467	471	382	335	766
(5) Coal							
9. Coal	860	481	308	306	—	14,276	28,657
(6) Other Minerals							
10. Metallic Ores	39	70	222	412	410	757	1,507
11. Nonmetallic Minerals	6,550	7,989	8,320	8,311	7,744	10,359	25,255
12. Salt	—	284	193	—	152	3,327	7,442
(7) Processed Foods							
13. Meat & Dairy Products	5	5	11	13	9	19	29
14. Vegetable & Fruit Processing	15	9	8	12	11	20	112
16. Grain Milling	2	4	—	—	—	—	—
18. Sugar Refining	0	0	0	0	0	0	1
19. Seasonings	13	12	10	6	74	255	391
20. Other Processed Foods	20	18	76	77	73	106	331
(10) Fibre Spinning							
26. Woolen Yarn	0	0	0	0	0	1	0
(11) Textile Fabrics							
29. Cotton Fabrics	—	—	—	3	1	1	585

Table A. 17. (Continued)

In Thousand U.S. Dollars

I-O 117 Sector Classification	1968	1969	1970	1971	1972	1973	1974
(12) Textile Products							
37. Apparels & Accessories	—	6	1	11	9	0	0
38. Misc. Textile Products	6	11	28	57	122	20	53
(13) Lumber & Plywood							
39. Lumber & Plywood	0	0	0	0	0	0	0
(14) Wood & Furniture							
40. Wood Products	—	—	—	—	91	0	0
(15) Paper & Products							
42. Pulp	6,710	4,066	3,836	1,954	749	9,407	9,215
43. Paper	13	29	72	62	42	59	51
44. Paper Products	604	884	1,190	1,976	1,882	3,390	3,880
(17) Leather Products							
46. Leather & Fur	78	110	129	287	809	2,483	9,590
(18) Rubber Products							
48. Rubber Products	1	4	6	1	3	2	0
(19) Basic Chemicals							
49. Inorganic Chemicals	6,075	9,438	11,113	13,551	11,447	20,904	32,978
50. Organic Chemicals	12,449	45,249	65,037	90,342	92,261	163,053	321,854
(20) Other Chemical Products							
51. Explosives	213	261	301	326	368	506	567
52. Paint	24	40	47	61	81	98	222
53. Drugs	8,220	9,853	13,345	11,867	10,483	15,621	21,172
54. Soap	285	370	460	475	523	1,045	1,007
57. Other Chemical Products	19,304	26,079	34,881	46,159	54,390	78,162	98,358

(21) Chemical Fertilizer						
58. Chemical Fertilizer	10,333	3,888	1,309	778	2,084	2,556	2,843
(22) Petroleum Products						
59. Petroleum Products	2,419	2,542	2,611	3,036	2,386	3,879	7,912
(23) Coal Products						
60. Coal Products	—	28	96	45	1	14	12
(24) Nonmetallic Mineral Products						
61. Cement	5	13	26	33	11	0	0
65. Other Stone & Clay	584	1,342	1,605	1,339	1,493	2,830	5,805
(25) Iron & Steel						
66. Pig Iron	11	—	—	—	—	109	125
67. Steel Ingots	—	—	—	4	1,102	1,685	3,053
(26) Steel Products						
68. Rolled Steel	15,519	23,080	31,755	49,364	85,628	148,661	212,226
69. Pipes & Plated Steel	—	2	4	19	1	0	0
(27) Nonferrous Metals						
71. Nonferrous Smelting	40	26	122	175	83	1,245	1,365
72. Primary Nonferrous	624	606	804	669	653	1,657	2,471
(28) Finished Metal Products						
73. Structural Metallic	1,689	—	—	—	—	—	—
74. Other Metallic Products	54	81	63	258	120	351	556
(29) Machinery						
75. Prime Movers & Boilers	13,326	26,663	20,529	21,982	9,087	14,408	46,173
76. Working Machinery	147	29	33	71	191	69	802
77. Industrial Machinery	16,869	14,486	11,515	6,932	4,172	12,480	22,961
78. Other Machinery	107	7	73	407	100	2,840	2,479
79. Office Machines	3,686	5,506	6,233	11,384	17,985	31,967	31,659

Table A.17. (Continued)

In Thousand U.S. Dollars

I-O 117 Sector Classification	1968	1969	1970	1971	1972	1973	1974
(30) Electrical Machinery							
82. Electrical Machinery	15,889	22,583	19,625	19,651	20,537	9,960	29,948
83. Electronic & Comm. Eq.	14,467	23,696	29,811	50,583	78,669	156,558	222,912
84. Household Electric Appliances	51	23	27	24	74	48	95
85. Other Electric Equipments	214	349	1,176	1,171	1,436	6,133	7,255
(31) Transport Equipments							
86. Shipbuilding	2,203	4,347	1,582	5,436	7,728	227	6,542
87. Railroad Transport Eq.	—	4,050	2,056	12,846	14,879	15,558	50,096
88. Motor Vehicles	7,380	7,566	9,648	12,213	12,950	16,517	13,013
89. Other Transport Equipments	1,396	11,632	20,097	26,962	34,089	106,693	72,803
(32) Misc. Manufacturing							
90. Measuring & Optical	4,787	5,679	5,681	8,392	8,742	19,113	24,763
91. Synthetic Resin Products	38	25	98	233	274	2,434	2,942
92. Other Manufactures	8	4	15	6	23	0	343
(42) Scrap							
115. Iron Scrap	1	17	5	93	75	1,506	1,931
116. Other Scrap	2,777	2,389	2,094	2,093	1,155	3,190	3,477
Whole Industry	402,417	571,959	670,705	880,416	999,513	895,317	1,349,843

Source: The same as Table. A.8.
Note: Excluding the non-competitive natural-resource-intensive imports.

Table A.18. *Amount of Commodities Transferred from 1963 Non-Competitive Imports to 1966 Competitive Imports*

In Thousand U.S. Dollars

I–O Code	1964	1965	1966	1967	1968	1969	1970	1971	1972	1973	1974
5	23	24	46	90	119	233	178	101	124	164	314
6	1	3	2	3	4	4	6	7	13	31	44
7	1,704	406	1,156	989	1,890	1,139	987	591	680	979	1,094
8	50	286	155	1,365	63	17	0	5	11	19	580
10	174	103	29	16	32	40	32	37	0	19	13
13	1,605	3,048	2,093	534	6,635	3,398	6,625	9,136	3,501	632	1,339
19	3	7	44	71	240	134	68	120	56	174	185
26	5	—	2	—	0	90	12	31	7	30	133
27	—	—	—	0	7	5	49	55	49	151	188
28	4,875	4,580	6,161	6,056	2,614	1,501	1,708	3,221	98	936	871
42	574	415	1,038	1,454	1,706	1,483	1,663	1,081	521	751	5,705
44	95	139	226	260	62	100	194	320	478	1,587	2,461
48	548	727	1,136	3,824	5,290	6,497	6,817	9,344	11,269	9,234	19,627
49	671	579	937	1,760	2,786	1,406	517	1,058	179	256	502
50	296	298	450	788	1,961	2,233	2,224	2,310	3,502	5,289	7,382
52	34	51	188	69	201	339	385	388	471	644	1,049
55	1	2	1	0	1	4	14	16	4	1	0
57	1,162	2,108	2,549	3,128	1,514	1,615	1,394	1,642	1,618	4,452	8,801
59	10,981	3,306	8,150	19,381	13,587	5,483	6,269	10,362	7,251	8,647	33,961
60	1,136	1,700	1,442	276	365	335	668	558	382	907	806

Table A.18. (Continued)

In Thousand U.S. Dollars

I-O Code	1964	1965	1966	1967	1968	1969	1970	1971	1972	1973	1974
63	101	59	252	223	183	159	295	328	472	621	869
65	25	24	70	4	23	122	113	85	114	182	72
67	3,019	1,249	4,755	2,233	1,105	3,865	2,409	6,507	14,060	46,997	21,808
68	17	1	92	3	555	455	977	286	248	329	228
69	—	—	—	18	69	372	674	636	112	237	305
70	12	91	51	135	135	408	378	522	961	1,249	1,290
71	1,362	3,981	3,228	1,628	2,363	2,700	3,755	2,614	3,979	8,546	17,205
72	107	138	379	480	378	464	997	1,257	1,184	2,893	7,109
74	724	572	578	1,165	1,972	2,046	1,843	2,441	2,452	4,022	7,708
75	167	522	1,295	3,519	1,525	5,980	4,150	2,388	3,759	3,337	14,027
76	878	1,447	2,419	5,486	6,021	5,272	7,216	16,703	13,573	20,426	23,580
77	7,588	4,233	17,107	16,073	41,450	42,747	44,459	59,643	31,387	76,068	95,013
78	3,486	4,553	12,035	15,096	16,134	16,478	19,459	20,503	29,963	24,929	45,763
82	52	344	229	444	121	189	383	541	2,795	972	753
83	4,736	749	3,055	3,183	975	1,080	1,519	4,442	3,497	8,783	18,181
84	98	51	65	101	211	122	121	265	150	300	306
86	173	261	374	1,252	1,684	624	920	962	1,071	819	1,227
88	2,304	1,831	3,392	9,624	32,911	21,811	21,841	22,294	11,506	5,275	9,709
90	247	143	37	569	718	1,093	1,364	2,875	1,430	1,500	1,736
Total	49,034	38,031	75,218	101,300	147,610	132,043	142,683	185,675	152,927	242,388	351,944

Source: The same as Table A.8.

Table A.19. Amount of Commodities Transferred from 1966 Non-Competitive Imports to 1968 Competitive Imports

In Thousand U.S. Dollars

I-O Code	1964	1965	1966	1967	1968	1969	1970	1971	1972	1973	1974
18	4	—	0	0	177	218	293	417	447	974	1,175
19	1	1	1	1	3	0	0	0	3	0	0
28	23	102	112	86	155	350	446	265	293	312	1,110
50	167	78	4	0	5	0	—	0	0	25	0
57	4,249	8,330	10,977	11,404	8,256	9,443	24,213	21,576	28,630	43,697	39,181
63	74	112	268	213	270	531	636	565	326	339	551
73	70	63	102	4	184	229	303	310	411	870	995
90	21	280	542	1,061	2,281	4,296	5,260	4,290	4,439	7,352	8,526
92	23	25	47	34	84	112	126	143	67	111	191
Total	4,632	8,991	12,053	12,803	11,415	15,179	31,277	27,566	34,616	53,680	51,729

Source: The same as Table A.8.

Table A.20. *Raw Material Imports for Export Production (Competitive Imports as of 1968): 1966-74*

In Thousand U.S. Dollars

I-O 43 Sector Classification	1966	1967	1968	1969	1970	1971	1972	1973	1974
1. Rice, Barley & Wheat	21	307	—	217	57	29	47	119	1,810
2. Other Agriculture	145	151	551	3,894	8,307	13,918	2,252	34,630	47,333
3. Forestry	136	70	538	48	90	292	315	1,827	2,334
4. Fishery	100	1,398	14	5	62	0	1,339	5,755	8,392
5. Coal Mining	—	0	—	—	—	—	—	—	—
6. Other Minerals	21	68	282	215	1,213	328	536	1,946	10,711
7. Food Processing	1,121	1,907	2,373	5,028	7,495	10,428	13,254	45,115	57,470
8. Beverages	98	395	383	643	755	244	106	55	65
9. Tobacco	—	55	64	183	256	160	82	67	57
10. Fibre Spinning	7,624	14,582	28,165	27,817	23,510	21,484	14,142	36,731	41,903
11. Textile Fabrics	9,628	14,516	28,050	38,970	61,112	79,328	63,350	156,936	153,444
12. Textile Products	521	698	1,682	2,683	3,787	13,925	30,270	42,023	36,475
13. Lumber & Plywood	320	368	115	419	157	237	87	253	658
14. Wood & Furniture	69	79	55	164	166	184	557	1,347	902
15. Paper & Products	980	1,126	2,625	3,294	4,971	6,102	5,652	8,548	14,470
16. Printing & Publishing	61	113	217	316	333	556	155	922	1,305
17. Leather Products	251	414	441	617	1,562	2,291	1,761	14,251	24,116
18. Rubber Products	275	174	108	564	1,781	927	1,091	3,332	10,528
19. Basic Chemicals	1,343	2,449	2,596	3,641	5,975	8,253	17,940	17,658	19,648
20. Other Chemicals	14,103	22,425	29,463	41,517	64,860	57,843	70,704	147,269	116,176

Table A.20. (Continued)

In Thousand U.S. Dollars

I-O 43 Sector Classification	1966	1967	1968	1969	1970	1971	1972	1973	1974
21. Chemical Fertilizer	0	0	5	1	0	1	0	740	103
22. Petroleum Products	65	55	91	150	597	1,885	1,341	2,265	4,031
23. Coal Products	1	49	11	30	262	14	105	561	1,327
24. Nonmetallic Mineral Products	635	525	749	1,063	1,221	1,522	1,555	4,548	6,763
25. Iron & Steel	176	78	114	466	51	2,705	7,215	7,854	10,226
26. Steel Products	4,513	1,211	1,258	2,030	1,312	1,404	6,648	33,393	82,745
27. Nonferrous Metal	1,611	618	672	587	1,046	1,731	4,974	17,477	36,301
28. Metal Products	2,963	6,267	8,949	6,269	5,452	5,436	5,601	15,511	23,264
29. Machinery	1,468	1,195	2,692	2,502	829	2,439	3,978	13,461	25,668
30. Electrical Machinery	2,139	1,330	2,944	7,353	7,316	9,825	21,490	69,125	107,950
31. Transport Equipments	2,308	44	110	121	206	245	1,095	8,724	12,006
32. Misc. Manufactures	401	1,110	11,639	12,209	6,564	7,150	11,030	18,509	42,931
41. Other Services	—	2	2	—	4	—	—	7	6
42. Scrap	734	405	180	443	501	1,460	1,926	4,032	2,853
43. Unclassifiable	1	—	—	—	—	—	7,728	—	—
Total (S)	53,832	74,184	126,894	163,459	211,810	252,347	298,326	714,991	903,971
(S)/Total Competitive Imports	11.9%	12.2%	14.6%	15.4%	19.1%	19.7%	23.7%	34.5%	23.9%
(S)/Total Exports	21.7%	23.2%	27.9%	26.3%	25.4%	23.6%	18.3%	22.2%	20.3%

Source: The same as Table A.8.

Table A.21. Raw Material Imports for Export Production (Non-Competitive as of 1968): 1966–74

In Thousand U.S. Dollars

I-O 43 Sector Classification	1966	1967	1968	1969	1970	1971	1972	1973	1974
2. Other Agriculture	9,084	7,418	11,749	12,623	29,297	45,190	51,371	90,432	100,115
3. Forestry	24,723	36,970	52,031	77,368	88,296	115,757	113,217	260,230	254,096
4. Fishery	5	15	20	74	215	249	202	568	885
5. Coal Mining	—	9	—	—	—	—	—	—	—
6. Other Minerals	37	0	2,968	11,445	7,955	3,497	4	21	104
7. Food Processing	639	683	856	667	552	868	1,435	8,480	40,757
10. Fibre Spinning	3,877	2,386	2,826	3,874	2,582	1,090	11,223	35,069	20,432
11. Textile Fabrics	—	—	—	—	—	3	—	—	504
12. Textile Products	—	—	—	—	—	—	2	2	4
13. Lumber & Plywood	—	—	5	—	—	5	—	60	62
14. Wood & Furniture	2	3	—	—	—	—	—	—	—
15. Paper & Products	68	136	118	139	232	990	1,847	3,846	5,693
17. Leather Products	28	16	56	85	80	213	732	2,410	9,380
18. Rubber Products	35	65	64	67	30	51	13	175	197
19. Basic Chemicals	1,904	3,488	4,525	8,026	12,096	21,687	26,909	60,879	145,525
20. Other Chemicals	2,643	4,202	4,259	6,159	10,866	16,261	22,237	52,657	77,669
21. Chemical Fertilizer	0	1	0	—	0	1	2	2	9
22. Petroleum Products	15	19	19	18	114	35	11	87	98
23. Coal Products	—	—	—	—	1	0	—	—	—
24. Nonmetallic Mineral Products	14	0	93	139	106	125	21	13	269

Table A.21. (Continued)

In Thousand U.S. Dollars

I-O 43 Sector Classification	1966	1967	1968	1969	1970	1971	1972	1973	1974
25. Iron & Steel	—	54	—	—	—	—	1	816	995
26. Steel Products	543	1,400	1,244	4,760	11,434	28,981	67,457	120,787	194,942
27. Nonferrous Metal	72	96	357	259	655	685	999	5,666	7,401
28. Metal Products	111	112	82	305	358	356	637	1,986	5,823
29. Machinery	570	457	98	814	154	808	1,081	36,682	46,190
30. Electrical Machinery	689	799	464	1,857	3,471	8,953	5,165	196,161	263,666
31. Transport Equipments	20	93	165	347	48	17	325	2,041	4,760
32. Misc. Manufactures	1,186	1,927	3,177	4,321	5,226	7,283	4,028	23,248	25,129
42. Scrap	14	6	285	401	739	848	721	3,156	3,280
Total (S)	46,279	60,355	85,461	133,748	174,507	253,953	309,640*	905,474	1,207,979
(S)/Total Non-Competitive Imp.	35.4%	28.0%	23.2%	29.0%	34.0%	39.3%	41.0%	41.7%	39.5%
(S)/Total Exports	18.7%	18.8%	18.8%	21.5%	20.9%	23.8%	19.0%	28.1%	27.1%

Source: The same as Table A.8.

*The sum of competitive and non-competitive raw material imports for export production in 1972 was $607,966 thousand. However, according to the *Statistical Yearbook of Foreign Trade*: 1972, the total amount of imports for export production in 1972 was $ 659,477 thousand, showing nearly 10 percent difference from the taped trade data of the Office of Customs Administration.

Table A.22. Industrial Origin of Gross National Product (At 1970 Constant Market Prices): 1953-74

In Million 1970 Dollars

	1953	1954	1955	1956	1957	1958	1959	1960	1961	1962	1963
Agriculture & Forestry	1,239.1	1,338.3	1,375.6	1,276.1	1,386.2	1,479.4	1,461.9	1,450.0	1,619.0	1,518.5	1,640.3
Fishery	40.3	38.2	36.5	52.1	63.1	59.9	59.5	52.2	62.3	66.1	72.7
Mining & Quarrying	30.6	21.6	23.8	25.1	31.5	31.6	36.0	47.7	51.4	62.3	64.8
Manufacturing	164.6	195.4	240.1	281.5	304.7	332.4	363.1	392.8	405.0	458.3	537.5
Construction	43.9	55.2	55.3	52.1	67.9	68.7	82.4	82.2	92.1	107.1	123.6
Electricity & Gas	7.9	9.6	9.6	11.5	13.4	16.2	18.8	19.4	20.0	24.3	28.1
Water & Sanitary Service	2.0	2.1	2.2	2.9	2.9	3.0	3.5	4.7	4.7	5.2	5.4
Transportation	35.9	46.4	53.3	68.4	69.8	77.3	89.0	97.5	96.6	106.2	124.1
Communication	4.0	5.8	6.2	7.4	8.4	10.0	12.9	15.3	17.2	21.5	25.8
Trade	304.0	320.7	360.3	374.2	425.6	447.3	500.6	541.1	526.2	587.7	629.0
Banking & Real Estate	48.8	39.3	53.0	51.0	55.7	67.4	73.2	80.3	76.1	85.5	88.7
Education	86.3	102.8	113.8	120.7	124.3	126.8	129.9	133.2	140.3	147.8	160.6
Other Services	160.1	171.2	171.6	200.7	216.5	238.0	263.2	249.0	236.5	256.0	274.0
Public Administration	390.0	364.2	360.3	348.0	330.5	309.5	304.3	300.2	296.6	308.8	321.6
Ownership of Dwellings	122.8	126.8	130.1	134.1	137.1	139.7	140.9	144.1	147.8	151.4	154.8
GNP	2,715.8	2,866.0	3,020.7	3,033.5	3,266.1	3,435.8	3,568.4	3,637.2	3,813.5	3,931.0	4,276.6

	1964	1965	1966	1967	1968	1969	1970	1971	1972	1973	1974
Agriculture & Forestry	1,891.8	1,850.2	2,051.0	1,930.3	1,965.2	2,220.8	2,183.4	2,230.0	2,215.3	2,276.9	2,356.9
Fishery	86.9	90.1	99.4	113.4	127.8	134.3	149.5	179.7	234.7	308.2	371.9
Mining & Quarrying	71.5	77.6	79.7	87.7	87.0	85.5	98.9	100.5	100.5	118.6	125.5
Manufacturing	572.6	686.9	804.5	987.7	1,254.6	1,523.0	1,803.0	2,122.4	2,455.9	3,215.6	3,777.0
Construction	133.8	163.3	205.1	232.8	330.4	462.4	483.6	484.8	478.0	581.8	586.8
Electricity & Gas	34.3	41.6	50.3	64.8	80.2	104.8	127.0	146.8	166.1	205.6	233.6
Water & Sanitary Service	5.4	6.8	6.6	9.5	11.4	14.3	17.9	20.7	20.4	21.3	23.6
Transportation	144.6	169.6	199.7	243.2	301.5	355.6	397.5	436.3	476.9	612.1	634.9
Communication	29.3	36.2	40.9	48.6	60.9	71.8	84.3	95.6	113.2	134.9	161.2
Trade	611.2	673.0	775.7	904.1	1,055.6	1,213.2	1,379.9	1,602.9	1,777.2	2,118.7	2,241.4
Banking & Real Estate	94.5	102.1	108.7	120.1	141.7	156.8	183.3	206.0	212.7	226.1	249.3
Education	169.5	181.5	196.9	206.5	220.2	234.1	250.9	267.2	281.0	295.9	310.3
Other Services	283.9	314.3	337.3	376.6	412.0	449.8	491.8	540.5	561.2	614.1	622.3
Public Administration	328.7	338.9	362.1	384.9	404.4	423.2	444.5	461.6	456.8	459.9	470.1
Ownership of Dwellings	159.9	164.1	167.9	174.6	183.0	192.3	202.4	212.7	224.1	237.9	257.3
GNP	4,642.6	4,925.0	5,535.0	5,965.9	6,719.6	7,728.6	8,336.3	9,101.2	9,734.8	11,341.7	12,316.5

Source: The Bank of Korea, *National Income Statistics Yearbook*. (GNP includes income from abroad.)

Table A.23. Sectoral Gross and Net Fixed Capital Stock: 1968

	Han's Gross Capital Stock (in million 1968 won) (A)	Han's Net Fixed Capital Stock		
		Uniform Net Adjustments (A x 0.6448) (B)	Net Stock in Million 1970 won (C)[1]	Net Stock in Million 1970 Dollar (C/310.6)
Agriculture, Forestry & Fishery	353,896	228,173	261,967	843.4
Mining & Quarrying	34,747	22,403	26,295	84.7
Manufacturing	720,190	464,339	522,316	1,681.6
Construction	53,036	34,195	38,814	125.0
Electricity, Water & Sanitary Service	145,448	139,019[2]	175,751	565.8
Transportation, Storage & Communication	730,945	471,273	580,386	1,868.6
Wholesale & Retail Trade	169,060	109,001	126,013	405.7
Banking, Insurance & Real Estate	24,955[3]	16,090	19,132	61.6
Public Administration	237,716	153,266	186,228	599.6
Services	574,982[4]	370,717	444,505	1,431.1
Ownership of Dwellings	1,791,441	1,155,024	1,588,754	5,115.1
Total Fixed Capital Stock	4,836,416	3,163,500	3,970,161	12,782.2

Source: K.C. Han, *Estimates of Korean Capital and Inventory Coefficients in 1968*, Seoul: Yonsei University, 1970 and Economic Planning Board, *Report on National Wealth Survey* (as of December 31, 1968) 1972.
[1] We applied the BOK's sectoral implicit price deflator for fixed capital formation in order to get 1970 won values.
[2] We applied the gross-to-net conversion rate of 0.9558. (See text.)
[3] 10,426.0 million won for real estate sector was added (which was obtained from the *Report on National Wealth Survey*.)
[4] Excluding 50,083.9 million won for agricultural service sector which was included in the agricultural sector. Includes 22.5 million won for unclassifiable sector.

Table A.24. Sectoral Gross Fixed Capital Formation (1953-74)

In Million 1970 Dollars

	1953	1954	1955	1956	1957	1958	1959	1960	1961	1962	1963
Agriculture & Fishery	19.9	17.2	21.9	24.9	32.7	26.9	30.5	35.7	45.9	36.2	56.2
Mining & Quarrying	0.5	1.3	3.7	5.8	9.2	6.3	3.8	5.3	1.8	3.4	6.0
Manufacturing	32.9	32.9	58.4	73.8	79.8	75.5	62.3	66.7	66.0	88.7	115.4
Construction	0.6	0.9	1.9	2.5	3.6	4.6	3.2	3.4	3.9	13.4	10.9
Electricity & Sanitary Service	3.8	6.0	12.9	8.2	7.4	14.5	10.7	10.7	26.3	45.0	69.1
Transportation & Comm.	28.1	41.1	37.1	43.1	72.7	62.4	73.4	54.9	76.8	99.6	124.8
Trade	13.5	11.9	16.8	14.3	12.4	17.6	21.1	18.6	15.3	25.9	27.2
Banking & Real Estate	0.2	0.3	0.4	1.3	1.1	1.4	1.7	1.1	0.3	0.7	0.7
Public Administration	3.3	7.4	6.5	7.0	7.7	8.6	9.0	8.7	5.5	5.1	7.6
Other Services	23.4	28.7	35.5	26.9	24.6	24.0	33.6	32.3	35.2	53.4	54.7
Ownership of Dwellings	38.3	61.9	42.9	45.4	42.0	39.9	51.0	75.0	59.4	58.1	67.6
Whole Industry	164.5	209.6	238.0	253.2	293.2	281.7	300.3	312.4	336.4	429.5	540.2

	1964	1965	1966	1967	1968	1969	1970	1971	1972	1973	1974
Agriculture & Fishery	62.0	76.4	112.9	101.4	113.7	128.5	168.6	179.6	231.7	243.2	316.9
Mining & Quarrying	4.0	7.4	10.3	11.3	15.8	13.5	11.2	15.7	13.7	17.9	24.7
Manufacturing	113.9	157.1	267.7	265.9	357.0	405.2	414.3	424.8	415.9	767.8	626.4
Construction	7.6	9.5	11.2	10.6	43.5	43.5	25.5	29.9	27.6	44.8	26.2
Electricity & Sanitary Service	38.6	36.8	50.5	98.4	177.3	248.8	237.9	193.1	127.9	131.6	205.8
Transportation & Comm.	98.8	119.4	240.1	337.9	422.4	615.8	539.3	572.4	632.9	681.9	805.7
Trade	26.2	44.5	38.4	51.3	65.5	108.3	124.4	141.5	101.3	117.6	153.1
Banking & Real Estate	1.3	2.2	4.2	3.5	14.0	18.5	21.2	15.9	13.7	18.8	24.6
Public Administration	6.6	10.5	11.8	23.0	41.0	41.5	42.1	68.7	70.5	58.7	50.0
Other Services	63.6	79.9	85.9	116.0	138.5	204.4	225.9	240.3	198.9	272.3	238.7
Ownership of Dwellings	76.7	85.5	114.5	135.4	215.6	230.1	283.1	309.3	288.0	388.0	551.2
Whole Industry	499.3	629.2	947.5	1,154.7	1,604.3	2,058.1	2,093.5	2,191.2	2,122.1	2,742.6	3,023.4

Source: The Bank of Korea, *National Income Statistics Yearbook*.

Table A.25. Sectoral Provisions for the Consumption of Fixed Capital (1953–74)

In Million 1970 Dollars

	1953	1954	1955	1956	1957	1958	1959	1960	1961	1962	1963
Agriculture & Fishery	7.9	8.3	7.2	9.4	8.5	9.5	9.2	11.3	10.4	14.8	14.0
Mining & Quarrying	2.0	3.2	3.4	2.2	4.2	5.0	4.9	9.4	7.0	7.7	7.8
Manufacturing	11.3	13.8	17.7	19.5	24.8	25.1	24.4	29.8	24.8	32.7	48.9
Construction	3.4	4.7	8.4	5.2	6.3	5.9	6.2	1.6	3.3	4.8	7.3
Electricity & Sanitary Service	3.3	2.8	4.4	3.9	3.5	5.8	3.8	4.3	8.1	9.2	10.1
Transportation & Comm.	6.3	11.7	11.5	15.2	17.5	17.4	24.4	19.7	20.9	28.7	38.3
Trade	22.8	22.0	24.3	25.4	27.5	27.1	30.0	27.7	27.2	30.6	39.7
Banking & Real Estate	—	—	—	—	—	0.5	0.6	0.7	1.6	1.4	1.1
Public Administration	1.2	1.5	1.6	1.9	2.2	2.8	3.2	3.3	3.3	3.1	3.4
Other Services	4.9	8.8	9.3	8.9	10.6	11.5	13.0	11.8	11.5	12.2	13.0
Ownership of Dwellings	50.9	46.5	30.3	28.6	30.1	29.4	29.6	27.8	24.2	22.5	25.9
Whole Industry	114.0	123.3	118.1	120.2	135.2	140.0	149.3	147.4	142.3	167.7	209.5

	1964	1965	1966	1967	1968	1969	1970	1971	1972	1973	1974
Agriculture & Fishery	24.0	23.4	24.7	31.2	35.5	44.3	49.5	59.4	69.0	83.1	89.2
Mining & Quarrying	8.0	7.8	9.2	11.4	12.8	13.6	17.3	17.5	14.4	15.7	14.5
Manufacturing	63.1	72.1	66.0	83.1	131.4	168.8	194.9	212.1	308.6	417.1	441.4
Construction	7.6	7.4	5.5	9.6	14.3	20.5	21.9	21.5	21.1	28.6	37.3
Electricity & Sanitary Service	10.1	10.5	15.1	15.6	17.6	23.3	23.6	28.8	36.5	40.2	38.2
Transportation & Comm.	33.5	33.9	47.4	49.4	68.6	71.5	70.6	78.5	83.0	124.2	130.4
Trade	42.6	51.3	59.5	67.4	48.9	62.0	70.3	80.8	133.3	156.7	168.8
Banking & Real Estate	1.0	1.1	1.3	2.1	3.2	4.6	6.4	7.3	8.3	8.8	12.3
Public Administration	3.7	4.6	5.8	5.9	7.4	9.1	10.1	11.2	13.6	13.5	28.2
Other Services	11.3	9.8	12.4	15.5	19.3	22.6	26.4	30.2	32.3	37.0	35.8
Ownership of Dwellings	22.5	20.9	22.0	25.6	26.7	27.9	24.6	27.3	28.0	28.5	14.8
Whole Industry	227.4	242.8	268.9	316.8	385.7	467.8	515.6	574.6	748.1	953.4	1,010.9

Source: The Bank of Korea.
Note: We applied the sectoral implicit price deflator for fixed capital formation in order to get 1970 won values, and then applied the exchange rate of 310.6 won per dollar to get 1970 dollar values.

Table A.26. Sectoral Net Fixed Capital Formation (1953–74)

In Million 1970 Dollars

	1953	1954	1955	1956	1957	1958	1959	1960	1961	1962	1963
Agriculture & Fishery	12.0	8.9	14.7	15.5	24.2	17.4	21.3	24.4	35.5	21.4	42.2
Mining & Quarrying	-1.5	-1.9	0.3	3.6	5.0	1.3	-1.1	-4.1	-5.2	-4.3	-1.8
Manufacturing	21.6	19.1	40.7	54.3	55.0	50.4	37.9	36.9	41.2	56.0	66.5
Construction	-2.8	-3.8	-6.5	-2.7	-2.7	-1.3	-3.0	1.8	0.6	8.6	3.6
Electricity & Sanitary Service	0.5	3.2	8.5	4.3	3.9	8.7	6.9	6.4	18.2	35.8	59.0
Transportation & Comm.	21.8	29.4	25.6	27.9	55.2	45.0	49.0	35.2	55.9	70.9	86.5
Trade	-9.3	-10.1	-7.5	-11.1	-15.1	-9.5	-8.9	-9.1	-11.9	-4.7	-12.5
Banking & Real Estate	-0.3	-0.2	-0.1	0.8	0.6	1.1	1.1	0.4	-1.3	-0.7	-0.4
Public Administration	2.1	5.9	4.9	5.1	5.5	5.8	5.8	5.4	2.2	2.0	4.2
Other Services	18.5	19.9	26.2	18.0	14.0	12.5	20.6	20.5	23.7	41.2	41.7
Ownership of Dwellings	-12.6	15.4	12.6	16.8	11.9	10.5	21.4	47.2	35.2	35.6	41.7
Whole Industry	50.0	85.8	119.4	132.5	157.5	141.7	151.0	165.0	194.1	261.8	330.7

	1964	1965	1966	1967	1968	1969	1970	1971	1972	1973	1974
Agriculture & Fishery	38.0	53.0	88.2	70.2	78.2	84.2	119.1	120.2	162.7	160.1	227.7
Mining & Quarrying	-4.0	-0.4	1.1	-0.1	3.0	-0.1	-6.1	-1.8	-0.7	2.2	10.2
Manufacturing	50.8	85.0	201.1	182.8	225.6	236.8	219.4	212.7	107.3	350.7	185.0
Construction	0.0	2.1	5.7	1.0	29.2	23.0	3.6	8.4	6.5	16.2	-11.1
Electricity & Sanitary Service	28.5	26.3	35.4	82.8	159.7	225.5	214.3	164.3	91.4	91.4	167.6
Transportation & Comm.	65.3	85.5	192.7	288.5	353.8	544.3	468.5	493.9	549.9	557.7	675.3
Trade	-16.4	-6.8	-21.1	-16.1	16.6	46.3	54.1	60.7	-32.0	-39.1	-15.7
Banking & Real Estate	0.3	1.1	2.9	1.4	10.8	13.9	14.8	8.6	5.4	10.0	12.3
Public Administration	2.9	5.9	6.0	17.1	33.6	32.4	32.0	57.5	56.9	45.2	21.8
Other Services	52.3	70.1	73.5	100.5	119.2	181.8	199.5	210.1	166.6	235.3	202.9
Ownership of Dwellings	54.2	64.6	92.5	109.8	188.9	202.2	258.5	282.0	260.0	359.5	536.4
Whole Industry	271.9	386.4	678.6	837.9	1,218.6	1,590.3	1,577.9	1,616.6	1,438.0	1,789.2	2,012.5

Source: The same as Tables A.24. and A.25.

Table A.27. Sectoral Net Fixed Capital Stock (1953–74)

In Million 1970 Dollars

	1953	1954	1955	1956	1957	1958	1959	1960	1961	1962	1963
Agriculture & Fishery	290.3	299.2	313.9	329.4	353.6	371.0	392.3	416.7	452.2	473.6	515.8
Mining & Quarrying	93.3	91.4	91.7	95.3	100.3	101.6	100.5	96.4	91.2	86.9	85.1
Manufacturing	477.7	496.8	537.5	591.8	646.8	697.2	735.1	772.0	813.2	869.2	935.7
Construction	92.4	88.6	82.1	79.4	76.7	75.4	72.4	74.2	74.8	83.4	87.0
Electricity & Sanitary Service	78.2	81.4	89.9	94.2	98.1	106.8	113.7	120.1	138.3	174.1	233.1
Transportation & Comm.	402.2	431.6	457.1	485.1	540.3	585.3	634.3	669.5	725.4	796.3	882.8
Trade	549.9	539.8	532.3	521.2	506.1	496.6	487.7	478.6	466.7	462.0	449.5
Banking & Real Estate	44.0	43.8	43.7	44.5	45.1	46.0	47.1	47.5	46.2	45.5	45.1
Public Administration	487.3	493.2	498.1	503.2	508.7	514.5	520.3	525.7	527.9	529.9	534.1
Other Services	777.2	797.1	823.3	841.3	855.3	867.8	888.4	908.9	932.6	973.8	1,015.5
Ownership of Dwellings	4,356.8	4,372.2	4,384.8	4,401.6	4,413.5	4,424.0	4,445.4	4,492.6	4,527.8	4,563.4	4,605.1
Whole Industry	7,649.3	7,735.1	7,854.5	7,987.0	8,144.5	8,286.2	8,437.2	8,602.2	8,796.3	9,058.1	9,388.8

	1964	1965	1966	1967	1968	1969	1970	1971	1972	1973	1974
Agriculture & Fishery*	553.8	606.8	695.0	765.2	843.4	927.6	1,046.7	1,166.9	1,329.6	1,489.7	1,717.4
Mining & Quarrying	81.1	80.7	81.8	81.7	84.7	84.6	78.5	76.7	76.0	78.2	88.4
Manufacturing	986.5	1,071.5	1,273.2	1,456.0	1,681.6	1,918.4	2,137.8	2,350.5	2,457.8	2,808.5	2,993.5
Construction	87.0	89.1	94.8	95.8	125.0	148.0	151.6	160.0	166.5	182.7	171.6
Electricity & Sanitary Service	261.6	287.9	323.3	406.1	565.8	791.3	1,005.6	1,169.9	1,261.3	1,352.7	1,520.3
Transportation & Comm.	948.1	1,033.6	1,226.3	1,514.8	1,868.6	2,412.9	2,881.6	3,375.5	3,925.4	4,483.1	5,158.4
Trade	433.1	426.3	405.2	389.1	405.7	452.0	506.1	566.8	534.8	495.7	480.0
Banking & Real Estate	45.4	46.5	49.4	50.8	61.6	75.5	90.3	98.9	104.3	114.3	126.6
Public Administration	537.0	542.9	548.9	566.0	599.6	632.0	664.0	721.5	778.4	823.6	845.4
Other Services	1,067.8	1,137.9	1,211.4	1,311.9	1,431.1	1,612.9	1,812.4	2,022.5	2,189.1	2,424.4	2,627.3
Ownership of Dwellings	4,659.3	4,723.9	4,816.4	4,926.2	5,115.1	5,317.3	5,575.8	5,857.8	6,117.8	6,477.3	7,013.7
Whole Industry	9,660.7	10,047.1	10,725.7	11,563.6	12,782.2	14,372.5	15,950.4	17,567.0	18,941.0	20,730.2	22,742.7

Source: The same as Table A.26.
* Includes capital stock for agricultural service sector.

Table A. 28. Age Structure of Fixed Capital Stcok: 1953-74

In Million 1970 Dollars

	1952	1953	1954	1955	1956	1957	1958	1959	1960	1961	1962	1963
1952	7,599	7,485	7,364	7,251	7,140	7,019	6,898	6,774	6,656	6,546	6,421	6,273
1953		165	162	159	156	153	150	147	144	142	139	136
1954			210	207	204	201	197	194	191	188	184	180
1955				238	234	230	226	222	218	214	210	205
1956					253	249	245	240	236	232	228	223
1957						293	288	283	278	273	268	262
1958							282	277	272	268	263	257
1959								300	295	290	284	277
1960									312	307	301	294
1961										336	330	322
1962											430	420
1963												540
1964												
1965												
1966												
1967												
1968												
1969												
1970												
1971												
1972												
1973												
1974												
Total	7,599	7,650	7,736	7,855	7,987	8,145	8,286	8,437	8,602	8,796	9,058	9,389
Depreciation		1.50%	1.61%	1.53%	1.53%	1.69%	1.72%	1.80%	1.75%	1.65%	1.91%	2.31%

	1964	1965	1966	1967	1968	1969	1970	1971	1972	1973	1974
1952	6,121	5,967	5,807	5,636	5,448	5,249	5,060	4,878	4,670	4,435	4,219
1953	133	130	127	123	119	115	111	107	102	97	92
1954	176	171	166	161	156	150	145	140	134	127	121
1955	200	195	190	184	179	172	166	160	153	145	138
1956	218	212	206	200	193	186	179	172	165	157	149
1957	255	249	242	235	227	219	211	203	194	184	175
1958	251	245	238	231	223	215	207	200	192	182	173
1959	270	263	256	249	241	232	224	216	207	197	187
1960	287	280	273	265	256	247	238	229	219	208	198
1961	314	306	298	289	279	269	259	250	239	227	216
1962	410	400	389	378	365	352	339	327	313	297	283
1963	527	514	500	485	469	452	436	420	402	382	363
1964	499	486	473	459	444	428	413	398	381	362	344
1965		629	612	594	574	553	533	514	492	467	444
1966			948	920	889	856	825	795	761	723	688
1967				1,155	1,116	1,075	1,036	999	956	908	864
1968					1,604	1,545	1,490	1,436	1,375	1,306	1,242
1969						2,058	1,984	1,913	1,832	1,740	1,655
1970							2,094	2,019	1,933	1,836	1,747
1971								2,191	2,098	1,992	1,895
1972									2,122	2,015	1,917
1973										2,743	2,609
1974											3,023
Total	9,661	10,047	10,725	11,564	12,782	14,373	15,950	17,567	18,940	20,730	22,743
Depreciation	2.42%	2.51%	2.68%	2.95%	3.34%	3.66%	3.59%	3.60%	4.26%	5.03%	4.88%

Table A. 29. Age Structure of Fixed Capital Stock (Excluding the Ownership of Dwellings): 1953-74

In Million 1970 Dollars

	1952	1953	1954	1955	1956	1957	1958	1959	1960	1961	1962	1963
1952	3,230	3,167	3,093	3,012	2,932	2,846	2,762	2,676	2,596	2,521	2,435	2,335
1953		126	123	120	116	113	110	107	104	101	97	93
1954			148	144	140	136	132	128	124	120	116	111
1955				195	189	183	177	172	167	162	156	150
1956					208	202	196	190	184	179	173	166
1957						251	243	235	228	222	215	206
1958							242	235	228	222	215	206
1959								249	242	235	227	218
1960									237	230	222	213
1961										277	268	257
1962											371	356
1963												473
1964												
1965												
1966												
1967												
1968												
1969												
1970												
1971												
1972												
1973												
1974												
Total	3,230	3,293	3,364	3,471	3,585	3,731	3,862	3,992	4,110	4,269	4,495	4,784
Depreciation		1.95%	2.33%	2.61%	2.64%	2.93%	2.96%	3.10%	3.00%	2.87%	3.40%	4.08%

	1964	1965	1966	1967	1968	1969	1970	1971	1972	1973	1974
1952	2,235	2,136	2,037	1,937	1,832	1,727	1,633	1,547	1,452	1,347	1,253
1953	89	85	81	77	73	69	65	61	57	53	49
1954	106	101	96	91	86	81	77	73	69	64	60
1955	143	137	131	124	117	110	104	98	92	85	79
1956	159	152	145	138	131	124	117	111	104	96	89
1957	197	188	179	170	161	152	144	136	128	119	111
1958	197	188	179	170	161	152	144	136	128	119	111
1959	208	199	190	181	171	161	152	144	135	125	116
1960	204	195	186	177	167	157	149	141	132	123	114
1961	246	235	224	213	202	190	180	171	160	148	138
1962	341	326	311	296	280	264	250	237	222	206	192
1963	453	433	413	393	372	351	332	314	295	274	255
1964	423	404	385	366	346	326	308	292	274	254	236
1965		544	519	493	466	439	415	393	369	342	318
1966			833	792	749	706	668	633	594	551	513
1967				1,019	964	909	860	815	765	710	660
1968					1,389	1,309	1,238	1,173	1,101	1,022	951
1969						1,828	1,729	1,638	1,537	1,426	1,326
1970							1,810	1,714	1,609	1,493	1,389
1971								1,882	1,766	1,639	1,524
1972									1,834	1,702	1,583
1973										2,355	2,190
1974											2,472
Total	5,001	5,323	5,909	6,637	7,667	9,055	10,375	11,709	12,823	14,253	15,729
Depreciation	4.28%	4.44%	4.64%	4.93%	5.41%	5.74%	5.42%	5.28%	6.15%	7.21%	6.99%

Table A.30. *Direct Factor Requirements Per $1,000 (1970 Dollar Prices) of Outputs: 1960, 1963, 1966, 1968 & 1970*

In Thousand 1970 Dollars & Persons

I-O 117 Sector Classification	Direct Labor Coefficients					Direct Capital Coefficients				
	1960	1963	1966	1968	1970	1960	1963	1966	1968	1970
(1) Rice, Barley & Wheat										
1. Rice, Barley & Wheat	0.9317	0.9317	1.0549	1.0543	0.9563	0.2538	0.2538	0.2538	0.3252	0.3421
(2) Other Agriculture										
2. Other Cereals	2.6650	2.6650	2.4420	2.7719	2.1123	0.2720	0.2720	0.2720	0.3450	0.3278
3. Vegetables	1.4310	1.4310	1.5534	1.4909	1.2653	0.2208	0.2208	0.2208	0.2835	0.2812
4. Fruit	2.8583	2.8583	2.1336	1.6048	1.6733	1.0324	1.0324	1.0324	1.8030	2.4989
5. Industrial Crops	2.8583	2.8583	2.1336	1.6048	1.6733	0.2162	0.2162	0.2162	0.2497	0.2762
6. Livestock & Sericulture	2.7983	2.7983	1.5719	0.8982	0.8053	0.8435	0.8435	0.8435	0.7474	0.6829
(3) Forestry										
7. Forestry	0.7363	0.7363	0.7363	0.7363	0.7363	0.1777	0.1777	0.1777	0.1777	0.1777
(4) Fishery										
8. Fishery	0.8396	0.8396	0.8396	0.8396	0.8396	1.5933	1.5933	1.5933	1.5933	1.5933
(5) Coal										
9. Coal	0.7792	0.5942	0.5119	0.4246	0.3751	0.2866	0.2075	0.5478	0.4913	0.6217
(6) Other Minerals										
10. Metallic Ores	0.8482	0.8485	0.4997	0.4362	0.2824	0.3852	0.6273	0.4113	0.5437	0.4969
11. Nonmetallic Minerals	1.5833	1.0909	0.5980	0.5808	0.5640	0.2506	0.4416	0.2781	0.3913	0.3429
12. Salt	0.3367	0.3367	0.7831	2.3048	1.5050	0.1446	0.1446	0.6698	0.4565	0.2516
(7) Processed Foods										
13. Meat & Dairy Products	0.1429	0.1896	0.1896	0.1589	0.1181	0.4406	0.4406	0.4406	0.2070	0.2035
14. Veg. & Fruit Processing	0.6667	0.5000	0.5998	0.3506	0.3682	0.3714	0.3714	0.8112	0.4517	0.3175
15. Processing of Sea Foods	1.0294	0.6591	0.6484	0.7328	0.3509	0.3816	0.5492	0.4141	0.5765	0.2611
16. Grain Milling	0.2456	0.2432	0.3240	0.2970	0.1269	0.2991	0.4902	0.3747	0.3972	0.2063
17. Bakery & Confectionery	0.5180	0.3158	0.4626	0.3530	0.2192	0.2110	0.2110	0.2637	0.1766	0.1553
18. Sugar Refining	0.0176	0.0270	0.0413	0.0281	0.0355	0.1870	0.1870	0.3184	0.1248	0.1222

19. Seasonings	0.3333	0.2156	0.2974	0.2280	0.1652	0.2471	0.3020	0.3925	0.3637	0.4636
20. Other Processed Foods	0.3878	0.2986	0.3440	0.2436	0.1581	0.4091	0.4329	0.4172	0.3662	0.2943
(8) Beverages										
21. Alcoholic Beverages	0.2962	0.1877	0.1828	0.1370	0.1119	0.3126	0.2640	0.2125	0.1575	0.1561
22. Soft Drinks	0.2143	0.2143	0.1919	0.1938	0.1721	0.1557	0.2976	0.3145	0.3145	0.1728
(9) Tobacco										
23. Tobacco	0.0873	0.0873	0.0973	0.0583	0.0490	0.2781	0.2781	0.2781	0.1543	0.0996
(10) Fibre Spinning										
24. Cotton Yarn	0.3167	0.3180	0.2571	0.2541	0.2616	0.5662	0.4256	0.9206	0.4712	0.9874
25. Silk Yarn	0.9250	0.7093	0.4733	0.2799	0.2974	0.5174	0.4163	0.3920	0.3103	0.3956
26. Woolen Yarn	0.2527	0.2903	0.2542	0.2439	0.5150	0.4906	0.8391	0.5604	0.6352	1.3959
27. Hemp & Flax Yarn	0.2527	0.2903	0.2542	0.2439	0.5150	0.4906	0.8391	0.5604	0.6352	1.3959
28. Chemical Fibre Yarn	0.4848	0.3699	0.5758	0.2390	0.1845	0.3886	0.3217	0.2972	1.8496	1.3486
(11) Textile Fabrics										
29. Cotton Fabrics	0.4736	0.5078	0.3961	0.4378	0.3235	0.2907	0.2912	0.1433	0.3879	0.3138
30. Silk Fabrics	0.7621	0.5538	0.5237	0.4161	0.2385	0.5501	0.4173	0.2913	0.2913	0.5201
31. Woolen Fabrics	0.2047	0.3128	0.5913	0.3229	0.1908	0.2948	0.5612	1.3740	0.4359	0.3540
32. Hemp Fabrics	0.4615	0.6667	1.5763	0.8125	0.4346	0.9709	1.6910	0.1017	0.2086	0.2103
33. Chemical Fibre Fabrics	0.5237	0.5237	0.5237	0.4020	0.3910	0.3452	0.3452	0.3452	0.4093	0.6858
34. Dyeing & Finishing	0.3579	0.3727	0.3734	0.3400	0.2578	0.4755	0.5614	0.5939	0.4181	0.3684
(12) Textile Products										
35. Knit Products	0.4934	0.5527	0.5493	0.7503	0.4785	0.2743	0.4155	0.3791	0.4051	0.4201
36. Rope & Fishing Nets	0.3846	0.3684	0.3865	0.3545	0.3397	0.1950	0.4146	0.1623	0.2346	0.2866
37. Apparels & Accessories	0.4276	0.5690	0.5620	0.3685	0.3516	0.1285	0.1476	0.2942	0.1864	0.2077
38. Misc. Textile Products	0.7581	1.3947	0.9801	0.5856	0.3481	0.4151	0.3985	0.4862	0.4736	0.4152
(13) Lumber & Plywood										
39. Lumber & Plywood	0.2506	0.1904	0.1875	0.1754	0.1576	0.2056	0.2104	0.2007	0.2583	0.3136
(14) Wood & Furniture										
40. Wood Products	0.5556	0.8387	0.7655	1.1800	0.8276	0.1610	0.6752	0.3218	0.2342	0.4936
41. Furniture	0.6912	0.6279	0.7062	0.5547	0.5174	0.2574	0.4984	0.3016	0.2266	0.3106

Table A. 30. (Continued)

In Thousand 1970 Dollars & Persons

I-O 117 Sector Classification	Direct Labor Coefficients					Direct Capital Coefficients				
	1960	1963	1966	1968	1970	1960	1963	1966	1968	1970
(15) Paper & Products										
42. Pulp	0.4126	0.2208	0.1996	0.1761	0.1366	0.4534	0.4133	0.5987	0.4618	0.2684
43. Paper	0.4126	0.2208	0.1996	0.1761	0.1366	0.4534	0.4133	0.5987	0.4618	0.2684
44. Paper Products	0.4468	0.3231	0.2673	0.3131	0.2832	0.2768	0.2743	0.2803	0.6163	0.4741
(16) Printing & Publishing										
45. Printing & Publishing	0.4920	0.4127	0.4446	0.3607	0.3225	0.7621	0.3132	0.5168	0.4047	0.4457
(17) Leather Products										
46. Leather & Fur	0.1731	0.2708	0.2865	0.2548	0.3182	0.2914	0.3205	0.1921	0.4196	0.3432
47. Leather Products	0.6774	0.7111	0.5434	0.4274	0.4087	0.1668	0.3632	0.3041	0.1911	0.3052
(18) Rubber Products										
48. Rubber Products	0.2691	0.3983	0.4244	0.3618	0.2872	0.1885	0.1927	0.2111	0.2583	0.2773
(19) Basic Chemicals										
49. Inorganic Chemicals	0.2000	0.1884	0.2956	0.2233	0.1789	0.9163	0.4226	1.8909	1.5252	1.0702
50. Organic Chemicals	0.3300	0.1894	0.2476	0.2304	0.2148	0.7303	0.7303	0.4842	0.4326	0.3010
(20) Other Chemical Products										
51. Explosives	0.2500	0.2500	0.2297	0.1897	0.1266	0.3704	0.3704	0.3704	0.2450	0.3582
52. Paint	0.1176	0.1486	0.1438	0.1069	0.0841	0.1620	0.2653	0.2084	0.1389	0.0992
53. Drugs	0.2604	0.2786	0.2310	0.1864	0.1479	0.2673	0.2465	0.2262	0.1674	0.1378
54. Soap	0.1486	0.1317	0.1796	0.1541	0.1230	0.2582	0.1502	0.2233	0.2316	0.2137
55. Cosmetics	0.3279	0.2500	0.2990	0.1814	0.1383	0.2695	0.2184	0.2783	0.1745	0.1105
56. Pesticides	0.3279	0.2500	0.1495	0.1812	0.2285	0.2695	0.2184	0.1463	0.1227	0.1370
57. Other Chemical Products	1.1111	0.9310	0.4528	0.2186	0.1493	0.2649	0.2354	0.2290	0.9429	1.2835
(21) Chemical Fertilizer										
58. Chemical Fertilizer	0.2072	0.2072	0.1657	0.0629	0.0582	1.3476	1.3476	1.3476	1.3476	1.1502
(22) Petroleum Products										
59. Petroleum Products	0.1154	0.1154	0.0240	0.0183	0.0117	0.2481	0.2481	0.3073	0.2405	0.2386

(23) Coal Products											
60. Coal Products	0.3640	0.3098	0.2337	0.1579	0.1183	0.1626	0.1731	0.1392	0.1430	0.1583
(24) Nonmetallic Mineral Products											
61. Cement	0.0769	0.0809	0.0779	0.0931	0.0519	0.6435	0.7719	3.1199	2.7880	1.7949
62. Ceramic Products	0.7581	0.7273	0.5430	0.5564	0.4210	0.3277	0.4086	0.4980	0.3314	0.3675
63. Glass Products	0.3929	0.4362	0.4125	0.3401	0.2868	0.5321	0.4997	0.3855	0.3003	0.6561
64. Pottery	0.8906	1.1053	0.9884	1.2365	0.9199	0.4729	0.5121	0.3527	0.4063	0.6128
65. Other Stone & Clay	0.4154	0.4251	0.3745	0.5874	0.5992	0.4325	0.3389	0.4205	0.4205	0.3437
(25) Iron & Steel											
66. Pig Iron	0.3019	0.1422	0.1929	0.2479	0.2919	0.6213	0.4189	0.9749	0.9749	0.9749
67. Steel Ingots	0.3019	0.1422	0.1929	0.2479	0.2919	0.6213	0.4189	0.9749	0.9749	0.9749
(26) Steel Products											
68. Rolled Steel	0.2037	0.1401	0.1552	0.1807	0.1009	0.2536	0.2356	0.1713	0.2828	0.2065
69. Pipes & Plated Steel	0.1538	0.1000	0.1058	0.1271	0.0542	0.2936	0.2885	0.2885	0.2885	0.3101
70. Cast & Forged Steel	0.6000	0.4135	0.3166	0.1947	0.2854	0.4997	0.3395	0.7050	0.2543	0.5609
(27) Nonferrous Metals											
71. Nonferrous Smelting	0.2308	0.2308	0.1310	0.1198	0.1037	0.4581	0.4773	0.2802	0.2854	0.1648
72. Primary Nonferrous	0.2632	0.1909	0.3411	0.2756	0.2521	0.3856	0.6706	0.3188	0.3188	0.9615
(28) Finished Metal Products											
73. Structural Metallic	0.2836	0.5049	0.6205	0.4132	0.2794	0.3277	0.4432	0.4408	0.3112	0.2941
74. Other Metallic Products	0.5342	0.5297	0.5323	0.4489	0.4006	0.2643	0.4176	0.4257	0.4138	0.4428
(29) Machinery											
75. Prime Movers & Boilers	0.5758	0.6081	0.4708	0.4235	0.3820	0.4172	0.9184	0.2867	0.4139	0.6332
76. Working Machinery	0.4545	0.6875	0.6466	0.5419	0.4056	0.7185	0.6799	0.7484	0.6040	0.5205
77. Industrial Machinery	0.7368	0.5593	0.5286	0.4147	0.3974	0.6296	0.4387	0.4796	0.3907	0.3754
78. Other Machinery	0.2917	0.5385	0.4562	0.3861	0.2796	0.3717	0.6139	0.4920	0.4075	0.3995
79. Office Machines	0.7000	0.5000	0.6096	0.4905	0.3551	0.3961	0.3704	0.3764	0.3760	0.5306
80. Household Machines	0.7000	0.5000	0.6096	0.4905	0.3551	0.3961	0.3704	0.3764	0.3760	0.5306
81. Machine Spare Parts	0.7273	0.6667	0.6213	0.4124	0.4160	0.6990	0.4866	0.4866	0.4797	0.4130

Table A.30. (Continued)

In Thousand 1970 Dollars & Persons

1-O 117 Sector Classification	Direct Labor Coefficients					Direct Capital Coefficients				
	1960	1963	1966	1968	1970	1960	1963	1966	1968	1970
(30) Electrical Machinery										
82. Electrical Machinery	0.6000	0.3069	0.3435	0.2135	0.2277	0.4607	0.6000	0.9795	0.3208	0.5162
83. Electronic & Comm. Eq.	0.6000	0.4648	0.3692	0.2664	0.2063	0.3232	0.5693	0.8642	0.2806	0.2715
84. Household Elec. Appl.	0.7333	0.5143	0.4195	0.4612	0.2371	0.2895	0.3373	0.1614	0.3719	0.1784
85. Other Electric Equipments	0.1429	0.2128	0.1983	0.1767	0.2468	0.2025	0.1407	0.4453	0.3017	0.3707
(31) Transport Equipments										
86. Shipbuilding	0.5424	0.3571	0.3184	0.3979	0.2897	0.9416	0.9206	0.4878	0.7674	0.5944
87. Railroad Transport Eq.	0.6000	0.3534	0.1867	0.1574	0.3064	0.4764	0.2364	0.2364	0.2801	0.4531
88. Motor Vehicles	0.7077	0.6063	0.3881	0.1653	0.1422	0.4936	0.5872	0.3617	0.1985	0.2185
89. Other Transport Eq.	0.5833	0.4462	0.4405	0.7253	0.1431	0.3676	0.3092	0.1691	0.4192	0.0961
(32) Misc. Manufacturing										
90. Measuring & Optical	0.6154	0.6207	0.6330	0.2905	0.3424	0.5016	0.4427	0.8252	0.2789	0.3416
91. Synthetic Resin Products	0.4746	0.4746	0.3060	0.2257	0.1942	0.5847	0.5847	0.3806	0.3806	0.2923
92. Other Manufactures	0.6250	0.5764	0.7393	0.5516	0.4720	0.3386	0.2749	0.3230	0.2379	0.2484
(33) Building & Maintenance										
93. Residential Building	0.6036	0.4550	0.2716	0.2763	0.3020	0.2562	0.1463	0.0823	0.0656	0.0551
94. Non-Residential Building	0.6036	0.4550	0.2716	0.2763	0.3020	0.1390	0.0794	0.0446	0.0356	0.0299
95. Building Maintenance	0.6036	0.4550	0.2716	0.2763	0.3020	0.0293	0.0167	0.0094	0.0075	0.0063
(34) Other Construction										
96. Public Construction	0.6036	0.4550	0.2716	0.2763	0.3020	0.9016	0.5151	0.2895	0.2309	0.1938
97. Other Construction	0.6036	0.4550	0.2716	0.2763	0.3020	0.7677	0.4385	0.2465	0.1966	0.1650
(35) Electricity										
98. Electricity	0.1960	0.3421	0.2650	0.1730	0.1331	1.7098	4.1246	3.5175	3.5196	4.5716
(36) Banking & Dwelling										
99. Banking & Insurance	0.1509	0.2132	0.2666	0.2604	0.2361	0.3123	0.2682	0.2204	0.2291	0.1666
100. Dwelling & Real Estate	0.0376	0.0390	0.0384	0.0567	0.0573	31.3385	26.9174	22.1193	22.9906	16.7188

(37) Water & Sanitary Service									
101. Water & Sanitary Service	0.3524	0.3486	0.2910	0.2085	0.2953	1.7132	4.1327	3.5244	3.5265	4.5806
(38) Communication									
102. Communication	0.6066	0.6264	0.4324	0.4190	0.4080	1.8053	1.8567	1.5659	1.7179	1.6420
(39) Transportation									
103. Railroad Transportation	0.7803	0.6548	0.3877	0.3897	0.3300	5.4794	5.6353	4.7526	5.2140	4.9835
104. Other Transportation	0.7803	0.6548	0.3877	0.3897	0.3300	3.1451	3.2346	2.7279	2.9928	2.8605
105. Storage	0.7803	0.6548	0.3877	0.3897	0.3300	0.5032	0.5175	0.4364	0.4788	0.4576
(40) Trade									
106. Trade	1.1858	1.0116	0.9513	0.7468	0.6549	1.0048	0.6777	0.4837	0.3330	0.3191
(41) Other Services									
107. Education	0.4679	0.5244	0.5661	0.6485	0.5521	2.5711	2.5685	2.8105	2.9294	2.4938
108. Medical Service	0.4679	0.5244	0.5661	0.6485	0.5521	0.7927	0.7919	0.8665	0.9032	0.7689
109. Social Service	0.4679	0.5244	0.5661	0.6485	0.5521	0.7525	0.7517	0.8225	0.8573	0.7298
110. Agricultural Service	0.7298	0.7298	0.7298	0.7298	0.7298	8.3691	8.3691	8.3691	8.3691	8.3691
111. Business Service	2.1871	1.3909	0.7031	1.1270	0.6146	0.3738	0.3734	0.4086	0.4259	0.3626
112. Recreation	0.2610	0.2605	0.2570	0.2957	0.3372	0.5915	0.5909	0.6465	0.6739	0.5737
113. Personal Service	2.8515	2.1967	2.3773	2.0167	1.4402	1.2981	1.2968	1.4190	1.4790	1.2591
114. Office Supplies	0.	0.	0.	0.	0.	0.	0.	0.	0.	0.
(42) Scrap									
115. Iron Scrap	0.	0.	0.	0.	0.	0.	0.	0.	0.	0.
116. Other Scrap	0.	0.	0.	0.	0.	0.	0.	0.	0.	0.
(43) Unclassifiable									
117. Unclassifiable	0.0046	0.0136	0.0095	0.0264	0.0950	0.	0.	0.	0.	0.

Source: See text. (Chapter 7)
Notes to Table A.30.:
We will use the following notations: for example, k(53–1968) represents the direct capital coefficient of 53rd sector in 1968, and n(69–1970) represents the direct labor coefficient of 69th sector in 1970.
1. n(1–1963) through n(6–1963) were applied to n(1–1960) through n(6–1960); and k(1–1966) through k(6–1966) were applied to k(1–1963, 1960) through k(6–1963, 1960).

2. n(7–1970) was applied to n(7–1960) through n(7–1968) and k(7–1970) was applied to k(7–1960) through k(7–1968).
3. n(8–1970) was applied to n(8–1960) through n(8–1968) and k(8–1970) was applied to k(8–1960) through k(8–1968).
4. n(12–1963) and k(12–1963) were applied to n(12–1960) and k(12–1960) respectively.
5. n(13–1966) was applied to n(13–1963).
6. k(13–1966) was applied to k(13–1963) and k(13–1960).
7. k(14–1963) was applied to k(14–1960).
8. k(17–1963) was applied to k(17–1960).
9. k(18–1963) was applied to k(18–1960).
10. n(22–1963) was applied to n(22–1960).
11. k(22–1968) was applied to k(22–1966).
12. n(23–1963) was applied to n(23–1960).
13. k(23–1966) was applied to k(23–1963) and k(23–1960).
14. k(28–1966) was derived from the 1966 Mining and Manufacturing Census itself.
15. k(30–1968) was applied to k(30–1966).
16. n(33–1966) was applied to n(33–1963) and n(33–1960).
17. k(33–1966), k(33–1963) and k(33–1960) were derived from the 1966 Mining and Manufacturing Census itself.
18. k(50–1963) was applied to k(50–1960).
19. n(51–1963) was applied to n(51–1960).
20. k(51–1966) was applied to k(51–1963) and k(51–1960).
21. n(58–1963) was applied to n(58–1960).
22. k(58–1968) was applied to k(58–1960), k(58–1963) and k(58–1966).
23. n(59–1963) was applied to n(59–1960).
24. k(59–1963) was applied to k(59–1960).
25. k(65–1968) was applied to k(65–1966).
26. k(66–1966), k(66–1968) and k (66–1970) are Han's (net) capital coefficient in 1968.
27. k(67–1966), k(67–1968) and k(67–1970) are Han's (net) capital coefficient in 1968.
28. k(69–1968) was applied to k(69–1966) and k(69–1963).
29. n(71–1963) was applied to n(71–1960).
30. k(72–1968) was applied to k(72–1966).
31. k(81–1966) was applied to k(81–1963).
32. k(87–1966) was applied to k(87–1963).
33. n(91–1963) was applied to n(91–1960).
34. k(91–1968) was applied to k(91–1966) and k(91–1963) to k(91–1960).
35. n(110–1960) was applied to n(110–1963) through n(110–1970).
36. Han's (net) capital coefficient was applied to k(110–1960) through k(110–1970).
37. k(72–1971) was applied to k(72–1970).

Table A.31. *Direct plus Indirect Factor Coefficients (Applying the A^d Matrix): 1966–70*
In Thousand 1970 Dollars or Persons Per Thousand 1970 Dollars of Output

I-O 117 Sector Classification	Direct plus Indirect Capital Coefficients 1966	1968	1970	Direct plus Indirect Labor Coefficients 1966	1968	1970
(1) Rice, Barley & Wheat						
1. Rice, Barley & Wheat	0.4579	0.5857	0.7198	1.1892	1.1962	1.0638
(2) Other Agriculture						
2. Other Cereals	0.3665	0.4983	0.7800	2.7310	3.1880	2.2933
3. Vegetables	0.3549	0.4939	0.5123	1.8615	1.7930	1.4616
4. Fruit	1.2322	2.0340	2.7483	2.3966	1.8806	1.8225
5. Industrial Crops	0.3697	0.4740	0.7171	2.3506	1.8229	1.9171
6. Livestock & Sericulture	1.1164	1.0608	1.1602	2.2037	1.4823	1.4204
(3) Forestry						
7. Forestry	0.2587	0.2550	0.2852	0.8614	0.8487	0.8260
(4) Fishery						
8. Fishery	1.7686	1.7231	1.8927	1.0163	0.9603	1.0348
(5) Coal						
9. Coal	0.9239	1.0882	1.0085	0.7312	0.7247	0.4901
(6) Other Minerals						
10. Metallic Ores	0.7862	0.9591	0.9464	0.6444	0.5754	0.3919
11. Nonmetallic Minerals	0.5628	0.8995	0.5723	0.7533	0.8215	0.6446
12. Salt	0.9896	0.7980	0.4275	1.0747	2.5500	1.6104
(7) Processed Foods						
13. Meat & Dairy Products	1.3551	1.0754	1.0693	1.9138	1.3252	1.1550
14. Vegetable & Fruit Processing	1.2576	1.0846	1.0224	1.4860	1.2417	0.9800
15. Processing of Sea Foods	1.5171	1.8408	1.2985	1.3070	1.4533	0.9626
16. Grain Milling	0.8231	0.5304	0.6423	0.4978	0.3482	0.3246
17. Bakery & Confectionery	0.9602	0.8150	0.6738	1.1602	0.9667	0.5747
18. Sugar Refining	0.4521	0.2947	0.2819	0.1344	0.1269	0.1331

Table A.31. (Continued)
In Thousand 1970 Dollars or Persons Per Thousand 1970 Dollars of Output

I-O 117 Sector Classification	Direct plus Indirect Capital Coefficients			Direct plus Indirect Labor Coefficients		
	1966	1968	1970	1966	1968	1970
19. Seasonings	0.9114	1.0177	1.0805	1.3192	1.1916	0.8751
20. Other Processed Foods	0.9899	1.0143	0.8328	1.4691	1.2999	0.7662
(8) Beverages						
21. Alcoholic Beverages	0.6303	0.6183	0.5821	0.7272	0.6607	0.4285
22. Soft Drinks	0.8742	0.5780	0.6179	0.6013	0.3793	0.4262
(9) Tobacco						
23. Tobacco	0.5759	0.4939	0.3096	1.0169	0.7607	0.3759
(10) Fibre Spinning						
24. Cotton Yarn	1.1340	0.6586	1.2595	0.3478	0.3232	0.3775
25. Silk Yarn	1.2265	1.1489	1.2189	1.9261	1.3425	1.1716
26. Woolen Yarn	0.7709	0.6725	1.7474	0.3864	0.2629	0.6411
27. Hemp & Flax Yarn	0.9046	1.1046	1.7901	1.4902	1.1606	0.7781
28. Chemical Fibre Yarn	0.5545	1.9051	1.9091	0.7736	0.2665	0.3536
(11) Textile Fabrics						
29. Cotton Fabrics	1.0747	1.0884	1.3551	0.7093	0.7621	0.6365
30. Silk Fabrics	0.9003	0.5966	1.3722	1.2013	0.6958	0.7484
31. Woolen Fabrics	1.9659	0.9908	1.2140	0.9063	0.5750	0.4862
32. Hemp Fabrics	0.6969	0.8492	1.2264	2.2051	1.3387	0.8559
33. Chemical Fibre Fabrics	0.6693	0.6839	1.5077	0.7788	0.4917	0.5943
34. Dyeing & Finishing	1.2086	1.0076	0.9190	0.6843	0.5814	0.4448
(12) Textile Products						
35. Knit Products	1.0543	1.2743	1.2741	0.9207	1.0302	0.7334
36. Rope & Fishing Nets	0.6769	0.7840	0.9976	0.8470	0.8769	0.6232
37. Apparels & Accessories	0.9773	0.8035	0.9388	1.0591	0.7617	0.6735

38. Misc. Textile Products	0.9419	0.9118	1.1024	1.5404	1.1068	0.7540
(13) Lumber & Plywood						
39. Lumber & Plywood	0.4369	0.4293	0.5068	0.4059	0.3193	0.2444
(14) Wood & Furniture						
40. Wood Products	0.7216	0.6078	0.9314	1.1347	1.4803	1.0639
41. Furniture	0.7535	0.6793	0.8758	1.0736	0.8868	0.7725
(15) Paper & Products						
42. Pulp	1.2673	1.1506	0.6804	0.5456	0.4804	0.4051
43. Paper	1.1302	0.8548	0.7288	0.4702	0.3404	0.2945
44. Paper Products	0.8892	1.1781	1.0051	0.6694	0.6147	0.5163
(16) Printing & Publishing						
45. Printing & Publishing	1.1958	1.0087	1.0137	0.7897	0.6536	0.5393
(17) Leather Products						
46. Leather & Fur	0.9968	0.8477	0.7111	1.2537	0.6762	0.6302
47. Leather Products	0.8871	0.7500	0.7461	1.1535	0.8493	0.7314
(18) Rubber Products						
48. Rubber Products	0.5898	0.5326	0.8071	0.6924	0.5103	0.4886
(19) Basic Chemicals						
49. Inorganic Chemicals	2.7943	2.2049	2.1210	0.5734	0.4217	0.4292
50. Organic Chemicals	0.8536	0.7041	0.7705	0.5787	0.4666	0.5139
(20) Other Chemical Products						
51. Explosives	0.7804	0.6889	0.8976	0.5573	0.4577	0.3706
52. Paint	0.5893	0.5548	0.4669	0.4321	0.3510	0.2630
53. Drugs	0.6388	0.5618	0.5120	0.6319	0.5507	0.3779
54. Soap	0.5830	0.4020	0.5590	0.4087	0.2508	0.2965
55. Cosmetics	0.7566	0.5235	0.5361	0.6700	0.4450	0.3663
56. Pesticides	0.4268	0.3331	0.6079	0.3155	0.2955	0.4425
57. Other Chemical Products	0.6398	1.2867	1.7141	0.7054	0.3911	0.2778
(21) Chemical Fertilizer						
58. Chemical Fertilizer	2.4805	2.4895	1.9882	0.4572	0.2973	0.2105
(22) Petroleum Products						

Table A.31. (Continued)
In Thousand 1970 Dollars or Persons Per Thousand 1970 Dollars of Output

I-O 117 Sector Classification	Direct plus Indirect Capital Coefficients			Direct plus Indirect Labor Coefficients		
	1966	1968	1970	1966	1968	1970
59. Petroleum Products	0.4129	0.4467	0.3674	0.0658	0.0879	0.0851
(23) Coal Products						
60. Coal Products	1.3679	1.6259	1.5975	0.7694	0.7325	0.5134
(24) Nonmetallic Mineral Products						
61. Cement	3.7949	3.7678	2.9213	0.3763	0.4476	0.2902
62. Ceramic Products	1.5139	1.8365	1.3525	0.8708	0.9390	0.6583
63. Glass Products	0.7528	0.6292	1.3081	0.6624	0.5420	0.5014
64. Pottery	0.8912	1.0091	1.4141	1.3365	1.5313	1.2038
65. Other Stone & Clay	1.3023	1.4737	1.2103	0.6961	0.8649	0.8032
(25) Iron & Steel						
66. Pig Iron	1.7418	2.0001	1.6696	0.5337	0.7122	0.4900
67. Steel Ingots	1.7795	1.5614	1.6428	0.4921	0.4736	0.4230
(26) Steel Products						
68. Rolled Steel	1.3893	1.4979	1.0791	0.5403	0.5977	0.3236
69. Pipes & Plated Steel	0.5866	0.5418	0.7625	0.2984	0.2726	0.2269
70. Cast & Forged Steel	1.3245	0.9904	1.2445	0.5882	0.4890	0.4666
(27) Nonferrous Metal Products						
71. Nonferrous Smelting	0.9201	0.6666	1.0168	0.5040	0.2948	0.2921
72. Primary Nonferrous	0.6935	0.5829	1.4929	0.5687	0.4102	0.4149
(28) Finished Metal Products						
73. Structural Metallic	1.0458	0.9731	0.9623	0.9369	0.7160	0.5064
74. Other Metallic Products	0.8701	0.7477	1.0806	0.7940	0.6175	0.6135
(29) Machinery						
75. Prime Movers & Boilers	0.9015	0.6577	1.3088	0.7853	0.5340	0.6163
76. Working Machinery	1.3944	1.2064	1.2373	0.9495	0.8173	0.6529

77. Industrial Machinery	1.0695	1.0001	1.0281	0.8516	0.7234	0.6549
78. Other Machinery	1.0466	0.6409	0.9521	0.7407	0.4940	0.4979
79. Office Machines	0.8662	0.8645	1.2198	0.9414	0.7691	0.5982
80. Household Machines	0.8626	0.9062	1.1716	0.9277	0.8511	0.6454
81. Machine Spare Parts	0.8196	0.6767	0.9852	0.8277	0.5174	0.6222
(30) Electrical Machinery						
82. Electrical Machinery	1.5021	0.8229	1.0687	0.6721	0.4882	0.4487
83. Electronic & Comm. Eq.	1.2936	0.6795	0.5662	0.6665	0.5211	0.3561
84. Household Elec. Appl.	0.6195	0.8048	0.6441	0.7440	0.7259	0.4615
85. Other Electric Eq.	1.0516	0.8465	0.9816	0.5615	0.4613	0.4604
(31) Transport Equipments						
86. Shipbuilding	0.8805	1.2736	1.0725	0.5654	0.6828	0.4797
87. Railroad Transport Eq.	0.8401	0.7646	1.1283	0.6455	0.4600	0.6155
88. Motor Vehicles	0.8382	0.7222	0.5589	0.7272	0.4653	0.3114
89. Other Transport Eq.	0.6771	1.0385	0.5501	0.8350	1.2533	0.3604
(32) Misc. Manufacturing						
90. Measuring & Optical	1.3649	0.7484	0.6848	0.9962	0.5710	0.4988
91. Synthetic Resin Products	0.6837	0.7543	0.7481	0.5546	0.4320	0.3467
92. Other Manufactures	0.7619	0.7323	0.6197	1.1143	0.9403	0.6663
(33) Building & Maintenance						
93. Residential Building	0.7001	0.8716	0.7258	0.6344	0.6498	0.5549
94. Non-Residential Bldng.	0.7684	0.9160	0.7282	0.5967	0.6045	0.5255
95. Building Maintenance	0.8066	1.0672	0.7660	0.7900	0.8501	0.6696
(34) Other Construction						
96. Public Construction	0.9260	0.9534	0.7954	0.5042	0.4873	0.4989
97. Other Construction	0.7023	0.5747	0.6515	0.5463	0.4783	0.5087
(35) Electricity						
98. Electricity	3.8568	3.9901	4.8515	0.4160	0.3527	0.2282
(36) Banking & Dwelling						
99. Banking & Insurance	0.4359	0.4235	0.3676	0.4003	0.3699	0.3205

Table A.31. (Continued)
In Thousand 1970 Dollars or Persons Per Thousand 1970 Dollars of Output

I-O 117 Sector Classification	Direct plus Indirect Capital Coefficients			Direct plus Indirect Labor Coefficients		
	1966	1968	1970	1966	1968	1970
100. Dwelling & Real Estate	22.2352	23.1192	16.8250	0.1513	0.1589	0.1490
(37) Water & Sanitary Service						
101. Water & Sanitary Service	4.2811	4.2159	5.3939	0.5522	0.4635	0.4870
(38) Communication						
102. Communication	1.7727	1.9152	1.8213	0.5402	0.5147	0.4812
(39) Transportation						
103. Railroad Transportation	5.0201	5.5022	5.2680	0.5166	0.5083	0.4445
104. Other Transportation	2.9772	3.2243	3.1344	0.5845	0.5267	0.4551
105. Storage	0.5620	0.6919	0.7122	0.4801	0.4877	0.4225
(40) Trade						
106. Trade	0.6339	0.5081	0.4774	1.0280	0.8228	0.7139
(41) Other Services						
107. Education	3.0387	3.0929	2.7047	0.7439	0.7624	0.6611
108. Medical Service	1.1697	1.1212	1.0636	0.8367	0.8067	0.7663
109. Social Service	1.1959	1.2480	1.1006	0.7596	0.8311	0.6855
110. Agricultural Service	8.7443	8.7952	8.6105	0.8474	0.8479	1.0239
111. Business Service	1.3946	1.3262	1.0093	1.3121	1.6743	0.9788
112. Recreation	1.1356	1.1760	1.2152	0.5365	0.6055	0.5999
113. Personal Service	1.6593	1.7625	1.5124	2.5021	2.1453	1.5229
114. Office Supplies	0.7883	0.7450	0.8415	0.8816	0.7081	0.5890
(42) Scrap						
115. Iron Scrap	0.2201	0.2475	0.3690	0.1340	0.1283	0.1520
116. Other Scrap	0.3985	0.5648	0.3342	0.6018	0.7122	0.2253
(43) Unclassifiable						
117. Unclassifiable	0.5372	0.5369	0.6232	0.8100	0.7135	0.6142

Table A.32. *Direct plus Indirect Factor Coefficients (Applying the A Matrix): 1960–70*
In Thousand 1970 Dollars or Persons Per Thousand 1970 Dollars of Output

I-O 117 Sector Classification	Direct plus Indirect Capital Coefficients					Direct plus Indirect Labor Coefficients				
	1960	1963	1966	1968	1970	1960	1963	1966	1968	1970
(1) Rice, Barley & Wheat										
1. Rice, Barley & Wheat	0.4906	0.5726	0.5771	0.6634	0.7391	1.1196	1.2048	1.2282	1.2369	1.0865
(2) Other Agriculture										
2. Other Cereals	0.3622	0.4797	0.4336	0.5413	0.7881	3.0599	3.0820	2.7468	3.2013	2.3009
3. Vegetables	0.3082	0.3565	0.4458	0.5486	0.5225	1.5908	1.6307	1.8814	1.8075	1.4686
4. Fruit	1.2469	1.7460	1.3219	2.0921	2.7631	3.0791	3.4957	2.4215	1.8995	1.8312
5. Industrial Crops	0.3686	0.4829	0.4902	0.5441	0.7324	3.0507	3.4062	2.3768	1.8377	1.9254
6. Livestock & Sericulture	1.0023	1.2041	1.1647	1.1346	1.2439	3.1637	3.4225	2.2285	1.5571	1.5223
(3) Forestry										
7. Forestry	0.1930	0.2426	0.2889	0.2754	0.2940	0.7523	0.8411	0.8724	0.8573	0.8308
(4) Fishery										
8. Fishery	1.9604	1.9177	1.8357	1.8131	1.9738	1.2088	1.1980	1.0930	1.0574	1.0749
(5) Coal										
9. Coal	0.5268	0.6048	0.9714	1.1443	1.0449	0.9715	0.8487	0.7562	0.7570	0.5145
(6) Other Minerals										
10. Metallic Ores	0.7438	1.1471	0.8201	0.9947	0.9909	1.0419	1.1117	0.6666	0.5931	0.4098
11. Nonmetallic Minerals	0.4437	0.8153	0.6140	0.9566	0.5949	1.7223	1.3647	0.7811	0.8525	0.6565
12. Salt	0.3767	0.3713	1.0147	0.8402	0.4508	0.6607	0.6581	1.0955	2.5822	1.6209
(7) Processed Foods										
13. Meat & Dairy Products	1.2581	1.3702	1.3947	1.1350	1.1474	2.6998	2.5827	1.9341	1.3832	1.2400
14. Veg. & Fruit Processing	1.6364	1.0553	1.3427	1.1528	1.0942	1.6057	1.8424	1.5293	1.2789	1.0201
15. Processing of Sea Foods	1.8350	1.9047	1.5625	1.9090	1.3649	1.9960	1.5807	1.3537	1.5226	0.9994
16. Grain Milling	0.8181	1.1472	1.0267	0.9128	0.9362	0.8751	1.0478	0.9124	1.0503	0.7423
17. Bakery & Confectionery	0.8405	1.0734	1.0379	0.9234	0.8344	1.2662	1.1826	1.2692	1.1301	0.7276
18. Sugar Refining	0.3030	0.4329	0.4857	0.3211	0.3023	0.1368	0.2653	0.1467	0.1406	0.1483

Table A.32. (Continued)
In Thousand 1970 Dollars or Persons Per Thousand 1970 Dollars of Output

I-O 117 Sector Classification	Direct plus Indirect Capital Coefficients					Direct plus Indirect Labor Coefficients				
	1960	1963	1966	1968	1970	1960	1963	1966	1968	1970
19. Seasonings	0.7910	0.8964	0.9768	1.0828	1.1541	1.4851	1.4123	1.3518	1.2467	0.9529
20. Other Processed Foods	0.9368	1.2069	1.0715	1.1436	1.0210	1.7123	1.7030	1.5701	1.5140	1.0690
(8) Beverages										
21. Alcoholic Beverages	0.7384	0.8640	0.6901	0.6767	0.6424	0.8311	0.8559	0.7744	0.7194	0.4947
22. Soft Drinks	0.6170	0.8523	0.9150	0.6133	0.7411	0.7424	0.8149	0.6298	0.4119	0.5178
(9) Tobacco										
23. Tobacco	0.5173	0.5287	0.6348	0.5378	0.3539	0.8054	0.8205	1.0361	0.7792	0.4012
(10) Fibre Spinning										
24. Cotton Yarn	1.0285	0.9331	1.1579	0.7009	1.3269	2.0863	2.3290	0.3655	0.3410	0.3951
25. Silk Yarn	1.3200	1.3866	1.2634	1.2088	1.2942	2.7560	3.1148	1.9453	1.4004	1.2548
26. Woolen Yarn	0.5999	1.0515	0.9010	0.9929	1.8580	0.3276	0.4542	0.5013	0.3713	0.6736
27. Hemp & Flax Yarn	0.7943	1.2133	1.0047	1.1778	2.0172	1.0383	2.3090	1.6627	1.2701	1.0372
28. Chemical Fibre Yarn	0.5628	0.8149	0.8473	2.7005	2.3980	0.6187	0.6970	1.0453	0.5194	0.4470
(11) Textile Fabrics										
29. Cotton Fabrics	1.1098	1.1528	1.1173	1.1556	1.4284	1.9129	2.4102	0.7357	0.8044	0.6624
30. Silk Fabrics	1.3785	1.0146	1.0088	1.5613	1.5729	2.4292	1.3869	1.3065	0.9084	0.8301
31. Woolen Fabrics	0.7886	1.3527	2.0574	1.1768	1.5316	0.5032	0.8161	0.9806	0.6470	0.5806
32. Hemp Fabrics	1.3733	2.5205	0.7503	0.8984	1.3565	1.5282	1.9038	2.2772	1.3982	0.9803
33. Chemical Fibre Fabrics	0.6961	0.8917	0.9619	1.8891	1.9913	0.8220	0.9313	1.0664	0.7486	0.6883
34. Dyeing & Finishing	0.8987	0.5614	1.3921	1.1776	1.1100	0.6121	0.3727	0.7744	0.6797	0.5534
(12) Textile Products										
35. Knit Products	1.0384	1.0213	1.1434	1.5353	1.6109	1.8266	1.4483	0.9960	1.1213	0.8113
36. Rope & Fishing Nets	0.5567	1.1064	0.8591	0.9202	1.3095	0.8372	1.2222	1.2475	1.1081	0.6903
37. Apparels & Accessories	0.7833	1.0200	1.1108	1.1612	1.3775	1.0196	1.5164	1.1777	0.8942	0.8204

38. Misc. Textile Products	0.7722	0.7602	1.0130	1.0494	1.2417	1.7501	2.1361	1.5851	1.1615	0.7978		
(13) Lumber & Plywood												
39. Lumber & Plywood	0.5437	0.5151	0.4595	0.4482	0.5426	0.7708	0.4359	0.4314	0.3337	0.2820		
(14) Wood & Furniture												
40. Wood Products	0.9843	1.1656	0.7551	0.6339	0.9985	1.2798	1.2716	1.1659	1.4978	1.1097		
41. Furniture	0.9261	1.0827	0.8672	0.7806	1.0352	1.2791	1.1031	1.1372	0.9462	0.8553		
(15) Paper & Products												
42. Pulp	0.4534	0.4133	1.2926	1.1767	0.8073	0.4126	0.2208	0.5579	0.4948	0.6814		
43. Paper	0.9203	0.8588	1.2797	0.9385	1.0365	0.7953	0.5176	0.5387	0.3883	0.5530		
44. Paper Products	1.0238	0.9555	0.9808	1.2495	1.2073	1.1020	0.8563	0.7106	0.6529	0.6626		
(16) Printing & Publishing												
45. Printing & Publishing	1.3872	0.9146	1.3271	1.1214	1.1702	0.9889	0.8313	0.8520	0.7132	0.6500		
(17) Leather Products												
46. Leather & Fur	1.2302	1.0775	1.0983	1.2228	1.1407	1.9473	1.3161	1.3014	1.0714	1.0897		
47. Leather Products	0.8024	1.1496	0.9844	0.9182	0.9569	1.4951	1.5938	1.2305	0.9996	0.9181		
(18) Rubber Products												
48. Rubber Products	0.6834	0.7101	0.7547	1.0898	0.9583	0.7079	0.9263	0.8113	0.6667	0.5348		
(19) Basic Chemicals												
49. Inorganic Chemicals	1.6527	1.2736	2.8609	2.2579	2.2314	0.6258	0.6311	0.6044	0.4548	0.5187		
50. Organic Chemicals	1.4186	1.2581	0.9456	0.7750	0.9042	1.2942	0.7373	0.6188	0.5058	0.5983		
(20) Other Chemical Products												
51. Explosives	1.0155	1.1536	1.0914	0.9289	1.0753	0.7280	0.8305	0.6888	0.5804	0.4455		
52. Paint	0.5773	0.8246	0.6727	0.6327	0.6745	0.4623	0.6679	0.4683	0.3877	0.3620		
53. Drugs	0.8398	0.7731	0.6934	0.6133	0.5651	0.9444	0.8422	0.6700	0.5857	0.4104		
54. Soap	0.7881	0.6689	0.7342	0.4962	0.6242	0.6313	0.5556	0.4617	0.2917	0.3323		
55. Cosmetics	0.8802	0.8142	0.8111	0.5773	0.6686	1.0245	0.7945	0.7018	0.4820	0.4282		
56. Pesticides	0.6400	0.7102	0.5087	0.4000	0.6505	0.6499	0.6584	0.3474	0.3275	0.4664		
57. Other Chemical Products	1.0095	0.7842	0.7665	1.3841	1.9256	1.7795	1.4670	0.7556	0.4329	0.3248		
(21) Chemical Fertilizer												
58. Chemical Fertilizer	2.0300	2.4521	2.7421	2.6428	2.0235	0.6661	0.6361	0.5203	0.3359	0.2306		
(22) Petroleum Products												
59. Petroleum Products	0.2481	0.8657	0.4307	0.4777	0.3795	0.1154	0.5908	0.0726	0.1033	0.0911		

Table A.32. (Continued)
In Thousand 1970 Dollars or Persons Per Thousand 1970 Dollars of Output

I-O 117 Sector Classification	Direct plus Indirect Capital Coefficients							Direct plus Indirect Labor Coefficients					
	1960	1963	1966	1968	1970	1960	1963	1966	1968	1970
(23) Coal Products										
60. Coal Products	1.2733	1.4761	1.4091	1.6740	1.6334	1.1306	1.0658	0.7915	0.7604	0.5345
(24) Nonmetallic Mineral Products										
61. Cement	1.1504	1.5549	3.8400	3.8291	2.9769	0.6308	0.4717	0.4042	0.4845	0.3170
62. Ceramic Products	1.1051	1.2150	1.5776	1.9059	1.4248	1.2646	1.2186	0.9108	0.9804	0.6918
63. Glass Products	1.0455	0.9129	0.7880	0.6687	1.3623	0.8149	0.7886	0.6846	0.5675	0.5317
64. Pottery	0.9813	1.1715	0.9514	1.0886	1.5245	1.3439	1.5659	1.3774	1.5841	1.2479
65. Other Stone & Clay	1.0427	1.1642	1.4796	1.7209	1.3709	0.9848	1.0065	0.8399	1.0549	0.9646
(25) Iron & Steel										
66. Pig Iron	1.4084	1.1610	2.1372	2.0495	2.1941	0.7857	0.6454	0.7504	0.7362	0.6911
67. Steel Ingots	0.8764	1.0637	2.1701	1.8436	1.9816	0.4295	0.4962	0.6624	0.6018	0.5601
(26) Steel Products										
68. Rolled Steel	1.1755	1.2000	1.8477	1.7033	1.3121	0.7603	0.6091	0.7157	0.6982	0.4155
69. Pipes & Plated Steel	1.1328	0.7394	1.2325	1.0350	1.1595	0.7406	0.4094	0.5666	0.4825	0.3606
70. Cast & Forged Steel	0.9478	0.8859	1.5784	1.1885	1.4780	0.8887	0.7081	0.6966	0.5767	0.5615
(27) Nonferrous Metals										
71. Nonferrous Smelting	0.9200	1.1455	0.9899	0.9638	1.2543	0.7387	0.7617	0.5437	0.4712	0.3897
72. Primary Nonferrous	0.7453	1.1371	0.7872	0.6893	1.9424	0.5706	0.5079	0.6227	0.4808	0.5682
(28) Finished Metal Products										
73. Structural Metallic	1.1658	1.1148	1.3549	1.1854	1.2616	0.8361	0.9235	1.0817	0.8128	0.6158
74. Other Metallic Products	0.8552	1.0483	1.0832	0.9130	1.2862	0.9861	0.8926	0.8855	0.6931	0.6955
(29) Machinery										
75. Prime Movers & Boilers	0.9628	1.4864	1.1527	1.2271	1.5538	1.0004	0.9828	0.9051	0.9262	0.7190
76. Working Machinery	1.3203	1.4194	1.7137	1.4201	1.4684	0.9247	1.1443	1.0793	0.9233	0.7428

77. Industrial Machinery	1.1894	1.1545	1.3529	1.2047	1.2581	1.1678	1.0261	0.9760	0.8238	0.7535
78. Other Machinery	1.0712	1.2911	1.2764	1.0851	1.2398	0.8353	0.9585	0.8476	0.7980	0.6217
79. Office Machines	0.9820	0.7118	1.0192	0.9923	1.4988	1.1255	0.7413	1.0086	0.8290	0.6983
80. Household Machines	0.8786	1.0630	1.1003	1.1143	1.3594	1.1660	1.1646	1.0913	0.9810	0.7303
81. Machine Spare Parts	1.0711	0.9751	0.9941	0.8251	1.2923	1.0312	1.0314	0.9172	0.6190	0.7449
(30) Electrical Machinery										
82. Electrical Machinery	1.0793	1.3536	1.6560	0.9823	1.4681	1.1127	0.8051	0.7531	0.5801	0.6034
83. Electronic & Comm. Eq.	0.8787	1.2989	1.4959	0.8440	0.9017	1.0318	0.9781	0.7715	0.6138	0.5392
84. Household Elec. Appl.	0.8492	0.9423	0.7283	0.9044	0.8800	1.2112	1.0184	0.8078	0.7880	0.5665
85. Other Electric Eq.	0.6890	0.8760	1.1876	1.0208	1.3065	0.5930	0.7812	0.6316	0.5542	0.5747
(31) Transport Equipments										
86. Shipbuilding	1.6063	1.5566	1.3324	1.6503	1.3867	1.0045	0.7731	0.7688	0.8636	0.6093
87. Railroad Transport Eq.	1.0668	1.0558	1.2871	1.1997	1.4307	1.0395	0.9959	0.8825	0.7065	0.7525
88. Motor Vehicles	1.0513	1.3676	1.1051	0.9890	0.6850	1.1242	1.1048	0.8515	0.6063	0.3681
89. Other Transport Eq.	1.1828	1.0721	0.8228	1.2239	0.6858	1.1657	0.8952	0.9065	1.3492	0.4157
(32) Misc. Manufacturing										
90. Measuring & Optical	0.9821	0.9977	1.4976	0.8724	1.1096	1.1437	1.2813	1.0669	0.6387	0.7481
91. Synthetic Resin Products	0.8858	1.1548	0.7138	0.7828	0.8957	0.7580	0.8773	0.5697	0.4475	0.3850
92. Other Manufactures	0.9533	1.0187	0.8317	0.8702	1.0049	1.2024	1.4105	1.1689	1.0466	0.7574
(33) Building & Maintenance										
93. Residential Building	1.0550	0.8150	0.8064	0.9559	0.8469	1.2587	0.9851	0.6954	0.6972	0.6151
94. Non-Residential Bldng.	0.9444	0.9405	0.9477	1.0347	0.9182	1.1934	1.0212	0.6865	0.6676	0.6128
95. Building Maintenance	0.7700	0.6691	0.9573	1.1578	0.8466	1.2534	1.0193	0.8776	0.9005	0.7172
(34) Other Construction										
96. Public Construction	1.5224	1.1786	1.0689	1.0805	0.8844	1.0406	0.8919	0.5615	0.5430	0.5377
97. Other Construction	1.3061	1.1480	0.9284	0.7284	0.9334	1.0543	0.9217	0.6706	0.5885	0.6324
(35) Electricity										
98. Electricity	2.1218	4.5123	3.8793	4.0297	4.8711	0.5746	0.6208	0.4290	0.3795	0.2376
(36) Banking & Dwelling										
99. Banking & Insurance	0.5913	0.5273	0.4574	0.4509	0.3887	0.3462	0.4042	0.4143	0.3899	0.3317

Table A. 32. (Continued)
In Thousand 1970 Dollars or Persons Per Thousand 1970 Dollars of Output

I-O 117 Sector Classification	Direct plus Indirect Capital Coefficients					Direct plus Indirect Labor Coefficients				
	1960	1963	1966	1968	1970	1960	1963	1966	1968	1970
100. Dwelling & Real Estate	31.4077	26.9793	22.2566	23.1301	16.8360	0.1488	0.1309	0.1638	0.1649	0.1555
(37) Water & Sanitary Service										
101. Water & Sanitary Service	2.2775	5.0665	4.3568	4.2665	5.4423	0.5623	0.7354	0.5840	0.4864	0.5085
(38) Communication										
102. Communication	1.9774	2.1000	1.7950	1.9403	1.8784	0.7397	0.7857	0.5525	0.5307	0.4989
(39) Transportation										
103. Railroad Transportation	5.7541	6.0176	5.0417	5.5300	5.3053	0.9892	0.9548	0.5309	0.5293	0.4620
104. Other Transportation	3.5330	3.6051	3.0482	3.3210	3.1800	1.0908	0.9816	0.6239	0.5880	0.4776
105. Storage	0.7009	0.6668	0.5774	0.7107	0.7284	0.9263	0.7772	0.4895	0.4991	0.4308
(40) Trade										
106. Trade	1.1855	0.8766	0.6513	0.5337	0.4959	1.2949	1.1582	1.0375	0.8384	0.7234
(41) Other Services										
107. Education	2.7347	2.7974	3.0722	3.1237	2.7382	0.5810	0.7420	0.7645	0.7844	0.6800
108. Medical Service	1.0509	1.2017	1.2223	1.1847	1.1029	0.7658	1.0699	0.8755	0.8546	0.7959
109. Social Service	1.1397	1.1958	1.2223	1.2783	1.1332	0.7909	0.8820	0.7767	0.8486	0.7008
110. Agricultural Service	8.5060	8.7480	8.7556	8.8086	8.6366	0.8080	1.0496	0.8541	0.8565	1.0453
111. Business Service	1.5095	1.1725	1.4914	1.4157	1.0728	2.9876	2.1059	1.3588	1.7216	1.0149
112. Recreation	1.0983	1.2040	1.2097	1.2360	1.2718	0.7483	0.7102	0.5743	0.6400	0.6232
113. Personal Service	1.6612	1.7050	1.6751	1.7856	1.5325	3.1732	2.5593	2.5121	2.1596	1.5327
114. Office Supplies	0.0000	0.9897	0.9141	0.9143	1.0864	0.0000	1.1748	0.9689	0.8224	0.6952
(42) Scrap										
115. Iron Scrap	0.0404	0.1010	0.2962	0.3000	0.4533	0.0212	0.0670	0.1646	0.1514	0.1857
116. Other Scrap	0.1832	0.3733	0.4245	0.5850	0.3785	0.4396	0.5868	0.6387	0.7273	0.2480
(43) Unclassifiable										
117. Unclassifiable	1.1772	1.2597	0.6266	0.6442	0.7282	0.7788	1.7847	0.8551	0.7719	0.6664

236

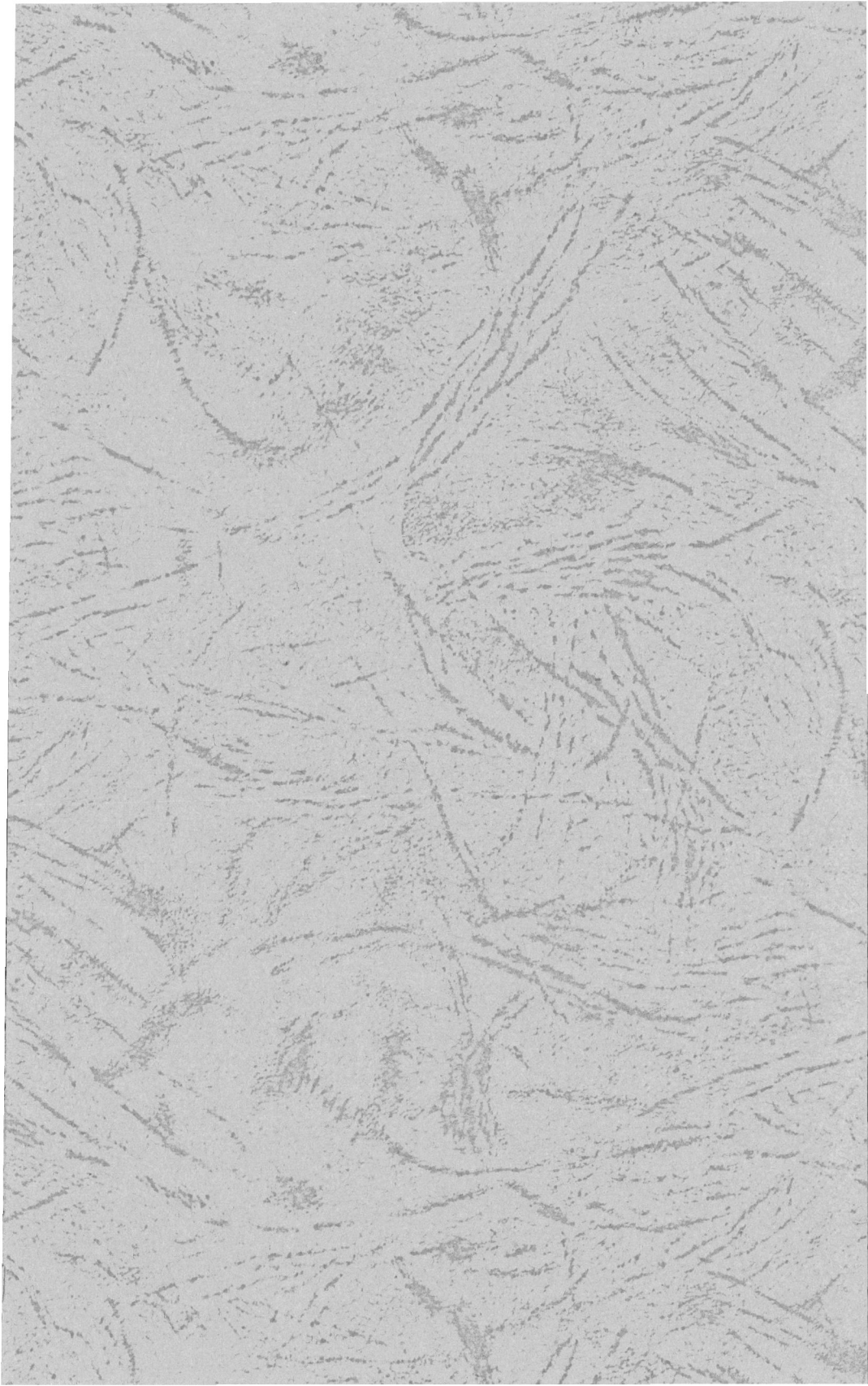